Cost-Benefit Analysis
and the
Economics of Investment in
Human Resources

i

Cost-Benefit Analysis and the Economics of Investment in Human Resources

An Annotated Bibliography

by

W. D. WOOD

H. F. CAMPBELL

INDUSTRIAL RELATIONS CENTRE
QUEEN'S UNIVERSITY
AT KINGSTON, ONTARIO

1970

iii

COST-BENEFIT ANALYSIS AND THE ECONOMICS OF
INVESTMENT IN HUMAN RESOURCES: An Annotated Bibliography

PREFACE

The past decade has witnessed increasing interest in both the theory and practical application of cost-benefit analysis. Our experience suggested that it would be a useful and time-saving service to publish an annotated bibliography surveying some of the literature in this field. The study has been designed to serve as an analytical reference for both the academic scholar and the policy-maker in this area. The first four sections of the bibliography deal with the theoretical aspects of cost-benefit analysis, and the remaining four sections cover various practical applications of this technique to the evaluation of investment in human capital.

Cost-benefit analysis is a method of investment appraisal. It can be applied to any expenditure which is capital-forming and, consequently, is expected to yield a future return. When cost-benefit analysis is applied to expenditures which purchase some kind of treatment for human beings, it is assumed that these expenditures represent human capital formation. The first section of the bibliography deals with the theory and measurement of human capital.

Cost-benefit analysis involves identifying and measuring the costs associated with and the benefits expected from an investment, and comparing them. The benefit/cost ratio is only one of a number of investment criteria which are used to decide whether a proposed investment project offers an increase in economic welfare. Since benefits and costs normally take a number of different forms, the analyst attempts to make them commensurable with one another by reducing them all to money terms.

An investment, by definition, incurs costs and yields benefits at more than one point in time. Costs incurred and benefits accruing at different times must be reduced to a common point in time, usually the present, before they can be compared. An interest rate is used to discount benefits and costs to present values. Where society bears the costs and reaps the benefits, the social discount rate is the appropriate interest rate.

Section 3 of the bibliography deals with theoretical problems encountered in identifying and measuring the costs and benefits of an action, while section 4 covers the choice of an investment criterion and the identification of the social discount rate. Before the sections dealing with specific theoretical issues, however, section 2 introduces the reader to general aspects of the theory and application of cost-benefit analysis. This section contains a variety of material ranging from theoretical surveys to applications of cost-benefit analysis to government decision making within the framework of Planning-Programming-Budgeting Systems. The last four sections of the bibliography deal with attempts to evaluate investments in schooling, training, retraining, and worker mobility, health, and investments aimed at reducing poverty and increasing social welfare in some way.

For a few of the studies examined, the decision as to which section they belonged was arbitrary. To a certain extent also the decision as to which references should be included in a bibliography covering such a wide area of economic research is necessarily arbitrary; the authors have attempted to include recent significant contributions to the theory and practice of cost-benefit analysis, but in many cases accessibility was the deciding factor.

The structure of the annotations is as follows: the "headings" of the various sections of a study provide a brief indication of its content; where the study is divided into sections but no headings are provided, we have supplied our own. Many of the works annotated provide references to further reading and this is indicated in the headings section. Cross references are identified by their entry number in this volume.

Most of the references annotated are articles or monographs, but there are a number of books. On the grounds of space and time, the authors have not attempted to give a reference representation in proportion to its length or to its importance. We have made no comments about the studies annotated, but have tried simply to give a brief description of their content.

The authors wish to express their sincere appreciation to the Canadian Department of Manpower and Immigration for their financial support for this study. We are also grateful to Professor David Sewell of the Queen's Economics Department for his valuable comments and suggestions on many aspects of the project. Finally, we wish to thank Mrs. Carol Williams and Centre staff for their usual meticulous editorial supervision and proofreading.

W. DONALD WOOD*

HARRY F. CAMPBELL*

December, 1969.

---

* Dr. Wood is Professor of Economics and Director of the Industrial Relations Centre, Queen's University. He is a graduate of McMaster, Queen's, and Princeton Universities. Mr. Campbell, a graduate of St. Andrew's University, is currently completing his Ph.D. programme in economics at Queen's where he also is associated in research with the Industrial Relations Centre.

CONTENTS

1. HUMAN CAPITAL

1. ARROW, KENNETH J. "The Economic Implications of Learning by Doing." *Review of Economic Studies,* Vol. 29 (1961-62), pp. 155-173.

Headings: Introduction; The model; Wages; Profits and investment; Rational expectations in a macroeconomic growth model; Divergence of private and social product; Some comments on the model; References (15).

Abstract: The author puts forward an endogenous theory of the changes in knowledge which underlie intertemporal and international shifts in production functions. Learning is assumed to take place only as a by-product of experience in production, although the model could be extended to include institutional forms of learning. The role of experience in increasing productivity has been observed in empirical studies on airframe production, national outputs, and iron production, and "learning curves" have been constructed to relate increases in output to increases in experience. The economic variable used to represent "experience" in this study is cumulative gross investment — each new machine produced and put into use provides new stimuli to learning. Learning is assumed to take place only in the capital goods industry, *i.e.*, technical change is completely embodied in new capital goods; the empirical studies, on the other hand, suggest that learning takes place in the use of a capital good once built. The hypothesis advanced is that technical change in general can be ascribed to experience. The implications of a simplified mathematical model incorporating this hypothesis are examined for wage earners, profits, the inducement to invest, and the rate of interest. It is pointed out that the presence of learning means that an act of investment benefits future investors but that this benefit is not paid for by the market. This externality causes the amount of investment in the competitive model to fall short of the socially optimal level.

2. BALOGH, T., and P. P. STREETEN. "The Coefficient of Ignorance." *Bulletin of the Oxford University Institute of Economics and Statistics,* Vol. 25, No. 2 (May, 1963), pp. 99-107.

Abstract: This paper discusses attempts to isolate the contribution to growth made by expenditure on research, education, health, provision of information, and other forms of non-physical social investments. These factors are generally incorporated in a residual term — the "coefficient of our ignorance" — in the production function. The author argues that estimates of the importance of investment in human capital in advanced Western economies may not have obvious implications for underdeveloped countries. He discusses the incorporation of educational programs into long-term economic development plans, and the quantitative measures required.

3. BECKER, GARY S. "Investment in Human Capital: a Theoretical Analysis." *Journal of Political Economy,* Vol. 70, No. 5, Part 2 (October, 1962, Supplement), pp. 9-49.

Headings: Introduction; Different kinds of investment; Relation between earnings, costs, and rates of return; The incentive to invest; Some effects of human capital; Summary and conclusions.

Abstract: The author sets out the theoretical arguments concerning investment in human capital. He makes an extensive examination of various kinds of investment in human beings, including on-the-job training, schooling, information, and health. On-the-job training is dealt with intensively because it clearly illustrates the effect of human capital on earnings, employment, and other economic variables. The most important single determinant of the amount invested in human capital is the rate of return. If the present values of net earnings in different occupations are assumed to be the same, the costs of investment and the internal rate of return can be estimated from information about net earnings. The incentive to invest is also discussed with reference to such variables as expected lifespan, wage differentials and secular change, risk and liquidity, and imperfect capital markets and knowledge. The author emphasizes the empirical nature of his work: he believes that the analysis of human investment offers a unified explanation of a wide range of empirical phenomena including age-earnings profiles; the so-called "labour intensive" exports and "capital intensive" imports which have been recorded for the U.S.; the effect of factor proportions on wages; the mechanism of technical change; and the distribution of earnings.

4. BECKER, GARY S. *Human Capital.* New York: National Bureau of Economic Research, 1964. xiv + 187 p.

Headings: Introduction; Investment in human capital: effects on earnings; Investment in human capital: rates of return; Rates of return from college education; Underinvestment in college education; Rates of return from high school education and trends over time; Age, earnings, wealth, and human capital; Summary and conclusions; Appendices.

Abstract: Activities which influence future monetary and psychic income by increasing the resources in people are human capital forming. The many forms of investments in human capital include schooling, on-the-job training, medical care, migration, and information. Most investments in human capital raise observed earnings at older ages because returns are part of earnings then, and lower them at younger ages, because costs are deducted from earnings at that time. Since these common effects are produced by very different kinds of investment in human capital, a basis is provided for a unified and comprehensive theory. The general theory helps to explain such diverse phenomena as inter-personal and as inter-area differences in earnings, the shape of age-earnings profiles, and the effect of specialization on skill. Some investments in human capital do not affect earnings because costs are paid and returns are collected by the firms, industries, or countries employing the individuals involved. Such investments are "specific": completely specific training can be defined as training which has no effect on the productivity of trainees in any firm other than the one providing the training; completely general training, on the other hand, increases the marginal productivity of trainees by the same amount in other firms as in the firm providing the training. Specific training helps to explain the fact that unemployment is greater among unskilled than skilled workers, and may explain the use of completely vested pension plans. This type of investment is relatively more important in monopsonistic than in competitive firms. The second part of the book investigates empirically the effect of investment in formal education on earnings and productivity in the United States. The following topics are examined: the relation between earnings and college education, taking college costs and the greater "ability" of college persons into account; the social gain from college education as measured by its effects on national productivity; private rates of return from high school education; the effects of the increase in education upon earnings differentials and rates of return on education; and the steepening and increased concavity of age-earnings profiles caused by investment in education. The book concludes with some suggestions for future research in the field of human capital.

5.   BENEWITZ, MAURICE C., and ALBERT ZUCKER. "Human Capital and Occupational Choice — A Theoretical Model." *Southern Economic Journal,* Vol. 34, No. 3 (January, 1968), pp. 406-409.
Headings: The model; Qualifications.
Abstract: The authors adopt the following model of occupational choice: an individual chooses that occupation for which the present value of his expected income stream is a maximum. The rate of discount used by an individual is determined by his "time-preference" function. The sequence of investment activities undertaken for entry into an occupation can be conceived of as an ordered chain, each link of which has its own rate of return. Declining rates of return with further investment make determinate the amount of investment an individual on the investment chain will undertake. Declining rates of return to education are consistent with much of the available evidence, although the paper by Becker and Chiswick (189) presents an apparent exception. The authors agree that this apparent exception can be explained by a downward bias of rates of return on earlier units of schooling. This bias is caused by a positive correlation between years of schooling and ability. The qualifying remarks at the close of the paper concern diminishing marginal utility of income, non-monetary influences on choice of occupation, dynamic effects in the labor market, and the tendency for investment in oneself to decline with age.

6.   BEN-PORATH, YORAM. "The Production of Human Capital and the Life Cycle of Earnings." *Journal of Political Economy,* Vol. 75, No. 4 (August, 1967), pp. 352-365.
Headings: Introduction; The model; The production function; The model and aggregate earning profiles; Summary and some open questions; References (8).
Abstract: The development of the theory of human capital by Becker (3, 4) and Mincer (19, 313) provided a novel view of the life cycle of earnings by linking it to the time profile of investment in human capital. The present

3

paper combines the part of the argument concerning the individual's demand for human capital with an explicit treatment of the cost conditions facing the individual. The basic model generates some of the qualitative characteristics of the observed life cycle of earnings — typically, an initial period of no earnings followed by a period in which earnings rise at a declining rate and, eventually, decline. The model specifies the nature of the bias which, the author argues, may exist when earnings are used to infer changes in productive capacity with age. The production function is intended to provide a framework within which some of the characteristics of the technology facing the individual when he makes decisions about investing in himself can be considered. Within this framework, the author demonstrates the role played by increasing costs in the explanation of the gradually rising portion in the individual life cycle of earnings; an explanation of the cross-section profile of earnings can be provided *without* the assumption of rising costs. The paper concludes by focusing attention on some problems raised by the analysis: the definition of human capital; the speed of adjustment of the stock of human capital; the homogeneity of human capital; the possibility of producing human capital in addition to earnings; the rate of deterioration of human capital; the time horizon; possible effects of public policy; problems of measurement; uncertainty and capital rationing; and the introduction of consumption activities to the analysis.

7. BEN-PORATH, YORAM. "Lifetime Income and Economic Growth: Comment." *American Economic Review,* Vol. 56, No. 4, Part 1 (September, 1966), pp. 869-872.

Abstract: This paper is a comment on Miller's analysis (18) of the effects of economic growth upon earnings. Miller divided the relative rise of income of an age cohort of a decade into an age and a growth effect. A complete breakdown, the author argues, would be an age effect, a growth effect, and an interaction component. Miller's measure of the "growth" effect is the sum of the growth effect and the interaction component. As a result, his measure is generally higher than the pure growth effect and tends to show a decline of the growth effect with age. A comparison of Miller's growth effect and the author's measure demonstrates that it cannot be concluded that the growth effect declines with age. Neutral growth is essential if we wish to interpret the relation between income and age in cross-section data as the static life cycle.

8. BOWMAN, MARY JEAN. "Human Capital: Concepts and Measures." In *Economics of Higher Education,* edited by Selma J. Mushkin, pp. 69-92. Washington: U.S. Department of Health, Education, and Welfare, Office of Education, 1962.

Headings: Prefatory remarks; The treatment of quantity and quality in measuring a "unit" of human capital; Some special considerations in cost-based measurement of human-capital formation; Net human-capital formation; Effective current stock; Conclusions.

Abstract: Analysis of human capital concepts and measures is necessary as a basis for considering the following four questions. What have been the total human capital inputs into the productive system and how have these affected national output over time? What proportion of society's resources has gone to human capital formation in the past and how does this compare with the proportion devoted to physical capital formation? What rates of return have been realized from investments in human capital? How may past, present, and prospective investments in human capital be expected to affect the stream of national product in the future? Units of human capital defined in the limited sense of "education embodied in the labor force" may be measured in a number of ways: number of school years; efficiency equivalence units (school years weighted to account for changes in the productivity of schooling); base-year lifetime earned incomes; approximations to base-year real costs; and approximations to current real costs. Cost measures of gross human capital formation are not subject to the severe problems of aggregation faced by measures of physical capital formation, but they do encounter special difficulties: it is difficult to sort out investment in human producer capital versus immediate consumption, and investment in human consumer capital; the estimation of the opportunity costs of student time poses problems; and there is the question of whether to count as part of human capital formation the costs of schooling persons who leave school after only a few years. The adjustment of gross human capital formation is discussed. The "effective current stock", which is a direct measure of the potential current inputs of human capital, can be measured. The paper concludes by suggesting four further areas of research.

9. BOWMAN, MARY JEAN. "Schultz, Denison, and the Contribution of "Eds" to National Income Growth." *Journal of Political Economy*, Vol. 72, No. 5 (October, 1964), pp. 450-464.

Headings: Introduction; The rental-value model; Empirical assumptions of the Schultz and Denison measurements; Differences between the methods used by Schultz and Denison; Critical issues.

Abstract: The author uses the term "Eds" to refer to the units of inputs of productive services derived from "embodied education". These inputs constitute a *flow* whereas human capital is a *stock*. A rental-value formulation of the model for assessing contributions of education to growth is set up in a generalized form which permits detailed comparison of the Denison and Schultz treatments as special cases. It is pointed out that, even after adjusting for factors correlated with education and earnings, the observed base-year "rental values" may not measure base-year returns to schooling since on-the-job training and learning are also reflected in the data. The use of base-year rental values as a measure of what "Eds" contribute, as opposed to a measure of inputs of "Eds", is discussed.

10. BOWMAN, MARY JEAN. "The Human Investment Revolution in Economic Thought." *Sociology of Education*, Vol. 39, No. 2 (Spring, 1966), pp. 111-137.

Headings: Introduction; The investment orientation; In the aggregate; Investments in human beings and micro-decision theory; Human resource demands, supplies, and development; The economics of educational planning.

Abstract: An investment orientation to education entails cost-benefit assessments in human beings and micro-decision theory; Human resource demands, principal's point of view, and sometimes from the point of view of a government or of a society as a whole. The author demonstrates that the investment orientation to education has a place in the history of economic thought. In her study of recent research into the economics of education viewed as investment in human beings, she distinguished four main areas. In the first place, efforts have been made to measure the aggregate of human capital formation in an economy and to estimate its contribution to national income growth. Secondly, much research on the economics of education as an investment centres on decision theories (or micro cost-benefit analyses) framed as testable behavioural hypotheses: the kind of question which is asked is whether individuals behave in an economically rational manner with respect to investment in the acquisition of future potential earnings streams via schooling. The third area of research is that of the determinants of the demands for educated or trained people, changes in those demands with economic development, and interactions between human resource demands and supplies. Lastly, an increasing amount of attention has been devoted to the development and application of systemized procedures and criteria for use in educational planning. The author has provided a survey of the work which has been done, and an indication of the direction of future research in those four areas of the economics of investment in education.

11. BRUMMET, R. LEE, WILLIAM C. PYLE, and ERIC G. FLAMHOLTZ. "Accounting for Human Resources." *Michigan Business Review,* Vol. 20, No. 2 (March, 1968), pp. 20-25.

Headings: Introduction; The need for human resource accounting; The neglect of human resource accounting; Research in human resource accounting; Conceptual foundations of a human resource accounting system; Research in progress.

Abstract: In business, decisions involving recruiting, hiring, training, supervising, evaluating, rewarding, developing, promoting, transferring, replacing, and discharging people are made almost continuously. Human resource accounting is the process of identifying, measuring, and communicating information about human resources to promote effective decision-making. It involves measuring the acquisition cost, replacement cost, and economic value of human resources, and their changes through time. The neglect of human resource accounting stems from the traditional treatment of outlays on human resources as "consumption" rather than "capital" expenditures by economists, and as "expenses" rather than "assets" by accountants. The authors outline three research objectives: the development of a human resource accounting system; the application of such a system; and the development of a set of generalizations about the behavioural impact of the system on people. Human resources can be viewed in two broad categories — internal human resources employees), and external human resources (customers, suppliers, distributors, stockholders). At present, research efforts are being focussed on internal human resources. Trends in the value of human resources may provide an additional measure to supplement "net income" as an indicator of management performance.

12. BRUMMET, R. LEE, ERIC G. FLAMHOLTZ, and WILLIAM C. PYLE. "Human Resource Measurement — A Challenge for Accountants." *The Accounting Review,* Vol. 43, No. 2 (April, 1968), pp. 217-224.

Headings: Introduction; Inadequacy of conventional practice; Need for human resource accounting; Research in human resource accounting; Multiple measures of human resources.

Abstract: Human resource costs should be treated by accountants as "expenses" in the periods in which benefits result, but if benefits accrue in a future time period, they should be treated as "assets". Human resource information is essential for each of the several phases of management's planning and control functions: recognizing and defining problems; searching for alternative solutions; evaluating alternatives; selecting among the evaluated alternatives; and reporting on actions taken and results achieved. The authors are attempting to develop human resource accounting systems in a number of corporations and thereby to find out how this kind of system should be used within the firm and what its impact is on the people associated with the firm. Human resources are being measured in terms of their acquisition cost, replacement cost, and economic value. The method of measuring acquisition and replacement costs of human resources is similar to that of other assets. There are a number of ways of measuring economic value, some of which raise interesting possibilities. Many of the concepts and much of the terminology being used are being adopted from conventional accounting. Human resource accounting, however, is not being designed for use in published financial statements. It is intended as a managerial tool.

13. CHAMBERLAIN, NEIL W. "Some Second Thoughts on the Concept of Human Capital." In *The Development and Use of Manpower, Proceedings of the Twentieth Annual Winter Meeting,* Washington, D.C., December 28-29, 1967, pp. 1-13. Madison: Industrial Relations Research Association, 1967.

Abstract: This paper discusses the evolution of the concept of human capital. Human capital is formed through investment in education, retraining, health, and environmental conditioning. The author feels that the application of an economic calculus is an inappropriate way of evaluating expenditure on human capital formation. In addition he points out that uncertainty and the dynamic nature of the social environment make rate of return calculations unreliable allocative criteria.

14. CHAMBERLAIN, NEIL W. "Some Further Thoughts on the Concept of Human Capital." In *Cost-Benefit Analysis of Manpower Policies, Proceedings of a North American Conference, May 14-15 1969*, edited by G. G. Somers and W. D. Wood, pp. 230-248. Published jointly by the Industrial Relations Centre, Queen's University, Kingston, Ontario, and the Centre for Studies in Vocational and Technical Education, The University of Wisconsin, Madison, Wisconsin, 1969.

Abstract: The validity and desirability of the human capital concept depends upon how far the pecuniary calculus can be extended to people in their roles as producers. With respect to their function as factors of production, we treat people as part of society's capital stock. If people can be viewed as capital, training and education can be regarded as investment in human capital. Is it reasonable to value an investment in education according to its rate of return? There is a presumption that the rate of return on investment in human capital can be compared with rates of return on other forms of investment to determine priorities. Does the human capital analyst merely seek to provide information? Although the analysis purports to be ethic and value free, it does harbor some ethical persuasions. If the concept of human capital is intended to have precise analytical relevance, we are in danger of repeating the intellectual excesses of the scientific management movement. The education process is seen as a training ground for the production function. The analyst may argue that his aim is to channel necessary activity along lines which achieve as efficiently as possible the goals which society has set for itself. This approach, however, is not value free since our price and income data are based on the existing system of social, legal, and political relations. These relations lead to judgements as to which investments are more productive than others, and the form which human capital should take if it is to produce maximum returns. Nor can we identify producers with consumers. Rewards are distributed by a social process. Efficient economic performance is an efficiency geared to the advantage of some more than of others. We are not value free as long as we accept the values given by the system inside which we operate. While aware that there are contentious interests within society, the social scientist prefers to treat society as an integrated system. Once we adopt a systems approach we impute a purpose to the system with which we are dealing. We tend to evaluate all the subsystems in terms of the system's objective. Nevertheless we know that all parts of the system have their own purposes and objectives. To treat only the system objectives is to accept the values of the system as a whole. The argument that the present system is the best compromise of interests that can be achieved is only a partial escape. When the analyst computes a rate of return, he cannot avoid the question, return to whom? It is not permissable to ignore "incommensurable values" since the pecuniary measures themselves derive from a system of existing values. The costs and benefits of given programs differ depending on which point of view one looks at — the firm, government, society, or the individual. The incommensurability which is at the root of the problem arises out of a clash of interests which are fundamental and opposed — opposed partly because of the scarcity condition which concerns economists. The author identifies two types of incommensurability: the first consists of phenomena which can have no accepted means of valuation since they are values which we are not prepared to compromise; the second type arises out of an identification with a class interest or a status category. When either of these two incommensurabilities is present there is no logic in attempting to calculate a rate of return which has "objective" power. A monistic approach cannot serve pluralistic ends. Where these elements are absent, cost-benefit analysis can be useful, but the author feels that human capital analysis cuts too close to personal integrity and life style. In addition, it is impossible to calculate the return on an investment in human capital, the underlying purpose of which is to change the shape of society. This consideration is relevant to any such type of investment, but educational programs are an increasingly important arena of the political contest. The movement of society towards more concern for the collective environment rather than private profit will change the valuation of costs and benefits deriving from investment in education. Should policy recommendations extending beyond the near future take values as given? To a certain extent intellectuals are the challengers of an existing system by exploring it more objectively than others.

15. CULLATHER, JAMES L. "The Missing Asset: Human Capital." *Mississippi Valley Journal of Business and Economics,* Vol. 2, No. 2 (Spring, 1967), pp. 70-73.

Abstract: What is the significance of the concept of human capital to the accountant? Expensing rather than capitalizing the costs of training implies that these expenditures represent no future benefit. The fact that investment in human beings is almost always associated with a consumption element, however, indicates that a part of training costs at least will always be expensed. Furthermore, the fact that an asset is brought into existence does not mean that is belongs on the firm's balance sheet. In the case of the "general training" cited by Becker (4), increased productivity as a result of training is matched by increased wages and the human capital is, therefore, not the firm's asset. The case for capiitalization increases to the extent that training becomes more "specific", and the degree of specificity of training is related to the degree of market imperfection. By and large, as accountants become more aware of the concept of human capital, there will be less expensing and more capitalization. Capitalization will usually be partial, and expensing will cover consumption aspects and general training. Increasingly, the problem of rational treatment of human capital in taxation and public policy will be explored.

9

16. GRUBEL, HERBERT G., and ANTHONY D. SCOTT. "The International Flow of Human Capital." *American Economic Review, Papers and Proceedings,* Vol. 56, No. 2 (May, 1966), pp. 268-274.

Headings: Introduction; Concept of a "country"; The possibility of reduced welfare in the home country through emigration; Increases in the home country's welfare as a result of emigration; Conclusions.

Abstract: The argument that a country loses by the emigration of highly skilled individuals is almost always valid when we consider the "country" as a nation state whose national objective is to maximize its military and economic power. If, on the other hand, a country wishes to maximize the income available to all its people, emigration should be welcomed whenever two conditions are met: firstly, that the emigrant improves his own income; and, secondly, that his departure does not reduce the income of those remaining behind. The first condition is normally met when emigration is voluntary. In a market economy, where persons are paid their marginal product, the second condition will be met as long as there are no short-run adjustment costs or market failures. The authors argue that emigration reduces the welfare of the remaining people only under rare circumstances. Indeed, a good case can be made for the proposition that highly skilled emigrants tend to increase the welfare of their own countrymen. The authors conclude that a good case can be made for the free movement of human capital throughout the world. The paper is followed by a discussion.

17. MARTIN, LEE R. "Research Needed on the Contribution of Human, Social and Community Capital to Economic Growth." *Journal of Farm Economics,* Vol. 45, No. 1 (February, 1963), pp. 73-94.

Headings: Introduction; Evidence on the importance of other sources of economic growth; Human, social and community capital; Functional relations among capital concepts; Research problems; References (55).

Abstract: The author cites evidence that suggests the inadequacy of conventional explanations of economic growth. He defines the unconventional inputs as human, social, and community capital, resulting from investment in human beings, research, and facilities and organizations producing public services. The nature of the relations among the various influences on the aggregate capacity to produce is outlined, and the problems of estimating returns and costs for the unconventional inputs are discussed. This paper, with its extended list of references, provides a survey of the literature in this field and suggests the future course of research.

18. MILLER, HERMAN P. "Lifetime Income and Economic Growth." *American Economic Review,* Vol. 55, No. 4 (September, 1965), pp. 834-844.

Headings: Introduction; Shortcomings of cross-section estimates; Differential impact of economic growth on age groups; Graphic presentation of cohort and cross-section data; Summary of components of income change by age groups; References (3).

Abstract: Estimations of lifetime income based on cross-section surveys tend to produce underestimates because of the failure to take future growth into account. Estimates based on cohort analysis produce quite different results: the differences in real income for a given age cohort in two successive decennial censuses are far greater than those obtained for individuals in those age groups at the same point of time; in addition, the impact of growth appears to be greater for young men than for those past the prime working years. To illustrate his argument the author includes two extensive tables in the paper: table 1 gives the change in mean income for selected cohorts of males, by years of school completed, colour, and region for the United States, 1949 and 1959; table 2 gives the components of change in mean income for selected cohorts of males, by colour and years of school completed for the United States, 1949 and 1959. Table 2 demonstrates that the impact of economic growth is greater for younger men, and greater for nonwhites than for whites.

19. MINCER, JACOB. "Investment In Human Capital and Personal Income Distribution." *Journal of Political Economy,* Vol. 66, No. 4 (August, 1958), pp. 281-302.

Headings: Introduction; A simple model; Extension of the model; Implications; Theoretical concepts and their empirical counterparts; Life paths of income; Aggregative skewness; Age and income dispersion; Education and income dispersion; Occupation and income dispersion; Mixed component groups; Distributions by industry; Color, sex, family status and city size; Summary.

Abstract: The author uses the concept of human capital in a model intended to account for the observed skewness of the distribution of earnings. The assumption of rational choice of occupation implies an equalization of present values of life earnings at the time of choice. Since interoccupational differentials are a function of differences in length of training, the distribution of earnings must be positively skewed if the present values of lifetime earnings are to be equalized. Intraoccupational differences reflect the growth of experience and productivity with age: the increases in productivity are more pronounced in jobs requiring greater amounts of training. Incorporation of the positive relation between investment in human capital and the growth in productivity into the model increases interoccupational differences and makes vertical occupational groupings exhibit a positive correlation between income levels and income dispersion. Income dispersion in training and age "mixes" is positively related to the average amount of human investment they contain.

20. REDER, M. W. "Gary Becker's 'Human Capital': A Review Article." *Journal of Human Resources,* Vol. 2, No. 1 (Winter, 1967), pp. 97-104.

Abstract: The basic idea of human capital is that a human agent of production is produced by an application of productive resources to "raw labour". Because the training process takes time to complete and because its benefits accrue over a considerable time period, the value of the resources used in training may be considered as investment and the resulting increment in earnings power may be treated as its yield. A primary objective of Becker's (4)

11

theoretical analysis is to explain the determinants of the rate of return to human capital. Becker argues that the return on investment in skills and other knowledge is determined by absolute wage differences. The present author points out that the rate of return to human capital depends upon the relation of the wage of trained labour to the prices of *all* inputs used in its production, and not to that of untrained labour alone. Becker concentrates exclusively upon equilibrium positions. This causes difficulty in the analysis of specific training: even in equilibrium an employee can, by quitting, impose a loss on the employer of his share of the return to training; but the employer can, by discharge, impose a similar loss on the employee. There is, therefore, a zone of bargaining not explored by Becker. In estimating the rates of return from college education Becker recognizes that some of what appears to be a return on investment may actually be a return to superior ability. It is also possible that the earning advantage of college graduates over others reflects the prejudices of employers as well as enhanced productivity. If this is the case, part of the private return to college training involves a transfer payment. A final suggestion is that Becker might have given more extensive treatment to the concept of vintages of human capital.

21. SCHULTZ, THEODORE W. "Investment in Man: An Economist's View." *Social Service Review,* Vol. 33, No. 2 (June, 1959), pp. 109-117.

Headings: Introduction; The neglect of the study of human wealth; The omission of human wealth by economists; New economic horizons; Puzzles and a paradox; A human wealth hypothesis.

Abstract: The main stream of modern economics bypassed undertaking any systematic analysis of human wealth. The influence of the classical economists encouraged the tripartite treatment of factors of production as land, labour and capital. It was convenient to treat labour as a homogeneous input, free of any capital components. In addition, economists have restricted their definition of capital to include only those classes of wealth which are bought and sold in the market place. Once it is recognized that investments in man play an important role in economic development, underdeveloped countries may decide to allocate more of their resources to human capital as opposed to physical capital formation. Human capital may be the key to the explanation of Goldsmith's declining capital/income ratios for the U.S. in the twentieth century, and to the explanation of the Leontief paradox. The author advances the hypothesis that a rapid accumulation of human wealth explains a rate of growth of the U.S. economy three times as large as the rate of increase of labour and capital.

22. SCHULTZ, THEODORE W. "Investment in Human Capital." *American Economic Review,* Vol. 51, No. 1 (March, 1961), pp. 1-17.

Headings: Introduction; Shying away from investment in man; Economic growth from human capital; Scope and substance of these investments; A concluding note on policy; References (21).

Abstract: The author begins by explaining why most economists have avoided the explicit analysis of investment in human capital. Once human investment is taken into account, a number of questions about our economy are resolved: for example, the problems of wage differentials, migration, the decreasing reproducible capital/income ratio, the apparent faster growth of national income than of national resources, the large increases in the real earnings of workers, the post-war recovery of countries devastated by war, and the slow development of backward countries. Some examples of human investments are investment in health, on-the-job training, formal education, institutional training, and migration. The policy implications resulting from the recognition of the importance of human capital extend to such areas as taxation, unemployment, discrimination, the capital market, internal migration, poverty, costs and returns of human investments, and developing countries.

23. SCHULTZ, THEODORE W. "Reflections on Investment in Man." *Journal of Political Economy,* Vol. 70, No. 5, Part 2 (October, 1962, Supplement), pp. 1-8.

Abstract: The article provides an introduction to a number of papers concerned with investment in human resources in the October 1962 supplement to this Journal The author proposes three hypotheses: economic growth which is not explained by an increase in physical inputs is due mainly to the rise in the stock of human capital; earnings differentials are explained mainly by differences in the amounts of human capital invested in people; the increase in the ratio of human to non-human capital is the basic factor reducing inequality of income. He argues that the findings of the various papers support these hypotheses.

24. SHAFFER, HARRY G. "Investment in Human Capital: Comment." *American Economic Review,* Vol. 51, No. 5 (December, 1961), pp. 1026-1039.

Headings: Introduction; Education: consumption expenditure or investment; Education and income; Public policy in relation to expenditure on education; Expenditures on human beings other than for education; Conclusions; References (21); Reply by T. W. Schultz; References (7).

Abstract: The author prefers to regard education as a consumption good rather than as an investment good. He argues that it is not possible to show that income differentials result from differences in levels of education because of other factors which are correlated with education and with income. Such factors are intelligence, connections, residence, occupational and cultural level of parents, and health. The author questions whether any estimate of the return on investment in humans can be made. He concludes that the capital concept should not be applied to man. In his reply, Schultz defends the concept of human capital and its use in policy-making.

25. SINGER, H. W. "The Notion of Human Investment." *Review of Sociol Economy,* Vol. 24, No. 1 (March, 1966), pp. 1-14.

Abstract: Social and human factors are pre-conditions for economic development, and economic development is a pre-condition for social and human development. Experience and research has shown that a large part of economic progress can be attributed to the human factor — better quality of labour, better education, better training, more knowledge, better housing, better nutrition, and better organization. The author identifies a succession of models characteristic of the different modes of approach to economic and social growth: the classical puritan model; the Keynesian model; the human investment model; and, lastly, the model we need today — one of growth plus change, social, cultural and economic change, and qualitative as well as quantitative change. In addition to the interdependence of economic and social factors, social development has a dynamism of its own as evidenced by the strong intracorrelations among social factors.

26. WEISBROD, BURTON A. "The Valuation of Human Capital." *Journal of Political Economy,* Vol. 69, No. 5 (October, 1961), pp. 425-436.

Headings: Introduction; Estimating the present value of a man; Productivity, consumption, and the discount rate; Estimates of capital values.

Abstract: Assessment of various public policies would be enhanced by knowledge of the value to society of the capital preserved or created through public expenditures. The "value" of a person is defined as the value of his expected future productivity, i.e., as his discounted expected future earnings stream, gross or net of consumption depending upon whether or not society is defined to include the individual in question. Present value figures (gross and net) are developed for U.S. males of different age groups from data on money earnings, labour force participation rates, mortality rates, and consumption. Discount rates of 4 per cent and 10 per cent are employed to provide an indication of the sensitivity of the results to the interest rate chosen. The overall life pattern of the capital values of males in the U.S. is outlined: the "value" of a male in the U.S. is at a maximum around the age of thirty years. The author concludes by exploring some of the policy implications of these results.

27. WEISBROD, BURTON A. "Investing in Human Capital." *Journal of Human Resources,* Vol. 1, No. 1 (Summer, 1966), pp. 5-21.

Headings: Introduction; Health as an investment; Education as an investment; Public policy for educational investment in human capital; Conclusion.

Abstract: The diffusion of benefits from investments in health and education is so diverse and complex that it raises important issues as to how such investments should be financed. It is suggested that government has the responsibility of ensuring that people are fully informed about the long-run benefits from investments in education and health. Government should also help to overcome limitations in the private capital market through financial measures which facilitate investment in people. Thirdly, the government should assume responsibility for expanding investment in human capital until marginal social costs equal marginal social benefits. Reconsideration of tax policy would help to redress the imbalance between investment in physical assets and investment in human capital.

28. ZUCKER, ALBERT. "A Note on the Declining Tendency with Age for Investment in Human Capital." *Journal of Human Resources,* Vol. 2, No. 4 (Fall, 1967), pp. 538-540.

Abstract: This paper calculates a measure of riskiness, resulting from mortality factors, in a simple model of human investment. From the model, investment risk is observed to start to rise rapidly at the age of forty. This theoretical conclusion appears to be supported by Mincer's observation (313) that investment in training tends to cease around age forty.

2. THEORY and APPLICATION of COST-BENEFIT ANALYSIS

29. ALCHIAN, ARMEN A. "Cost-Effectiveness of Cost-Effectiveness." In *Defense Management,* edited by Stephen Enke, pp. 74-86. Englewood Cliffs: Prentice-Hall, 1967.

Headings: Introduction; Cost-effectiveness concept; Defects of old system; Obstacles to effectiveness of cost-effectiveness; Effectiveness of cost-effectiveness; Related readings (7).

Abstract: Cost-effectiveness studies under the old system of defense management had a number of correctible faults: the wrong span of costs of a weapon system was used; decisions were made independently about interdependent or component parts of a system; incremental gains and costs tended to be disregarded. In addition, the absence of a market and of private-property rights in the resources being allocated limits the effectiveness of cost-effectiveness analysis. It is suggested that program-budgeting introduces a reward-incentive system which, coupled with centralized control, compensates for the absence of market criteria. Program budgeting aids program definition, helps in the distribution of costs among program elements, and overcomes uncertainty about objectives. An increasing proportion of non-defense government activities will be submitted to cost-effectiveness evaluations.

30. ARROW, KENNETH J. "Criteria For Social Investment." *Water Resources Research,* Vol. 1, No. 1 (1965), pp. 1-8.

Headings: Introduction; Remarks on investment in general; The special category of social investment; Problems in the measurement of benefits; The rate of discount; The measurement of costs.

Abstract: The paper presents an elementary exposition of choice criteria for social investment. It is pointed out that an overall optimum for the economy requires that the discount of future benefits according to opportunity costs equal their discount according to time preference. Social investment is placed in a special category because its benefits are usually inappropriable and it is often subject to increasing returns. The author discusses a number of problems in the measurement of benefits: the uses and limitations of market prices; divergence between social and private benefits; shadow pricing; economies of scale and consumers' surplus; and production and consumption benefits. He expands his remarks on the rate of discount, and concludes by examining the measurement of costs. The two main difficulties in the analysis of costs are the existence of unemployed resources and of divergencies between social and private costs.

31. BAIN, JOE S. "Criteria for Undertaking Water-Resource Developments." *American Economic Review,* Papers and Proceedings, Vol. 50, No. 2 (May, 1960), pp. 310-320.

Headings: Introduction; The general investment criterion; The interest rate to be used; Intangible benefits and project design.

Abstract: Two investment criteria are examined, one of which aims at maximizing the ratio of discounted net benefits to given capital outlays, while the other aims at maximizing the ratio of gross benefits to all costs, both capital and operating. The author expresses a preference for the latter criterion. He outlines the difficulties attached to calculating the social rate of time preference, and suggests the social cost of governmental funds as a conservative approximation. The two investment criteria described can determine optimal project timing by choosing among mutually exclusive starting dates for a given project. It is suggested that the procedures adopted with respect to intangible benefits produce an unduly commercial bias. Project design is frequently biased by initial assumptions concerning the absolute and relative prices to be charged to recipients of various sorts of benefit. Although the paper is concerned with water-resource development projects, its principles have general application.

32. BAUMOL, WILLIAM J. *Welfare Economics and the Theory of the State.* 2nd ed. Cambridge, Mass.: Harvard University Press, 1965. x + 212 p.

Headings: Welfare and the state revisited: an introduction to the second edition; References (55); The extension of the external economies argument; Towards an economic theory of the state.

Abstract: The introduction surveys the theory of welfare economics and its application. The remainder of the book attempts to determine the circumstances in which a particular extension of government authority is necessary for the most efficient pursuit of the economic interests of the individuals comprising the economy. Baumol's economic theory of the state is based on the principle of external economies, using the assumption of relative rationality implemented by sufficient information for the formation of economic decisions. His conclusion is that unless we can measure the magnitude and effects of external economies, we cannot give objective advice on specific problems. The category of "external economies" tends to limit the application of welfare economics.

33. BRECKNER, NORMAN V., and JOSEPH W. NOAH. "Costing of Systems." In *Defense Management,* edited by Stephen Enke, pp. 42-59. Englewood Cliffs: Prentice-Hall, 1967.

Headings: Introduction; The role of cost; Synthesis of system costs; Topics in cost estimation; Some avenues for further work.

Abstract: In a nonmarket activity, such as defense, the various levels of achievement within a mission are not readily represented by dollar magnitudes. For this reason, the specified cost procedure is often used; this involves comparison of the effectiveness of two systems of equal cost. The comparison of nonmarketable projects also raises problems with respect to the application of a discount rate. The authors feel that there are two main types of decisions in which systems analyses assist: force-structure procurement and development planning. The following topics related to these decisions are outlined: the use of historical data, cost-quantity relationships, estimating procedures, early estimates for advanced systems, and sensitivity of results. It is suggested that further research is required on evaluating "support" activities, on spillovers, and on the problem of pricing resources whose observed prices are imperfect reflections of true alternative costs.

34. BROOKINGS INSTITUTION. *Applying Benefit-Cost Analysis to Public Programs.* Brookings Research Report No. 79. Washington, 1968. 8 p.

Headings: Introduction; Shadow prices and benefit-cost analysis; Evaluating travel time; Evaluating the reduced risk of death; The distributive effects of the cotton program; Conclusion.

Abstract: This report outlines the highlights of *Problems in Public Expenditure Analysis,* edited by Samuel B. Chase Jr. The five papers represent attempts to improve the state of benefit-cost analysis through conceptual refinement and through advancement in analytical technique. In the first paper Roland N. McKean (94) considers the use of imputed prices rather than market prices to measure benefits from government programs. James R. Nelson discusses methods of evaluating programs which reduce travel time, while T. C. Schelling (365) looks at ways of evaluating programs which reduce the risk of death. Burton A. Weisbrod (110) suggests that it may be possible to evaluate simultaneously both the efficiency and the distributive effects of public programs. James T. Bonnen identifies the distribution of benefits from the cotton price support program; his results indicate that this program is an inefficient method of supplementing low farm incomes.

17

35. CIRIACY-WANTRUP, S. V. "Benefit-Cost Analysis and Public Resource Development." *Journal of Farm Economics,* Vol. 37, No. 4 (November, 1955), pp. 677-689.

Headings: A crucial question; Abuse of benefit-cost analysis; Quantifying in benefit-cost analysis; Extramarket benefits and costs; Primary (direct) and secondary (indirect) benefits and costs; Secondary benefits "stemming from" a public project; Secondary benefits "induced by" a public project; Conclusions.

Abstract: The paper deals with the public policy aspects of benefit-cost analysis. The author favours the use of benefit-cost analysis as a guide to public investment in resource development for two main reasons: it is likely to restrain the abuse of economic arguments in the political process, and it may provide a stimulus to research and scientific understanding. The problems of accommodating intangible and indirect benefits and costs in the cost-benefit framework are discussed. It is suggested that intangibles such as recreational opportunities can be evaluated through indirect use of market data. Most indirect or secondary benefits and costs are evaluated directly in the market place; it is not, however, evident as to what extent they should be considered and added to direct benefits and costs. The author examines secondary benefits and costs "stemming from" a public project and those benefits "induced by" a project. In the light of his analysis, and in view of the two main reasons advanced in favour of benefit-cost analysis as a guide to public policy, he feels that all classes of secondary net benefits should be dropped from consideration if the problem area is project selection.

36. ECKSTEIN, OTTO. *Water Resource Development.* Cambridge, Mass.: Harvard University Press, 1958. xiii + 300 p.

Headings: Introduction; The theoretical basis of benefit-cost calculations; The benefit-cost criterion; The benefit-cost criterion, continued; Flood control; Navigation; Irrigation; Electric power; The allocation of joint costs; Conclusion; Bibliography (134).

Abstract: The author outlines the theory of cost-benefit analysis in his first four chapters, and examines its application to specific problems in water resource development in the latter part of the book. The problem of obtaining figures for benefits and costs is discussed against the background of welfare economics and the theory of perfect competition. The data on benefits and costs must be organized into some specific form which can serve as an investment criterion. Three possible criteria are: a comparison of benefits and costs; a comparison of rate of return on investment; and the ratio of benefits to costs. The first of these is rejected while the other two are examined and contrasted, and the benefit/cost ratio is selected as the investment criterion. Before this criterion can be applied, adjustments for risk and depreciation must be made, an interest rate which reflects social time preference and the opportunity cost of capital must be selected, and the appropriate

18

prices and period of analysis must be chosen. Although the author applies his cost-benefit analysis framework to water projects, it has general application in the field of investment appraisal.

37.   ECKSTEIN, OTTO. "A Survey of the Theory of Public Expenditure Criteria." In *Public Finances: Needs, Sources, and Utilization,* edited by James M. Buchanan, pp. 439-504. Princeton: Princeton University Press, 1961.

Headings: Introduction; The objective function; The constraints; Interest rates; Repercussion effects; The treatment of risk and uncertainty; A survey of some recent models; Concluding comments; Comment by Jack Hirshleifer; Comment by Benjamin Toren; Reply by Mr. Eckstein.

Abstract: This paper presents the elements of the theory of public expenditure: attention is largely confined to the evaluation of public works and development projects of a sort for which measures of value can be established empirically. The most fundamental consideration in a decision model is the choice of an objective function. The author suggests that the economist should interpret the desires of the policy people whom he is serving and express them in an analytical form as an objective function. He should then seek to maximize this function, given the empirical relations in the economy and the institutional constraints that may be appropriate to the analysis. Since the objective function must be suited to the problem at hand and must often be multiple in nature, the definition of benefits is a relative matter. The objective function is usually maximized under constraints which the economist is required to build into his analysis; the author distinguishes physical, legal, administrative, distributional, uncertainty, and financial or budget constraints. The choice of the interest rate for valuing outputs accruing at different points in time is a particularly difficult problem in the specification of an objective function and is examined in detail. In perfect competition there is no need to pursue the repercussions of any action beyond the most immediate market. Because the real world is not perfectly competitive, some repercussions must be pursued, and various categories of these are listed. In the real world some cognizance must be taken of risk and uncertainty and the author evaluates various methods of adjusting for these imperfections. The paper concludes with a survey of recent models for evaluating public expenditures. The authors of the work included in the survey are The Federal Inter-Agency River Basin Committee, Eckstein, Krutilla and Eckstein (147), McKean (50), Steiner (60), Tinbergen, Chenery, Galenson and Leibenstein, and Sen.

38.   FEDKIW, JOHN, and HOWARD W. HJORT. "The PPB Approach to Research Evaluation." *Journal of Farm Economics,* Vol. 49, No. 5 (December, 1967), pp. 1426-1436.

Headings: Introduction; Research in the USDA PPB structure; Research programming and RPDES; Current research information system (CRIS);

Evaluation of research alternatives; Research evaluation in PPB; Method of evaluation; Experience with results; Discussion: the PPB approach to research evaluation, by Willis L. Peterson.

Abstract: The paper begins by describing the U.S. Department of Agriculture's PPB system. Under this system each of the 91 research problem areas identified by a Long Range Study is assigned for programming and evaluation to one of 32 PPB research program elements. The Long Range Study developed a set of eight weighted criteria for use in judging the relative importance of research programs. The key to evaluation of research alternatives for planning and programming purposes, however, lies in the area of estimating benefits. Consequently, benefit-cost analysis promises to have wide applicability to research evaluation. The presence of uncertainty on both the benefit and cost side indicates that sensitivity testing of the benefit-cost ratio is required; in addition, subjective estimates of the probability of success for each project may be included. Where there are factors which are not accounted for in the benefit-cost calculation, additional constraints can be applied.

39. FISHER, G. H. *The World of Program Budgeting.* Santa Monica: The Rand Corporation, May, 1966. 30 p.

Headings: Introduction; A Department of Defense example; The major characteristics of a program budgeting system; Another format example: transportation; The role of analysis in program budgeting; Some examples; Considerations and problems in implementing a program budgeting system; Concluding remark; Selected bibliography (20).

Abstract: The primary considerations involved in program budgeting are as follows: structural aspects concerned with establishing a program and program element structure oriented toward "end-objective" activities that are meaningful from a long-range planning point of view; an analytical process that enables alternative courses of action to be examined systematically in terms of utility and cost; and, thirdly, an information system aimed at support of the first two items. The most important analytical approach used to support the program budgeting decision process is cost-utility analysis. Some important guidelines to be followed in carrying out this kind of analysis are presented. Some areas of possible application are identified, and some of the considerations and problems involved in implementing such a system are discussed.

40. GROSSE, ROBERT N. *An Introduction to Cost-Effectiveness Analysis.* McLean: Research Analysis Corporation, July, 1965. v + 27 p.

Abstract: This paper discusses the use of economic analysis as a conceptual framework in assisting military planners and decision-makers. The primary ingredients of cost-effectiveness analyses or systems analyses are: objectives; alternative means or systems; costs or resources required by each system; a set of relations among the objectives, alternative means, environment, and resources; and a criterion for choosing the preferred alternatives. The exposition consists of a series of thirty diagrams which illustrate the construction of cost/effectiveness curves from equal effectiveness curves (or isoquants) and budget lines. The paper concludes with examples of the models used to estimate effectiveness, initial investment costs, and operating costs.

41. GROSSE, ROBERT N., and ARNOLD PROSCHAN. "The Annual Cycle: Planning-Programming-Budgeting." In *Defense Management,* edited by Stephen Enke, pp. 23-41. Englewood Cliffs: Prentice-Hall, 1967.

Headings: Introduction; The defense budgetary process before 1961; The budget system and resource allocation; Department of Defense programming system: 1961-1965; Department of Defense program/budget system: 1966-; Prospects; Bibliography (8).

Abstract: The PPB system installed in the U.S. Department of Defence in 1961 established a five-year planning structure and process to guide the formulation of annual budgets. This structure classifies the entire scope of Defense activity into individual program elements (nearly 1,000 in all), grouped into major programs such as strategic forces and tactical forces. An imporatnt part of the planning process is the performance of systems or cost-effectiveness analysis. This analysis involves defining objectives, calculating how effectively each alternative accomplishes a given objective, and computing the cost of each alternative. The paper concludes by describing the restructuring of the system undertaken in 1966.

42. HAMMOND, RICHARD J. "Convention and Limitation in Benefit-Cost Analysis." *Natural Resources Journal,* Vol. 6, No. 2 (April, 1966), pp. 195-222.

Headings: Benefit-cost analysis as an administrative device; Contradictory doctrines of benefit maximization; The debilitating assumption of perfect foresight; The indispensability of policy presuppositions; The inherent limitations of benefit-cost procedures; Conclusion.

Abstract: The report of the U.S. Federal Inter-Agency River Basin Committee's Sub-Committee on Benefits and Costs (the "Green Book") published in 1950 has shaped official thinking on public project evaluation. The most influential error in the Green Book was the criterion of maximizing net benefits: if this criterion is applied it is impossible to choose on economic grounds between projects having identical net benefits and differing costs. The use of benefit-cost ratios, on the other hand, would give the correct answer. The criterion for government should be that employed by the ordinary investor — to seek the maximum return on investment. Benefit-cost analysis depends at every point on judgement in the choice of assumptions. It is assumed that future benefits and costs can be predicted with certainty. Assumptions are made about "national secondary benefits". Perfect foresight and perfect competition are assumed when the market price of resources is

21

used as a measure of the opportunity cost of a project: under those assumptions the opportunity cost (or forgone benefits) would also measure the benefits from the project under evaluation, and benefit-cost analysis would be futile. We may adopt the benefit-cost ratio as a basis of comparison among projects in the belief that the prospect of error in all instances is broadly identical. Since the prospect of error is high, however, fine distinctions should not be drawn between projects solely on the basis of the benefit-cost ratio. Because benefit-cost analysis involves so much judgement in the choice of assumptions, it is really a creature of policy. To treat it as a determinant of policy is to argue in a circle. Many critics of benefit-cost procedures — for example, those who advocate the use of "opportunity cost" interest rates in discounting costs and benefits — are really putting forward policy proposals in the guise of changes in analytical technique. There is a temptation to substitute supposedly impersonal calculation for personal responsible decision, and to rely on the expert rather than the administrator. Benefit-cost analysis made its first appearance as an administrative tool and it ought to be judged by its contribution to the administration of public funds. A benefit-cost analysis of benefit-cost analysis is called for.

43. HELMER, OLAF. *The Application of Cost-Effectiveness to Non-Military Government Problems.* Santa Monica: The Rand Corporation, September 1966. 21 p.

Headings: Introduction; Mandatory allocations; Programs; Nomination and aggregation; Reasonable adoption bounds; Costs; Benefits; Composition of the First-Approximation Program; Refinement of the Program; The use of panels of experts.

Abstract: The author believes that panels of experts should be used to ascribe costs and benefits to proposed program measures. For each measure, value is represented as a function of cost on a two-dimensional diagram. A ray from the origin is used to help select the degree to which each measure should be adopted: all points above the ray have a larger benefit/cost ratio than those below. The nature of the entire program, which is composed of a number of measures, is determined by an iterative procedure. Since the reliance on expert judgement is an indispensable part of budgetary planning, the author believes that the use of experts should be institutionalized. He outlines an anonymous debating procedure aimed at contriving an eventual group position.

44. HEYMONT, I., O. BRYK, H. LINSTONE, and J. SURMEIER. *Guide for Reviewers of Studies Containing Cost-Effectiveness Analysis.* McLean: Research Analysis Corporation, 1965. v + 67 p.

Headings: Foreword; General background; Key questions; Glossary; Selected questions; Bibliography (13).

Abstract: This book provides a general introduction to the use of cost-effectiveness studies in military decision-making. It contains a list of 73 key questions grouped under the following headings: statement of the problem; assumptions; alternatives; documentation; cost; relationships (models); effectiveness; criteria; and conclusions and recommendations. Those questions which are considered to be of particular importance in evaluating a cost-effectiveness analysis are listed as selected questions (fifteen in all) and are underlined in the text. The book serves as an elementary text as well as providing a practical manual.

45. HINES, LAWRENCE G.. "The Hazards of Benefit-Cost Analysis as a Guide to Public Investment Policy." *Public Finance,* Vol. 17 (1962), pp. 101-117.

Headings: Introduction; The mechanics of benefit-cost analysis; The comparability of private and public costs; The limitations of market data as criteria for public investment.

Abstract: It is pointed out that the problem of resource allocation assumes greater significance in the present-day context of full employment and rising prices than it did during the expansion of the public sector in the 1930's. The paper considers the implications of the implementation of a report submitted by a sub-committee of the U.S. Federal Inter-Agency River Basin Committee in 1950 (reissued 1958), entitled "Proposed Practices for the Economic Analysis of River Basin Projects". Among the questions considered are the nature of benefits, the appropriate interest rate, the period of analysis, the treatment of taxes, and the ability of the market system to reflect and achieve certain objectives. The limitations of benefit-cost analyses are discussed and the author concludes that benefit-cost analysis must be confined to a sub-optimizing role.

46. HIRSHLEIFER, JACK, JAMES C. DeHAVEN, and JEROME W. MILLIMAN. *Water Supply, Economics, Technology and Policy.* Chicago: University of Chicago Press, 1960. xii + 378 p.

Headings: The water problem; Our water resources: the present picture; The economics of utilization of existing water supplies; Criticisms of market allocations: the political allocation process; Municipal water rates; Investment in additional water supplies; The practical logic of investment efficiency calculations; Technological features and costs of alternative supplies of water; Water law: Government discretion or property rights ?; New York's "water crisis": a case study of a crucial decision; Water for Southern California: a case study of an arid region; Some controversial conclusions and their implications.

Abstract: The authors point out that much of the analytical attention paid to the technology and economics of water supply has been directed to the problem of developing additional water supplies and not to the question of whether existing supplies are being well utilized. The economic theory which should govern the allocation of water supplies is outlined, and it is suggested that marginal-cost pricing is the appropriate principle for determining the level and structure of water rates. The following aspects of the theory of investment decision, which has general relevance, are discussed: intertemporal economic decision; extra-financial considerations in the cost-benefit calculation; intangible effects; the investment criterion; risk; taxes; inflation; and the discount rate. A chapter is devoted to the practical details of computing an economic solution for investment decisions. The remainder of the book is concerned with other aspects of water supply.

47. KRUTILLA, JOHN V. "Welfare Aspects of Benefit-Cost Analysis." *Journal of Political Economy.* Vol. 69, No. 3 (June, 1961), pp. 226-235.

Headings: Introduction; Initial conditions and side effects; Implications of redistributive effects for the measurement of welfare; The welfare status of the status quo; Welfare implications of non-optimal initial conditions of production and exchange; Conclusions for practical choices "in the public interest"; References (39).

Abstract: The introduction defines benefit-cost analysis and places it in the perspective of welfare economics. Three main problems are studied. The problem of assessing the welfare implication of changes in income distribution is considered in the light of the Kaldor-Hicks-Scitovsky-Samuelson criteria. Secondly, the problem of using the prevailing income distribution as a yardstick is examined with particular reference to the work of Samuelson and Little. Thirdly, the fact that a Pareto optimum may only be approximated in practice makes market prices unreliable as indicators of opportunity cost. This raises problems of the second best. The conclusion is that although benefit-cost analysis is not free from distribuitonal value judgements and other theoretical problems, it is useful to the policy maker as a "perforated rationale".

48. MARGLIN, STEPHEN A. *Public Investment Criteria: Benefit-Cost Analysis for Planned Economic Growth.* Cambridge, Mass.: The M.I.T. Press, 1967. 103 p.

Headings: Introduction; A capsule history of benefit-cost analysis; Benefit-cost analysis in a planned economy; Objectives; Benefits; Costs; Time and interest; Budgetary constraints; Risk and Uncertainty; Dynamics; Secondary benefits; Private alternatives and alternative costs; Pricing policy for public enterprise; A selective summary; References (30).

Abstract: The author describes benefit-cost analysis as a tactical rather than a strategic weapon in economic development. For benefit-cost analysis to fulfil this role, economic planning must proceed through successive stages of setting objectives, allocating resources among sectors, and deriving criteria for designing individual projects. The goal of project design is the maximization of net benefits under constraints. The meaning of the terms "benefits" and "costs" depends upon the program's objectives. The problem of comparing benefits with respect to different objectives is similar to the problem of comparing benefits in different years: in both cases we use weights; in the latter case the discount rate is the weighting system. The marginal internal rate of return in the private sector is not an appropriate rate of discount for the public sector because there exists no market by means of which the economy, as opposed to the individual Fisherian investor, can divorce the decisions of choosing an investment program and distributing consumption over time. A value judgement about the intertemporal distribution of benefits must be incorporated into the investment criteria. While the present value criterion is recommended for intertemporal comparisons, it can lead to errors in the timing of projects when benefit rates increase over time. The author puts forward a criterion which can be applied in a fairly wide variety of such cases. Risk aversion is not necessarily the appropriate attitude for a government: the government should concentrate on expected values instead of worrying about the dispersion of outcomes. Secondary benefits are defined separately for each objective as indirect contributions not reflected in the direct consumption of goods and services produced by public enterprises. The discussion of specific criteria concludes with an outline of the principles of pricing decisions for public enterprise. Throughout the book the author illustrates his remarks with examples drawn from his experiences in Indian economic planning.

49. McCULLOUGH, J. D. *Cost Analysis for Planning-Programming-Budgeting Cost-Benefit Studies.* Santa Monica: The Rand Corporation, 1966. 64 p.

Headings: Introduction; The role of cost-benefit analysis; The role of cost in cost-benefit analysis; Features of systems cost analysis; Steps of cost analysis; Concluding remarks; Appendix — costing guidelines for Department of Defense cost-effectiveness studies; References (20).

Abstract: The author, a military systems cost analyst, presents a hypothetical cost analysis in the field of education in order to illustrate the techniques of cost-benefit analysis employed by the U.S. Department of Defense, and to explore the possibility of applying such techniques in non-defense agencies. He describes the role of cost analysis in support of cost-benefit studies, and examines the appraisal both of individual competing systems and of total programs. The study also deals with the problem of organizing a planning-programming-budgeting system.

50. McKEAN, ROLAND N. *Efficiency in Government Through Systems Analysis.* New York: John Wiley & Sons, 1958. x + 336 p.

Headings: Introduction; Some general problems of analysis; Special problems in the analysis of water-resource projects; The problems as illustrated by specific analyses; Other potential uses of analysis to increase governmental efficiency; Appendix on possible classifications of expenditures by programs, and indicators of performance; Bibliography (97).

Abstract: The study begins by examining some methodological problems common to the analysis of various kinds of alternative actions. Attention is given to the devising of criteria or tests of preferredness, the selection of the alternatives to be compared, the treatment of intangibles and uncertainty, and methods of taking time streams into account. Some special problems in the analysis of water-resource problems are discussed: the choice of criteria, spillover effects, secondary benefits, and the valuation of benefits. Two analyses of water-resource projects prepared by Federal agencies are used as case studies. These projects are the Green River Watershed (Kentucky and Tennessee), and the Santa Maria Project (California). Finally the study explores the potential use of cost-benefit analysis to increase efficiency in other government activities.

51. McKEAN, ROLAND N. "Remaining Difficulties in Program Budgeting." In *Defense Management*, edited by Stephen Enke, pp. 60-73. Englewood Cliffs: Prentice-Hall, 1967.

Headings: Introduction; Background; Shortcomings of program budgeting; Conclusions; Bibliography (9).

Abstract: Program budgeting stresses the full implications of choices when they are made, thus making it difficult for officials to start projects without calling attention to the full costs. The author is careful to point out the limitations of program budgeting: compartmentalization cannot illuminate all the relevant trade-offs and direct attention to all the important interdependencies; it is difficult to obtain accurate cost estimates, and the value of cost information may be fairly low if information about effectiveness is limited. Another criticism of the system concerns the possible deleterious effects of centralization. It is emphasized that program budgeting is no panacea.

52. MOOD, ALEX M. "Diversification of Operations Research." *Operations Research*, Vol. 13, No. 2 (March-April, 1965), pp. 169-178.

Headings: Introduction; Education; Health; Welfare; Agriculture; Urban affairs; To get started.

Abstract: The author outlines important areas in which operations analysis has the potential to make salient contributions. In the field of education, operations research may help us to determine what an education is worth, whether teaching machines should be introduced, which subjects should be included in curricula, and how vocational training programs should be designed. O.R. can be applied to the allocation of health budgets, the valuation of human life, and to expenditure on medical research. There is also scope for O.R. in designing welfare programs, allocating resources in agriculture, and in urban affairs such as fire prevention and traffic control.

53. MUSGRAVE RICHARD A. "Cost-Benefit Analysis and the Theory of Public Finance." *Journal of Economic Literature*, Vol. 7, No. 3 (September, 1969), pp. 797-806.

Headings: Introduction; Past approaches; Measuring benefits; Investment decisions; Allowing for distributional objectives; Conclusion; References (23).

Abstract: A theory of public finance remains unsatisfactory unless it comprises both the revenue and expenditure sides of the fiscal process. While the classical theory of "taxation-only" dealt with minimizing the costs of taxation without allowing for expenditure benefits, cost-benefit analysis by its very nature includes both the cost and benefit sides. All nonpecuniary benefits, whether internal, external, direct, indirect, tangible or intangible, should be included. In the case of final social goods, cost-benefit analysis is generally unable to solve the problem of evaluating benefits; an analysis based on arbitrary evaluation of final benefits may, nevertheless, be useful. In the case of intermediate social goods, such as education, that have a further output which is in the nature of a private good, market valuations may be used. The questions of the proper level of total investment and the proper mix between public and private investment are logically distinct. The analyst should use *two* policy instruments (equalization of the private rate of return with the social discount rate, and public investment) to achieve the proper level of total investment and the proper mix. Where capital markets are imperfect and the government uses the social rather than the private discount rate, the sources of finance should enter into the investment decision. Distributional considerations provide another instance where multiple targets are arrived at by use of a single instrument. The distributional and efficiency objectives should be separated: cost-benefit analysis can indicate the efficient investment while the distributional objectives can be satisfied by another instrument — transfer payments. There are some qualifications to this view. Revenue policy may enter cost-benefit analysis not only via its bearing on opportunity cost and the rate of discount but also through its distributional effects. The problem remains that the tax and expenditure sides of the budget continue to be determined independently.

54. NISKANEN, WILLIAM A. "The Defense Resource Allocation Process." In *Defense Management,* edited by Stephen Enke, pp. 3-22. Englewood Cliffs: Prentice-Hall, 1967.

Headings: Introduction; The defense program; The defense program — change process; Some problems and proposed solutions; Conclusion; Bibliography (5).

Abstract: This paper describes the establishment of the U.S. Defense Department's system of program control. The program-budget cycle is outlined and the three aspects of planning, programming, and budgeting are discussed. The author feels that there are three major problem areas — the problems of establishing priorities under a budget restraint, of overcentralization, and of resource pricing. The latter problem arises because the Department of Defense has access to several major resources at prices below full value, and in some cases pays more for resources than their value.

55. PEACOCK, ALAN T. "The Control and Appraisal of Public Investment in the United Kingdom." *Finanz Archiv,* Vol. 22 (1962 /63), pp. 79-91.

Headings: Introduction; The amount and composition of public investment; Investment by public corporation; Control of local authorities' investment; Central government capital expenditure; Some outstanding problems.

Abstract: The author mentions two of the most complex issues in cost-benefit analysis — the question of who should benefit by government decisions, and the problem of measuring costs and benefits. He emphasises the importance of public investment in the U.K., and suggests that closer scrutiny of the investment programs of public corporations and local authorities is evidence of more interest in the technical appraisal of investment programs. The difficulties inherent in the appraisal of public investment projects by means of cost-benefit analysis have important consequences for the methods of expenditure control. Since some benefits and costs are difficult to measure, and since some projects are not subjected to the test of the market, politics are given a fair amount of scope in determining the public investment program. The author advocates improvements in the method of presenting estimates to the parliamentary body, and better co-ordination of the different sectors comprising the executive.

56. PREST, A. R., and R. TURVEY. "Cost-Benefit Analysis: A Survey." *Economic Journal,* Vol. 75, No. 300 (December, 1965), pp. 683-735.

Headings: Introduction; Enumeration of costs and benefits; Valuation of costs and benefits; Choice of interest rate; Relevant constraints; Investment criteria and second best matters; Application to water projects; Application to transport projects; Application to land usage programs; Application to health programs; Application to investment in education; Application to other fields, e.g. defence, research and development; Conclusions; Bibliography (90).

Abstract: This article surveys a selection of the literature on the topics indicated by the chapter headings. Under the heading "Enumeration of costs and benefits" the authors examine the definition of a project, externalities, secondary benefits, and project life. Under "Valuation of costs and benefits" they examine studies relating to pricing problems, nonmarginal changes, market imperfection, taxes and controls, unemployment, collective goods and intangibles. The "Choice of interest rate" involves consideration of the social time preference rate, the social opportunity cost rate, the problem of uncertainty, the need for an interest rate, and some practical aspects. Constraints which must be taken into account by the analyst can be classified as physical, legal, distributional and budgetary. The other chapter headings are self-explanatory. The bibliography provides an extensive list of references to work in this field.

57. QUADE, E. S. *Systems Analysis Techniques for Planning-Programming-Budgeting.* Santa Monica: The Rand Corporation, 1966. 31 p.

Headings: Introduction; The essence of the method; The process of analysis; Principles of good anaylsis; The models; The virtues; The limitations; The future; Concluding remarks; References (17).

Abstract: The paper looks at the question of extending military systems analysis to the civilian activities of the government. It outlines the principles and methods of systems analysis which is described as an analytic study designed to help a decision-maker identify a preferred choice among possible alternatives. The use of scientific and, where possible, quantitative methods is stressed, and the role of the model is regarded as essential. The model forces the analyst to make explicit what elements of the situation he is considering, and thereby enables expert intuition and judgement to be applied efficiently. By providing the analytic framework for the plans, programs, and budgets of the various Government departments, systems analysis can help guide national policy.

58. SELIGMAN, DANIEL. "McNamara's Management Revolution." *Fortune,* Vol. 72, No. 1 (July, 1965), pp. 117-120 ff.

Headings: Introduction; A definition of the job; Lots of room at the top; The end of authority; The systems-analysis hop; How to get a defense budget; Looking through the funnel; When savers are heroes; What men are worth; The executive as reader; The spread of intelligence.

Abstract: Systems analysis is akin to operations research which is widely used in tackling complex business problems involving many variables. The "cost-effectiveness" calculation is made routinely by business, but the problem is more difficult in government because "effectiveness" cannot be measured in market terms and must be related to specific performance capabilities. The article provides a general description of the Defense Department's management system which is built on the cost-effectiveness concept. Planning-programming-budgeting techniques are being established in other government departments.

59. SEWELL, W. R. D., J. DAVIS, A. D. SCOTT, and D. W. ROSS. "Guide to Benefit-Cost Analysis." A paper prepared for the Resources For Tomorrow Conference, Montreal, October 23-28, 1961. 49 p.

Headings: Introduction; The benefit-cost analysis approach to project evaluation; Definition of terms; Principles of benefit-cost analysis; Dealing with some practical difficulties; Evaluation of benefits of selected project purposes; Steps in the analysis; A sample case; Joint or common costs; Bibliography (76).

Abstract: This survey outlines the general principles and procedure of benefit-cost analysis. Among the practical difficulties considered are the problems of pricing, project life, discount rate, secondary effects and intangibles, damages and compensation, employment, taxes, and conflicts between resource use. Procedures for evaluating benefits in the following areas are outlined: flood control; hydroelectric power; fisheries improvements or preservation; irrigation; domestic, municipal, and industrial water supply; navigation; recreation; and pollution abatement. The sample case relates to the economic merits of alternative hydroelectric projects. The section on joint costs describes the "Separable Costs — Remaining Benefits" method of accommodating common costs.

60. STEINER, PETER O. "Choosing Among Alternative Public Investments in the Water Resource Field." *American Economic Review,* Vol. 49, No. 5 (December, 1959), pp. 893-916.

Headings: Introduction; The model; Problems of solution; An application of the model; Methods of solution; Conclusion; Mathematical appendix; References (8).

Abstract: The policy of building every project for which benefits exceed costs, and developing every project to the point where marginal benefits equal marginal costs does not provide a satisfactory solution to the problem of resource allocation for four main reasons: firstly, the existence of budget constraints derived from other dimensions of public welfare; secondly, the technological and economic incompatibility of alternative projects; thirdly, the discretness of individual projects; and finally, the opportunity cost of the displacement of alternative private developments. A four sector model is developed, the objective function of which is the present value of the difference between total benefits (direct and indirect) and total costs in all sectors of the economy. Estimates for the opportunity cost of the given project in the public sector must be obtained for the other three sectors — the "slack activities" area of the public sector, the area embracing private alternatives to the public project, and the sector comprising marginal private opportunities. The author discusses the factors affecting the magnitude of these three parameters. The paper concludes with a simple application of the model: two methods of solution are discussed, an iterative method, and an algorithmic procedure which can be adapted to machine computation.

61. TOLLEY, G. S. "McKean on Government Efficiency." *Review of Economics and Statistics,* Vol. 41, No. 4 (November, 1959), pp. 446-448.

Abstract: This note argues that since there is an institutional restraint precluding internal investment of net receipts from most government expenditures, the ratio of present worth to investment cost may be superior, as a ranking device, to the internal rate of return. The internal rate of return criterion may discriminate against long-lived projects. The author suggests that McKean's book *Efficiency in Government through Systems Analysis* (50) should have concentrated on institutional impediments to efficiency and errors in the data and estimates used in appraising projects.

62.   TOLLEY, GEORGE S. and CLEON HARRELL, "Extensions of Benefit-Cost Analysis." *American Economic Review,* Papers and Proceedings, Vol. 52, No. 2 (May, 1962), pp. 459-473.

Headings: Introduction; What to do about fiction in economic evaluations; Irreplaceable assets; Time: interest rates, horizons, and interdependence; Conclusion; Discussion by Stephen A. Marglin and Jerome W. Milliman.

Abstract: The authors examine the problem of estimating project effects, using as an example a proposed irrigation scheme based on the Garrison Reservoir in North Dakota. The existence of slack in the economic system suggests that market valuations may overstate project costs and benefits. Overestimation tends to be greater in the short run than in the long run. An estimate of the value of agricultural production from a reclamation project is more easily obtainable than an estimate of the recreational enjoyment of a park because the latter has relatively poor substitutes. The problem of estimating the value of a National Park is considered on the assumption that the value of a good to a consumer is the area under his demand curve. A political solution to the problems of evaluating this kind of project is suggested as an alternative. The question of the appropriate discount rate is examined in relation to the rate of growth of national income.

63.   U.S. Bureau of the Budget. *Planning-Programming-Budgeting (PPB) System.* Bulletin No. 68-9. Washington, April, 1968.

Headings: Purpose and scope; Elements of the system; Major program issues; Program structure; The program memoranda; Special analytic studies; Program and financial plans; Timing and submission of PPB documents; Responsibility, staffing and training; Agencies to which this bulletin applies; Program and Financial Plan (PFP) guidance.

Abstract: This bulletin contains guidelines for the continued development of of integrated planning - programming - budgeting (PPB) systems in U.S. government. It also provides guidance on the preparation of program and financial plans (PFP's) which organize available program data in a way which is conducive to efficient decision-making. The need for more suitable and accurate program measures is stressed.

64.   U.S. Department of Labor, *Program Analysis Manual to Support a Planning-Programming-Budgeting System.* Prepared for the U.S. Department of Labor, Manpower Administration, Office of Manpower Policy, Evaluation and Research by the Planning Research Corporation, Los Angeles, California, and Washington, D.C. vii + 145 p.

Headings: Need for program analysis and relationship to PPB; Costs, benefits, and analytical techniques applicable to manpower programs; Information problems and presentation of results; Special studies in support of PPB.

Abstract: Planning-programming-budgeting (PPB) is an integrated management system incorporating various techniques of systems analysis employed by the U.S. Department of Defense in the choice of weapons systems. This type of analysis is usually called cost-effectiveness analysis; its object is to determine which program is most efficient in achieving a specific objective by relating the program's total costs to the anticipated effects. The effects may be measured in nonpecuniary terms. This manual provides the manpower analyst with a general guide to cost-effectiveness analysis. This approach can help him choose the appropriate level for a particular program, choose between alternative programs, and estimate the cost of various constraints upon the manpower program.

65.   U.S. Department of Labor. *Illustrative Cost-Goal Analysis in the U.S. Employment Service Area.* Prepared for the U.S. Department of Labor, Manpower Administration, Office of Manpower Policy, Evaluation and Research by the Planning Research Corporation, Los Angeles, California, and Washington, D.C. iv + 41 p.

Headings: Introduction; Summary; Background; A feasible evaluation design; Study results; Future research; Appendices.

Abstract: This study illustrates the use of cost-goal analysis (as described in the Planning Research Corporation's *Program Analysis Manual to Support a Planning-Programming-Budgeting System* (64)) to identify the cost-effectiveness curve associated with the operations of the U.S. Employment Service. The curve indicates the sensitivity of cost to changes in the program's desired level of effectiveness, and is important in establishing program levels. A detailed analysis of the functions of the U.S. Employment Service is provided, and the statistical procedures used in the analysis are described. The conclusion, given the limitations of the study, appears to be favourable to the extension of U.S.E.S. programs.

3. THEORETICAL PROBLEMS IN MEASURING BENEFITS and COSTS

66. ANDEL, NORBERT. "Some Notes on Equating Private and Social Cost: Comment." *Southern Economic Journal,* Vol. 33, No. 1 (July, 1966), p. 112.

Abstract: The author disagrees with the conclusion of Davis and Whinston (73) that there is no economic or efficiency argument to favour one of the status quo points identified by them over another. The two extreme status quo points are: the situation where there is no legal restriction upon an activity which imposes an externality; and the situation where the activity creating the externality is allowed only if the individuals affected agree to it. The author argues that the latter status quo point is preferable to the former; under the former status quo an activity might be undertaken in order to reduce the welfare of neighbours and thereby induce them to pay for having these activities stopped. While this kind of behaviour may be privately profitable, it represents social waste to be avoided from the point of view of efficiency. From this point of view, therefore, the second status quo point is preferable. This conclusion does not affect the argument that the parties involved should be free to determine a settlement by bargaining.

67. BATOR, FRANCIS M. "The Anatomy of Market Failure." *Quarterly Journal of Economics,* Vol. 72 (August, 1958), pp. 351-379.

Headings: Introduction; The conditions of market efficiency; Neoclassical external economies: A digression; Statical externalities: An ordering; Comments; Efficiency, markets and choice of institutions.

Abstract: The central theorem of modern welfare economics, the duality theorem, implies that decentralized market calculations correctly account for all economic costs and benefits to which the relevant social welfare function is sensitive. The paper examines a number of ways in which duality can fail: failure of existence; failure by signal; failure by incentive; failure by structure; and failure by enforcement. Some of the mutually reinforcing and overlapping descriptions of market failure are external economies, indivisibility, nonappropriability, direct interaction, and public goods. A threefold classification of the above causes of market failure is suggested: ownership externalities; technical externalities; and public good externalities. The author points out that these are not mutually exclusive and that most externality phenomena are blends.

68. BROOKINGS INSTITUTION. *Can Benefits and Costs of Public Investments be Measured?* Brookings Research Report, No. 32. Washington, 1965. 8 p.

Headings: Introduction; Incentives for government enterprise; Benefit-cost analysis; Highlights of project evaluation; Conclusions.

Abstract: This report presents some highlights from *Measuring Benefits of Government Investments*, edited by Robert Dorfman. The debate about cost-benefit analysis centres on the question of whether the social value of benefits can be estimated reliably enough to justify the trouble and effort involved in a benefit-cost computation. The seven papers included in the volume suggest how benefit-cost analysis can be applied in various contexts, what difficulties are encountered, what expedients can be used to overcome the difficulties, and the limitations of the approach. Frederic Sherer proposes a method of quantifying one aspect of the benefits of expenditures on technological development; Ruth Mack and Sumner Myers (92) attempt to develop procedures for estimating the benefits of investments in outdoor recreational facilities; Gary Fromm deals with government expenditures on civil aviation; Burton Weisbrod (239) analyzes the problem of high school dropouts; Herbert Mohring estimates the market value of highway investments; Jerome Rothenberg looks at the nature of benefits from urban redevelopment projects; and Herbert Klarman (359) attempts to measure the benefits of a syphilis control program.

69. BUCHANAN, JAMES M. "Politics, Policy, and the Pigovian Margins." *Economica,* Vol. 29, No. 113 (February, 1962), pp. 17-28.

Headings: Introduction; Self-interest model of political behaviour; Social interest model of political behaviour; Pigovian analysis and the "Bifurcated Man"; Restricted model; Conclusion.

Abstract: The author challenges the implication of Pigovian analysis that externalities are either reduced or eliminated by the shift of an activity from market to political organization. This implication can be supported only under certain restrictive assumptions. In the self-interest political model, externalities will be present in any solution using a less-than-unanimity voting rule. In the social-interest political model neither "real" nor "apparent" externalities can provide grounds for organizational changes since each market situation represents the decision-makers' estimates of genuine community interest. In each model, therefore, political changes will not improve the market solution. The implication of Pigovian analysis holds only on the assumption that individuals respond to a different set of motives when they participate in market activity than when they are involved in political activity. The analysis may be rescued if the range of possible political action is restricted to genuinely collective goods and services financed by taxes levied on the principle of incremental benefits enjoyed.

70. BUCHANAN, J. M., and W. C. STUBBLEBINE. "Externality." *Economica,* Vol. 29, No. 116 (November, 1962), pp. 371-384.

Headings: Definitions; Descriptive example with diagram; Implications of this approach.

Abstract: The authors formulate a mathematical expression of a vigorous and precise definition of externality which can be applied to technical economies of production and consumption. The concepts of marginal and inframarginal externality and of Pareto-relevant and Pareto-irrelevant externalities are developed. Since the latter may be found in Pareto equilibrium, there is no *prima facie* case for intervention in all cases where an externality exists. The analysis emphasizes that there are two parties involved in the externality relationship, and that the externally affected party must compensate the acting party for modifying his behaviour. Thus, unilaterally imposed taxes and subsidies which eliminate all Pareto-relevant externalities cannot attain full Pareto equilibrium. Taxes and subsidies should, accordingly, be bilateral in nature.

71.   COASE, R. H. "The Problem of Social Cost." *Journal of Law and Economics,* Vol. 3 (October, 1960), pp. 1-44.

Headings: The problem to be examined; The reciprocal nature of the problem; The pricing system with liability for damage; The pricing system with no liability for damage; The problem illustrated anew; The cost of market transactions taken into account; The legal delimitation of rights and the economic problem; Pigou's treatment in *The Economics of Welfare;* The Pigovian tradition; A change of approach.

Abstract: The problem of social cost and the interrelationship of law and economics is examined in the light of a number of hypothetical and documented cases.   The reciprocal nature of the problem of harmful affects is emphasized, and it is argued that both the offender and the aggrieved party should take the harmful effect into account. In this way, it is suggested, the total value of production with and without the action becomes the criterion for deciding whether the particular action should be allowed to continue. The author recommends the use of opportunity cost concept in the comparison of receipts obtained under alternative sets of circumstances. He criticizes Pigou's treatment of harmful effects in *The Economics of Welfare* and suggests that the failure of a number of economists to reach correct conclusions can be attributed to the concentration of attention on particular deficiencies, the rise of laissez faire and ideal states for purposes of comparison, and the failure to define a factor of production as the right to perform certain actions.

72.   DAVIS, OTTO A., and ANDREW WHINSTON. "Externalities, Welfare, and the Theory of Games." *Journal of Political Economy,* Vol. 70, No. 3 (June, 1962), pp. 241-262.

Headings: Introduction; Motivation and merger; Separability and dominance; Some possible approaches; Non-separable cost functions; Policy approaches and equilibrium; Concluding remarks.

Abstract: The problem of externalities in production is examined in the context of two firms in a competitive industry.   Such firms will be motivated to attempt to eliminate externalities in production through merger. The authors distinguish between "separable", and "non-separable" types of externalities. "Separable" externalities affect the overall profit position of the firm, but do not affect marginal cost. The welfare implications of "separable" externalities are considered in terms of game theory. Three policy approaches are examined — the imposition of direct constraints through planning, a tax-subsidy arrangement, and no government action. Games theory is then used to analyse the "non-separable" case. The policy approaches considered are the merger solution, the tax-subsidy arrangement, and the constrained game approach. The authors tend to discount the Pigovian tax-subsidy solution, and to emphasize the formation of "natural units" for decision-making through mergers.

73. DAVIS, OTTO A., and ANDREW B. WHINSTON. "Some Notes On Equating Private and Social Cost." *Southern Economic Journal,* Vol. 32, No. 2 (October, 1965), pp. 113-126.

Headings: Introduction; The setting of the problem; The basic analysis; The problem of convergence to a Pareto optimum; The spillover on to the tax-subsidy schemes; Bargaining when the status quo point is zero; The intermediate case; Concluding comments; References (10).

Abstract: If externalities which cause a divergence between private and social cost are present in the economic system, a decentralized pricing system may not achieve Pareto optimality. Given certain classes of consumption externalities, the paper considers bargaining between the affected parties as one of four possible policy alternatives. In bargaining theory the status quo point assumes an important position, and the status quo point can be determined by law. Two polar status quo points are posited: in the first position, there are no legal restrictions upon the choice of the item which imposes an externality upon other individuals; in the second position, the law does not allow the externality-creating activity unless affected individuals agree to allow it. An intermediate status quo position is one in which the law allows only a specified quantity of the externality-creating activity without the consent of affected parties. Under these three alternative legal arrangements, bargaining of a prescribed variety can lead to a Pareto optimum, but if certain preference patterns are present bargaining will lead to a non-Pareto optimal equilibrium. There appears to be no economic or efficiency argument to favour one status quo point over another; the choice of the status quo point upon which final settlements are to be based then depends upon society's view as to the desired distribution of income.

74. DAVIS, OTTO A., and ANDREW B. WHINSTON. "On Externalities, Information and the Government-Assisted Invisible Hand." *Economica,* Vol. 33, No. 131 (August, 1966), pp. 303-318.

Headings: Introduction; Some points at issue; Decentralization and the Wellisz proposal; A new proposal; Concluding comments; References (15).

Abstract: This article attempts to point out some errors in Wellisz's article (113) on the controversy over externalities. The authors claim that "separable externalities" do affect the pattern of resource allocation and that the authorities can calculate the appropriate tax-subsidy structure if the difficulties of obtaining information can be overcome. Wellisz's proposal for computing the appropriate taxes and subsidies is criticized as being as demanding as a centralized system in terms of needed information: the authorities require to know the firms' cost function, and must determine appropriate constants of integration. In addition, there is the problem of motivating firms to have their decision-making on the cost functions determined by the government tax-subsidy function. The paper puts forward an iterative procedure for computing "Pigou-like" bounties and penalties paid from one firm to the other. This procedure is informationally decentralized and circumvents the problems of uncertainty created by non-separable and reciprocal externalities. The firms themselves also have an incentive to request recomputation of the tax-subsidy scheme in the event of changes in the values of such parameters as prices and technologies.

75. DEVINE, E. J. "The Treatment of Incommensurables in Cost-Benefit Analysis." *Land Economics,* Vol. 42, No. 3 (August, 1966), pp. 383-387. (Reprinted by the Institute of Government and Public Affairs, University of California, Los Angeles, 1966.)

Abstract: In the author's illustration of an investment decision with respect to water reclamation and recreation, the benefits from recreation are specified as incommensurable in that they cannot satisfactorily be expressed in terms of the common unit, dollars. Recreation benefits are not, however, intangible: they can be measured in user-hours. The benefit streams of the recreation project (user hours), and of the water reclamation project (dollars) are discounted at some suitable rate. A project mix is constructed such that funds are allocated to the water project up to the point where incremental benefit equals incremental cost (present values), the remainder of the budget going to the recreation project. This project mix is varied by shifting resources from water to recreation, and a trade-off is developed between dollar benefits from water reclamation and user-hours of recreation. The different trade-off positions imply various minimum valuations of a user-hour of recreation. The author feels that this information can help narrow the choice of project mix down to a range of more or less acceptable solutions.

76. DUNN, ROBERT M., JR. "A Problem of Bias in Benefit-Cost Analysis: Consumer Surplus Reconsidered." *Southern Economic Journal,* Vol. 33, No. 3 (January, 1967), pp. 337-342.

Abstract: The benefit total for a project is the sum of what individuals would have been willing to pay for the output: in other words, the total area under the imagined demand curve is explicitly included. This principle, which is correctly applied to measuring benefits, is not carried over to the measurement of costs and hence a bias is created. The opportunity costs of resources will be accurately measured by their market prices only if the demand curve

37

for the alternative private output is horizontal. If the demand curve for the alternative private output is downward sloping, the consumers' surplus must be added to the private return to give an estimate of social opportunity cost. In competitive markets the problem of bias also exists if the effect of a public project's removal of resources from the private sector is to raise costs and reduce output in that sector. If the public project replaces not one private project of equal size but a number of smaller projects the bias is reduced in magnitude. The bias is similarly smaller if the affected private businesses are in imperfect markets. The point of the paper, therefore, is that some of the costs to society attributable to a public project will show up in the markets for goods which require the same inputs as the public project. The bias problem is of little relevance to an economy like that of the United States where there are a great many private firms. In an underdeveloped economy, however, capital and other markets are often extremely narrow and a significant downward bias may be imparted to the cost of a public project. It would be very difficult to adjust the benefit-cost ratio to take account of cost bias of this type: the most that can be said is that projects with marginally favourable benefit-cost ratios should be looked upon with doubt.

77. DUNN, ROBERT M., JR. "Problems of Bias in Input Pricing for Benefit-Cost Analysis: A Reply." *Southern Economic Journal,* Vol. 34, No. 4 (April, 1968), p. 571.

Abstract: This paper is a reply to criticisms of the author's article (76) on bias in input pricing for benefit-cost analysis. He concedes that Stober, Falk and Ekelund (103) are correct in pointing out that the bias he attributed to "profits in excess of a normal interest rate" is in fact caused by the market price of the resource failing to measure the value of its marginal products. Stober, Falk and Ekelund have provided a much broader treatment of the problem of input pricing in cost-benefit analysis, but they have failed to work out the implications of their third source of bias. In reply to Solo (101), the author points out that there is a systematic bias in benefit-cost analysis because, while the consumer surplus aspect of the benefits from a public project is generally included, the consumer surplus part of social opportunity cost is omitted. The answer to Solo's argument, therefore, is basically one of symmetry.

78. ELLIS, HOWARD S., and WILLIAM FELLNER. "External Economics and Diseconomies." *American Economic Review,* Vol. 33, No. 4 (September, 1943), pp. 493-511.

Headings: Introduction; Diminishing returns and rising transfer costs ("External Diseconomies"), without external economies; External economies; Summary.

Abstract: The paper examines the proposition that competition causes output under "diminishing returns" to exceed, and under "increasing returns" to fall short of a socially optimal output. This proposition is the basis of the Marshall-Pigou "tax-subsidy" argument. The authors show that there is no divergence between the ideal and competitive outputs under "diminishing returns"; and that the cost function which maximizes the total of consumers' and producers' surplus is marginal cost in the sense of costs of the marginal unit of output alone and not marginal cost including the total increment of rent. The authors agree that, where there are unexploited external economies, competitive output falls short of the optimum. Under certain circumstances, therefore, the "subsidy" argument may be upheld.

79. FOSTER, C. D., and M. E. BEESLEY. "Estimating the Social Benefit of Constructing an Underground Railway in London." *Journal of the Royal Statistical Society,* Vol. 126, Part 1 (1963), pp. 46-92.

Headings: Introduction; Results; Benefits and costs of the Victoria Line; Special problems; Uses of the calculations; Appendix; References (25); Discussion and authors' reply.

Abstract: This article tackles the problem of assessing the social benefits and costs associated with adding the Victoria Line to the London Transport Underground Railway System. Costs are the initial capital invested and the operating expenses of the Victoria Line; benefits consist of time savings, travel cost reductions, and increased comfort and convenience. The method of reaching values for these costs and benefits is described in detail in the Appendix. The authors present a table expressing the present value of net benefits as an annual rate of return, over the period of construction and operation, on the present value of the capital invested. The sensitivity of the results is measured by substituting in the calculation various values for the discount rate, project life, and construction period.

80. HANSEN, W. LEE, and BURTON A. WEISBROD. "The Distribution of Costs and Direct Benefits of Public Higher Education: The Case of California." *Journal of Human Resources,* Vol. 4, No. 2 (Spring, 1969), pp. 176-191.

Headings: Abstract; Introduction; Subsidies students can receive; Subsidies students do receive; Distribution of amounts of subsidies through higher education; Distribution of subsidies by family income; Who pays the taxes; Conclusion.

Abstract: The maximum amount of subsidy a student can receive is fairly well determined by his ability as gauged by his high school performance. Not everyone, however, can or does choose to avail himself of the full amount of the subsidy for which he is potentially qualified. There are others who, through lack of interest in public higher education, receive no subsidy whatsoever. Although California prides itself on the wide access to higher education it provides, there is a highly unequal distribution of the amounts of subsidies actually received. Median family incomes are highest for parents of University students, followed by State College student families, Junior College student families, and families without children in the California system. Access to subsidies, therefore, is positively correlated with levels of family income. The patterns of subsidies identified by the authors raise questions about the equity of the current system for financing public higher education in California. In order to compare the subsidies received with the tax payments made, the authors develop estimates of state taxes and combined state and local taxes paid by families at each income level. When subsidies received through higher education alone are compared with the total tax payment, it becomes apparent that the current method of financing public higher education leads to a redistribution of income from lower to higher income families.

81. HAVEMAN, ROBERT H. "Benefit-Cost Analysis: Its Relevance to Public Investment Decisions: Comment." *Quarterly Journal of Economics,* Vol. 81, No. 4 (November, 1967), pp. 695-702.

Headings: Comment; Reply by Arthur Maass.

Abstract: The author agrees with Arthur Maass (90) that the redistribution consequences of public investment are of importance and must be incorporated into the decision process. Maass is, however, mistaken in implying that welfare economics has not been concerned with the redistribution consequences of public investments. He equates the distributional impact of public expenditure with the disbursement pattern of project benefits and thereby fails to recognize the concept of the net redistribution impact of an expenditure. Given the difficulty of estimating the true redistribution impact, the idea of a vote on trade-off rates is chimerical. Even if a vote were possible, trade-off ratios would be liable to costly changes since Congress is a transient group of policy makers. The author cites three empirical studies which indicate that the redistribution consequences of a number of public investments accentuate rather than ameliorate efficiency short-falls. In his reply, Maass argues that the three empirical studies do not prove that water resource developments should not be planned for the purpose of income redistribution: in the first place, the projects examined did not have redistribution as an explicit design objective and not all the redistribution effects appear to have been included; secondly, even if these projects were inefficient at redistributing income, the community need not prefer the most efficient method of redistribution — the results are not independent of the means. Maass also feels that his threefold process, involving the executive departments, the President, and Congress, is capable of setting standards for the redistributional effects of projects.

82. HAVEMAN, ROBERT, and JOHN KRUTILLA, "Unemployment, Excess Capacity, and Benefit-Cost Investment Criteria." *Review of Economics and Statistics,* Vol. 49, No. 3 (August, 1967), pp. 382-392.

Headings: Introduction; The model; The data; Breakdown of industrial and occupational demands; Nominal and opportunity costs; Conclusions; Notational appendix: The model of sectoral demand.

Abstract: The post-war years in the U.S. have been characterized by persistent unemployment conditions which would seem to require the adjustment of market prices to reflect the divergence of opportunity from money costs. The authors present a model which identifies the pattern of industrial and occupational demands imposed by various types of public water investments. The capital consumption component is maintained as an estimate of the social cost of capital use even in the presence of unused capacity. The remaining value-added components are adjusted for unemployment. A set of synthetic response functions is used to relate the probability that a given increment in the demand for labour and capital will be drawn from otherwise unemployed resources to the (measurable) level of occupational unemployment and industrial excess capacity. Using this analysis, real rather than nominal contract costs can be used in the cost-benefit calculation, and benefit-cost ratios which would be unacceptable under full employment assumptions may be deemed sufficient, given the pattern of unemployment.

83. JUDY, RICHARD W. "Costs: Theoretical and Methodological Issues." In *Cost-Benefit Analysis of Manpower Policies, Proceedings of a North American Conference, May 14-15, 1969,* edited by G. G. Somers and W. D. Wood, pp. 16-29. Published jointly by the Industrial Relations Centre, Queen's University, Kingston, Ontario, and the Center for Studies in Vocational and Technical Education, The University of Wisconsin, Madison, Wisconsin, 1969.

Headings: The concept of cost in cost-benefit analysis; Conceptual and methodological problems of cost estimation; Conclusion.

Abstract: Microeconomics, the science of rational choice, constitutes the basis of cost-benefit analysis. Choice can take either of two forms — constrained maximization or constrained minimization. There are a number of aspects of choice dealt with by the author: specification of the objective function, determination of the constraints, elaboration of feasible alternatives, measurement of costs and benefits of feasible alternatives, and evaluation and choice. The basic notion of opportunity cost should underly all cost measurement performed by cost-benefit analysis. Opportunity cost and accounting cost measures rarely give identical results. This point is illustrated by a simple example of cost calculation. Some conceptual and methodological problems of cost estimation are examined. Market prices can be used as indexes of social opportunity cost, but we must take into account violations of the assumptions of the basic theorems of welfare economics which accredit prices as a measure of costs. For example, the assumption of perfect competition is likely to be violated, present prices may not represent future scarcities in a dynamic system, and the "other things remaining equal" assumption may be violated. If we use market prices as measures of opportunity costs, we are assuming that income redistribution effects involve no benefits or costs. It is unusual to find explicit considerations of redistributional effects even when redistribution is included among the ostensible objectives of the program. The author gives an example of the calculation of the incidence of costs and benefits of higher education in Canada. The opportunity cost concept requires consideration only of the costs which are avoidable. Related to the concept of avoidable costs is that of incremental costs: when comparing two programs we should not assume that average and marginal costs are equal. When calculating costs we must be alert to the existence of externalities, and must also recognize that we cannot estimate costs and benefits with perfect certainty. The problem of uncertainty is particularly acute when an alternative involves an irreversible decision. When two or more objectives are furthered by the same process, we need some method of allocating costs to outputs. If we consider the outputs singly, we can deal with joint products by subtracting the value of the by-product associated with the increased output of the product we are interested in from the costs of that increased output. The analyst should not take it upon himself to relax constraints which are not self-imposed. He should compute the cost of observing constraints which he believes are relaxable, e.g. "imaginary constraints". Where a constraint can be marginally tightened or relaxed, the decision-maker should be provided with a set of shadow prices.

84.   JURGENSEN, HARALD. "Private and Social Costs." *German Economic Review,* Vol. 2, No. 4 (1964), pp. 273-288.

Headings: Additional social cost within the ambit of social costs; Additional social costs of production in the case of households and public authorities; Additional social costs between production processes; Additional social costs as an instrument of economic policy; Additional social costs as a responsibility of economic policy.

Abstract: The author describes "additional social costs" as social costs, defined as the sum total at market prices of goods and services made available to an economy by production, minus private costs, which include only the goods and services entered at market prices in the cost accounts of individual economic units including government-operated enterprises. He examines additional social costs caused to private households and public authorities by business enterprise, and those caused to enterprises by other enterprises. He discussed additional social costs as a policy instrument, and the implications of additional social costs for economic policy. The author feels that free market economies can function despite the disturbances caused by social costs, but that there is a need for improved methods of economic policy.

85.   KHATKHATE, D. R. "Opportunity Cost and Its Application to Underemployment." *Social Research,* Vol. 28, No. 1 (1961), pp. 60-70.

Headings: Introduction; The principle of opportunity cost; Opportunity cost of labour; Application of the concept in underdeveloped countries experiencing underemployment.

Abstract: The author contrasts the principle of real cost, which rests on objective physical or psychological units of input, with the principle of opportunity cost. Opportunity cost may be interpreted in two ways: the factor of production may be valued at what it would produce elsewhere, i.e. its marginal productivity; or it may be valued in terms of what it would "earn" elsewhere. There are two objections to the definition of opportunity cost with reference to productivity considerations: in the first place, there is a floor to the price of labour; and secondly, the opportunity cost principle requires full employment of resources. When opportunity cost is defined with reference to labour's alternative earnings, the principle becomes applicable to situations of unemployment and at any level of marginal productivity. Interpreted in this manner, the opportunity cost of labour is determined from the point of view of the individual employer, by the alternative compensation, and from society's point of view, by the alternative consumption. In terms of this definition, the private opportunity cost of labour is always positive, but social opportunity cost may be zero if the newly employed worker is willing to work at his previous level of consumption. This divergence between private and social opportunity cost of labour may have concealed the full need for labour intensive techniques in underdeveloped countries. This conclusion is in line with suggestions that over-populated countries should make intensive use of "surplus labour" or "disguised unemployed".

86. KNETSCH, JACK L. "Economics of Including Recreation as a Purpose of Eastern Water Projects." *Journal of Farm Economics,* Vol. 46, No. 5 (December, 1964), pp. 1148-1157.

Headings: Introduction; Recreation benefits at Kerr Reservoir; Recreation benefits and efficiency.

Abstract: In Federal water resource development activities, standards of recreation benefits have been adopted which yield a recreation benefit figure for projects on the basis of monetary unit values and visitor day totals. One alternative to this method of calculating recreation benefits is a measure based on a derived demand curve for recreation facilities using travel cost data as a proxy for prices: regression analysis is used to relate visit rates of several distance zones from the recreational area to total travel costs. From this relationship, a demand curve indicating total attendance as a function of price can be derived. This calculation is performed for the Kerr Reservoir on the Virginia-North Carolina Border. It is suggested that the failure to evaluate recreation developments other than those which occur as a by-product of water resource schemes can lead to a serious imbalance in recreational development.

87. KRUPP, SHERMAN. "Analytic Economics and the Logic of External Effects." *American Economic Review,* Papers and Proceedings, Vol. 53 (May, 1963), pp. 220-226.

Headings: Introduction; Composition laws and discontinuous deductive chains; Externalities and deduction; Conclusion; References (15).

Abstract: Among the axioms which govern the range of application of a theory are the composition laws. Composition laws govern the extension of relationships derived from micro-units. At certain levels of complexity or aggregation, composition laws may cease to apply. The laws and relationships which apply at the new level of analysis are frequently undefined. There are two ways of handling the inadequacy of composition rules: new variables, e.g. "external economies" can be added, or the composition rules can be modified for some level of aggregation or range of problems. This problem in logical analysis is illustrated by the following examples from the field of economics: externalities in relation to rising supply price; externalities in relation to the distinction between marginal private and marginal social cost; and externalities in relation to direct physical interdependence. The last field, where the activities of one sector contribute benefits or costs to third parties in the form of side effects which are not reflected in prices, presents microanalysis with its most intractable composition problem.

88. KUMAGAI, HISAO. "External Economies and the Problem of Investment Criteria." *Osaka Economic Papers,* Vol. 7, No. 2 (February, 1959), pp. 13-20.

Headings: Introduction; Social marginal productivity and mathematical programming; Rule of thumb.

Abstract: If the policy objective consists of maximizing real national income in a certain year, the investment criterion must be based on the social marginal productivity of capital. Apart from "technological" external economies, the attainment of general equilibrium under conditions of perfect competition would automatically ensure a maximization of national income. In the actual situation before us prices of goods may cease to represent their marginal opportunity costs, and various types of external economies may exist. These problems may be overcome by the use of mathematical programming and input/output tables. The author considers however, that Dupuit's classical test of the desirability of an investment project supplemented by consideration of external economies and marginal opportunity cost, can claim general validity as a rule of thumb to assess the marginal productivity of an investment project.

89. LEDEBUR, LARRY C. "The Problem of Social Cost." *American Journal of Economics and Sociology,* Vol. 26, No. 4 (October, 1967), pp. 399-415.

Headings: Introduction; Earlier discussions of social cost; Professor Coase's criticism; The Pigovian system — a critique; An extension of the argument; Summary.

Abstract: This paper examines the alternative approaches put forward by Pigou and Coase (71) to ensure the maximization of the national dividend in cases involving social cost. Pigou recommended a system of bounties and taxes which would equate private and social products at the margin. The approach advocated by Coase is based on the concept of opportunity cost: the decision for remedial action should take total product into account. The author demonstrates that the Pigovian *a priori* tax-subsidy approach to divergencies between marginal social and private products cannot be relied upon to maximize economic welfare. The Pigovian solution, however, is not, as Coase claims, incorrect in its entirety: in the case of an industry creating a social cost which is transferred directly to society, both approaches provide the correct solution. In cases involving single firms within competitive industries, Coase's analysis is inadequate.

90. MAASS, ARTHUR. "Benefit-Cost Analysis: Its Relevance to Public Investment Decisions." *Quarterly Journal of Economics,* Vol. 80, No. 2 (May, 1966), pp. 208-226.

Headings: Introduction; What is the problem; Have benefits been overestimated; How did we get to where we are; What changes in welfare economics theory are needed; What is the evidence that trade-offs can be determined; The lesson.

Abstract: The author argues that benefit-cost analysis may be relevant only to a small part of the problem evaluating public projects and programs since it has been adapted only to the single objective of economic efficiency. There may be a capacity of the legislative process to make trade-off decisions, e.g. between economic efficiency and income redistribution which can govern the design of projects and programs. It is argued that what is meant by a secondary benefit is mainly a benefit in support of an objective other than efficiency; if the objective function of a public program involves more than economic efficiency then the so-called "secondary" benefits can be included in the benefit-cost analysis without giving rise to accusations of consistent over-estimation of benefits. The preoccupation with efficiency is seen as a reflection of the new welfare economics. The author feels that two of the assumptions of the new welfare economics must be challenged: indifference to the distribution of income; and the doctrine of consumers' sovereignty. The paper concludes by demonstrating that there is a trade-off between efficiency and other objectives in Interstate Highway and Federal housing and urban renewal programs established by the legislative process. The executive should obtain such a trade-off value between efficiency and the most important non-efficiency objective for every agency program.

91. MacDONALD, JOHN S. "Benefits and Costs: Theoretical and Methodological Issues: Discussion." In *Cost-Benefit Analysis of Manpower Policies, Proceedings of a North American Conference, May 14-15, 1969,* edited by G. G. Somers and W. D. Wood, pp. 30-36. Published jointly by the Industrial Relations Centre, Queen's University, Kingston, Ontario, and the Center for Studies in Vocational and Technical Education, The University of Wisconsin, Madison, Wisconsin, 1969.

Abstract: The complaint that cost-benefit analysis has not taken account of more intangibles is not justified since these are not the proper business of econometricians. Sociologists and political scientists could have contributed more to the expansion and elaboration of comprehensive project appraisal. Politicians and administrators are wary about exposing the inner workings of an agency to external criteria. Cost-benefit analysis is equally disturbing for everyone when it is anchored to an abstract collective welfare. Weisbrod (112) proposes that benefits and costs should be measured for society as a whole whereas Judy (83) proposes measuring benefits for The Boss. Since welfare economics has posed the question of the distribution of costs and benefits, we must incorporate the economics of consumption into our analysis: this can be done by means of a sectoral model. It is not necessary for the economist to incorporate the political process into the benefit-cost model by identifying the political weight of the various sectors: the political process presents as many problems of monopoly, monopsony, oligopoly, and other rigidities as does the market. The identification of costs and benefits to particular sectors is necessary because there may be no equilibrium among interest groups: this calls into question the use of macro-indicators of collective welfare. Economists should not attempt, however, to replace their single-valued objective welfare function with multi-dimensional scales derived from sociology. Cost-benefit analysis has borrowed heavily from welfare economics and it is perhaps time to ask whether the compensation principle is necessary. It could be argued that society may sanction a net loss for some group, or that failure on the part of a group to mobilize itself as an interest group makes the net loss irrelevant to public policy. There has been a tendency to put all but the most easily monetized variables outside the social cost-benefit model. Putting variables and goals outside the analysis means that cost-benefit analysis cannot go beyond sub-optimization and cost-effectiveness to optimization and a rate of return. The author feels that shadow-pricing can hardly be avoided since it is a way of adjusting for the very market disequilibrium which a public project is supposed to correct. In conclusion, econometric analysis of costs and benefits tend to be politically naive: the remedy is to bring political power inside the model by translating costs and benefits into groups' interests. Leaving an econometric analysis in the hands of The Boss so that he can make up his mind in terms of other considerations is simply passing off an intellectual responsibility.

92. MACK, RUTH P., and SUMNER MYERS. "Outdoor Recreation." In *Measuring Benefits of Government Investments,* edited by Robert Dorfman, pp. 71-116. Washington: The Brookings Institution, 1965.

Headings: Introduction; Recreation and public expenditure decisions; Dollar measures; Merit-weighted user-days; Conclusion; Comments by Howard E. Ball and Lyle E. Craine.

Abstract: The government must make the following decisions bearing on outdoor recreation; how many dollars to spend on all public purposes vis à vis those of the private economy; how much to spend on outdoor recreation vis à vis other public purposes; and how to disttribute expenditure among various recreational projects. The benefits from outdoor recreation cannot, in the absence of appropriate market mechanisms, be measured by market prices, nor can other satisfactory dollar measures be contrived. The authors feel that benefits need to be measured in terms of merit-weighted user-days of outdoor recreation: a user-day of recreation is a crude unit of benefit and needs to be weighted according to a list of performance criteria derived from some value scheme. This utility scale can be used as a measure of effectiveness in analysing alternative program elements, but its value is limited with respect to inter-program decisions.

93. MARGOLIS, JULIUS. "Secondary Benefits, External Economies, and the Justification of Public Investment." *Review of Economics and Statistics,* Vol. 39, No. 3 (August, 1957), pp. 284-291.

Headings: Introduction; Secondary benefits; Employment effects; External economies.

Abstract: The paper examines the concepts of secondary benefits used by the U.S. Bureau of Reclamation and the Federal Inter-Agency River Basin Committee. Secondary benefits are defined as those "stemming from" and "induced by" the project: the former category includes net incomes in the secondary activities which transport, process or sell the products of the project area; the latter category includes net incomes in activities which sell to the project area. The author dismisses the arguments used to support this definition of secondary benefits, and claims that the existence of external economies is the only valid defense of the inclusion of secondary benefits in the benefit/cost ratio. Pecuniary external economies, however, are not social benefits since they are transfers of rent among specialized factors. The argument for technological external economies is based on the assumption that there exists a large volume of underemployed resources both human and natural. Major sources of external economies are the growth of market, and the use or expansion of social overhead capital. The analysis should investigate this kind of development when looking for secondary benefits.

94. McKEAN, ROLAND N. "The Use of Shadow Prices." In *Problems in Public Expenditure Analysis,* edited by Samuel B. Chase Jr., pp. 33-77. Washington: The Brookings Institution, 1968.

Headings: Introduction; Pareto optimality and limitations of market prices; Market prices and nonmarket values; Ways of deriving shadow prices; Comments on specific examples; Criteria in deciding what prices to use; A case in point: evaluating oil-shale R & D policies; Comments: Allen V. Kneese and Julius Margolis.

Abstract: When prices are explicitly used to exchange items freely they are called market prices. When they are implicit in exchanges that should be made to maximize a particular objective function or to minimize a cost function, they are called "shadow prices". If we assume that the government seeks economic efficiency or "Pareto optimality", market prices may not provide accurate information about substitution possibilities because of imperfect markets, constraints on resource use, price-support programs, anticipated changes in supply and demand conditions, unemployed resources, external effects, and products produced by government and not sold through markets. The author lists four methods by which the benefit-cost analyst can derive shadow prices: programming techniques which highlight appropriate trade-offs or substitutions; price relationships in markets for similar items or in markets for the same items in other countries; the prices implied by other governmental choices; and, finally, shadow prices can be derived by adjusting market prices to allow for considerations that are not reflected in those market prices. The gains and costs of using shadow prices are very uncertain. Any set of prices used in a benefit-cost analysis will be imperfect: one should ask how "bad" are market prices and how "bad" are shadow prices for the purpose, and which set is worth its cost? The author's view is that where market prices exist they will in general be more accurate than shadow prices.

95. MISHAN, E. J. "Welfare Criteria for External Effects." *American Economic Review,* Vol. 51, No. 4 (September, 1961), pp. 594-613.

Headings: Introduction; Appraisal of Little's welfare criteria; Resemblance and contrast between Little's criteria and those for external effects; Reformulation and a proposal for a single welfare criterion; A single welfare criterion for variable external effects; References (9).

Abstract: The author argues that the piecemeal analysis which attempts to find a better welfare position for society is of more practical value than the general allocation approach which defines an optimum. He examines Little's version of the dual welfare criterion involving the Kaldor-Hicks and reversal tests of hypothetical compensation. The apparent paradox observed in batch comparisons appears to arise in the case of external effects, but for a different reason — namely the possibility of evaluating the external effect either as a gain or as a loss. The concept of consumer's surplus or rent is used to extend the application of the usual compensation tests to cases in which the difference between two situations consists only of the amount of the good responsible for external effects. A single welfare criterion is formulated, and the welfare effects of the externality in question can be gauged from schedules representing its marginal social benefit and marginal social cost.

96. MISHAN, E. J. "Reflections on Recent Developments in the Concept of External Effects." *Canadian Journal of Economics and Political Science,* Vol. 31, No. 1 (February, 1965), pp. 3-34.

Headings: Introduction; Summary of twelve propositions; Survey of the recent literature; Conclusion; Appendix.

Abstract: Universal perfect competition does not in general meet the requirements of a Pareto optimum unless the condition is met that all relevant effects, as defined by the welfare economist, make their impact on the pricing system. Where there are external effects, the appropriate "corrections" of the relevant outputs should be made so that the values of the social marginal products of the factor classes are the same in all uses. The author lists twelve propositions argued in the paper, and then makes a summary and critical examination of the work of the following contributors: Scitovsky (100); Duesenberry; Ellis and Fellner (78); Meade; Davis and Whinston (72); Coase (71); and Buchanan and Stubblebine (70). He points out that as societies grow in material wealth, the incidence of external effects grows rapidly. This justifies the attention given to external effects.

97. MURAKAMI, Y., and T. NEGISHI. "A Note on a Formulation of External Economy." *International Economic Review,* Vol. 5, No. 3 (September, 1964), pp. 328-334.

Headings: Formulation of the problem; Socially optimal production and individual efficiency; An example of inefficient individual production; References (7).

Abstract: The authors present a mathematical treatment of the question as to whether socially optimum production necessarily requires the technical efficiency of individual production. They conclude that where all outputs concerned have external diseconomy and all inputs concerned have external economy this is not necessarily so. An example of this unusual situation is given.

98. NEENAN, WILLIAM B. "Efficiency and Distribution in Benefit-Cost Analysis." Mimeographed. Ann Arbor: Department of Economics, University of Michigan, 1969. 12 p.

Headings: Introduction; Recent efforts; Proposed approach; Benefit-cost analysis; Evaluation of distributional weights; Concluding remark; Footnotes (13).

Abstract: The purpose of this paper is to suggest a way in which the simple efficiency criterion of benefit-cost analysis, the maximization of net benefits "to whomsoever accruing", may be related to income distributional effects.

A brief review of recent efforts to relate efficiency and equity evaluations of government programs is provided and the relationship of this paper to these efforts is indicated. A traditional benefit-cost analysis is performed on the X-ray tuberculosis screening program conducted by the Michigan Department of Public Health. Three distinct investment benefits are produced by the earlier detection of tuberculosis: the direct benefit of the reduced hospitalization and other treatment costs associated with new active cases; the indirect benefit of the reduced productivity loss, measured by earnings, associated with the new active cases; and the external benefit of contagion reduction. In addition to these investment benefits the program produces several other benefits of positive economic value; the consumer benefit received by screenees; the "option value" future screenees derive from the continued existence of the program; and the value to some in the community from the maintenance of a public health service for others. The latter is a distributional benefit while the former five are efficiency benefits. At the grand efficiency level, the product of marginal investment benefits and marginal redistributive weights equals marginal cost. The paper demonstrates how this equation can be used to calculate shadow distributional weights for the program. These are the weights which are implicit in the actual allocation pattern of the program's services.

99.   RAYNAULD, ANDRE. "Benefits and Costs: Theoretical and Methodological Issues: Discussion." In *Cost-Benefit Analysis of Manpower Policies, Proceedings of a North American Conference, May 14-15, 1969,* edited by G. G. Somers and W. D. Wood, pp. 37-41. Published jointly by the Industrial Relations Centre, Queen's University, Kingston, Ontario, and the Center for Studies in Vocational and Technical Education, The University of Wisconsin, Madison, Wisconsin, 1969.

Abstract: The author feels that it may be more desirable to make decisions on the basis of a cost-benefit analysis which fails to satisfy all the theoretical requirements than on no measured basis whatsoever. The important factor is the ingenuity of the researcher in translating the issues into a meaningful economic framework. On this basis Weisbrod's paper (112) is to be commended although the author disagrees with its main conclusions. In the first place, while he agrees that it is not enough for manpower programs to reduce unemployment but that they must do so efficiently, it cannot be argued *a priori* that manpower programs are inefficient. Secondly, it does not follow that because the private market does not provide extensive training, placement, and relocation services, these activities cannot be profitable or efficient. Leaving aside the question of externalities, the lack of private activity in this field, as demonstrated by the unemployment rate, can still be attributed to a malfunctioning private market. The author argues that private market imperfections can be taken as a presumption in favour of government action rather than against it. Nevertheless, he agrees that, where manpower programs are not profitable, redistribution can provide an alternative rationale. Turning to some wider issues, he points out that the usual problem is to assess a single program with regard to a variety of goals: normally the more numerous the stated goals are the less efficient the program will prove to be. Secondly, when we examine the question of the level of optimization, we should realize that we are not entitled to the assumption of a perfect market since it is only the existence of market imperfections which yields our programs any kind of positive benefit at all. Thirdly, an obvious substitute for manpower programs is increasing aggregate demand: this has a price tag in terms of inflation and other costs and we must ask ourselves how we can compare the two alternatives. Finally, although transfer payments cannot be added to real benefits, they do affect the private behaviour and calculations of the beneficiaries. If individuals include transfer payments along with forgone earnings, public retraining programs will have to be more generous and consequently will appear less efficient.

100. SCITOVSKY, TIBOR. "Two Concepts of External Economies." *Journal of Political Economy,* Vol. 62, No. 2 (April, 1954), pp. 143-151.

Headings: Introduction; Equilibrium theory; External economies and the industrialization of underdeveloped countries.

Abstract: The paper describes four types of nonmarket interdependence and discusses their implications for equilibrium theory. It is argued that technological external economies, which can be defined as a peculiarity of the production function, are the only external economies that can arise because of direct interdependence among producers and within the framework of general equilibrium theory. The concept of external economies occurs frequently in connection with the problem of allocating savings among alternative investment opportunities in underdeveloped countries. While the private profitability of investment is, according to equilibrium theory, usually considered a good index of its social desirability, there are a number of exceptions to this rule, particularly in underdeveloped countries. The author outlines three special cases in which the principles of general equilibrium theory are incapable to the problems of investment.

101. SOLO, ROBERT A. "Benefit-Cost Analysis and Externalities in Private Choice: Comment." *Southern Economic Journal,* Vol. 34, No. 4 (April, 1968), pp. 569-570.

Abstract: The author agrees with Dunn (76) that neglect of consumer surplus may introduce bias into cost measurement. He points out, however, that consumer surplus is only one of many important external economies which need not be left out of the cost side of an analysis of a public project. There are also significant external diseconomies consequent upon entrepreneurial choice, and there is no *a priori* reason to suppose that the economies over-

balance the diseconomies or vice versa. In addition, there may be external effects stemming from the proposed public project as well as from the private activity that will be displaced. Only if the public authority takes account of all other external effects in its cost-benefit analysis can we assume a systematic bias resulting from the omission of consumer surplus.

102. STEINER, PETER O. "The Role of Alternative Cost in Project Design and Selection." *Quarterly Journal of Economics,* Vol. 79, No. 3 (August, 1965), pp. 417-430.

Headings: Introduction; The basic model; Choices only among explicit alternatives .... government choice pre-empting; Choices only among explicit alternatives — government choice determinatives; Addition of implicit alternative; Summary and conclusions.

Abstract: Unless there is legislative assertion of the need for the service, a specific governmental project requires a cost-benefit study. Where there is a viable private alternative which will be activated in the absence of government action, the costs of the government project can be compared with the costs of the private project, on the assumption that public and private funds have the same social opportunity cost. Where there is partial existence of viable alternatives to government investment, the calculation may be limited to incremental rather than total benefits of the government project. The evaluation of a public project may also be facilitated by taking implicit alternatives into account and comparing them with public and private projects. Where government choices are determinative it may be necessary to establish absolute merit, but, on the other hand, it may be possible to prescribe the private alternatives. The conclusion is that alternative cost limits the number of cases in which precise benefit measurement is required.

103. STOBER, WILLIAM J., L. H. FALK, and ROBERT B. EKELUND JR. "Cost Bias in Benefit-Cost Analysis: Comment." *Southern Economic Journal,* Vol. 34, No. 4 (April, 1968), pp. 563-568.

Abstract: The authors agree with Dunn (76) that the problem of cost bias has not been adequately treated, but they feel that there are certain defects in his analysis. Market prices of resources may fail to measure social opportunity costs in three ways: market prices of resources are changed as a result of the public project; resources are withdrawn from firms selling their output in imperfectly competitive product markets, or from firms having resources in imperfectly competitive factor markets. Dunn deals only with the first and second of the possible biases and his measures for these are inadequate. In the first instance of bias Dunn has omitted a loss in producers' surplus corresponding to the loss in consumers' surplus which he identified. While his conclusion regarding the disappearance of the bias when resources are drawn from a perfectly competitive economy is correct, Dunn has wrongly applied the same conclusion to an imperfect economy. The authors demonstrate that the bias can be reduced only as the degree of monopoly in the private sector is reduced. It should be recognized that the underlying source of all three types of bias is that the prices at which resources are evaluated in benefit-cost analyses fail to measure the value of their marginal products in the private sector. Three concluding points are made: the paper assumes that resources are inelastically supplied, and the questions of second best optima and the legitimacy of partial equilibrium analysis are ignored.

104. STOCKFISCH, J. A. "External Economies, Investment, and Foresight." *Journal of Political Economy,* Vol. 63 (October, 1955), pp. 446-451.

Headings: Introduction; External pecuniary economies and diseconomies; Externalities and foresight; Imperfect knowledge and economic planning; A reply by Tibor Scitovsky.

Abstract: The author challenges Scitovsky's view (100) that centralized investment planning is preferable to a system without central planning if there are significant external effects. In his reply Scitovsky points out that his policy implication would not apply to the U.S., but to underdeveloped countries where investment expenditure, in the absence of planning, tends to be spread over too wide an area.

105. STROTZ, ROBERT H. "Two Propositions Related to Public Goods." *Review of Economics and Statistics,* Vol. 40, No. 4 (November, 1958), pp. 329-331.

Abstract: This note examines the problem of output decisions with reference to public goods. It is suggested that this problem can be solved by using public goods as supplementary devices for controlling the distribution of income.

106. TURVEY, RALPH. "On Divergences Between Social Cost and Private Cost." *Economica,* Vol. 30, No. 119 (August, 1963), pp. 309-313.

Abstract: This article is a survey of papers by Coase (71), Davis and Whinston (72), and Buchanan and Stubblebine (70), concerning externalities. Optimum resource allocation involves maximizing the algebraic sum of gains and losses as against the situation where there are no externalities. Where the parties are able and willing to negotiate to their mutual advantage, state intervention is unnecessary to secure optimum resource allocation. Where negotiation cannot take place no *a priori* policy prescription is warranted.

107. WEISBROD, BURTON A. *External Benefits of Public Education.* Princeton: Industrial Relations Section, Department of Economics, Princeton University, 1964. xi + 143 p.

Headings: Introduction; Concepts and units of analysis; The nature of education benefits and their spill-overs; Production and spill-overs of educational capital; Geographic dispersion of spill-over of educational capital; External fiscal benefits: I; External fiscal benefits: II; External non-monetary benefits; Spill-over effects and the allocation of resources to education; Summary, policy implications, and concluding remarks; Appendix A — Estimating net and gross rates of annual migration for Clayton, Missouri, 1950-1960 — summary of methodology; Values of educational capital for various levels of educational attainment; Value of the option to obtain additional education.

Abstract: This study investigates the question of who receives the benefits created by education: the people within the school district providing the education (internal benefits) or people outside (geographical spill-over), the parents of, and the children who are educated, or others (external benefits)? The mobility of the U.S. population indicates that geographical spill-over effects will be significant, and there is a presumption that external benefits exist, otherwise education would not be provided publicly. When a community attempts to maximize its own economic welfare, to the extent that externalities exist, resources will be allocated in a non-optimal fashion. Spill-ins do not raise expenditure to compensate for the less than socially optimal expenditure due to spill-outs. Externalities can lead to inequity as well as to misallocation of resources: if the benefit principle of taxation is applied to education finance, costs should be borne by those who reap the benefits. The financial effects of education can be separated into four categories — direct income effects, tax effects, redistributive effects, and indirect income effects. The author demonstrates that spill-over effects of education can take a number of forms: additional lifetime income, and additional local taxes out of that income, may be lost to the community through outmigration; education may benefit persons other than those educated by reducing the social costs of other activities (such as law enforcement) and by reducing transfer payments; and non-monetary external benefits from education are lost to the community if out-migration occurs. Estimates of the spill-over component of the benefits of education are provided where possible for the case study city of Clayton, Missouri. The hypothesis that spill-overs exert some predictable marginal influence on the means and level of support for public education is tested. The welfare maximization model predicts that, in a multiple regression analysis in which other determinants of public education expenditures are held constant, states which anticipate outmigration will have expenditures per student lower than otherwise expected. The findings are consistent with the proposition that benefit spill-overs accompanying outmigration are tending to depress aggregate expenditures on education, and to shift financial responsibility for education to higher-level governments. The traditional economic remedies for the tendency of external economics to cause sub-optimal expenditures — subsidizing the producer of the external benefits, establishing minimum standards of performance, and enlarging the decision-making unit so as to internalize the benefits — are examined in a U.S. context.

108. WEISBROD, BURTON A. "Income Redistribution Consequences of Government Expenditure Programs." Mimeographed. Washington: The Brookings Institution, 1966. 57 p.

Headings: Introduction; Economic efficiency and distributional equity: a case for their integration; The separate presentation of distributional effects; Integrating efficiency and distributional equity; Summary; Appendix: Concepts of costs and benefits.

Abstract: This paper starts by considering the conceptual case for integrating income — distributional effects and allocative-efficiency effects in the evaluation of public expenditure projects. The author proposes two principal levels at which distributional effects might be introduced into a benefit-cost framework. The first level involves presenting to political decision-makers information about the distributional as well as the efficiency effects of alternative decisions. The second level involves a full integration of efficiency and distributional equity, and requires a Social Welfare Function. The Social Welfare Function makes explicit the value judgements concerning the distribution of income. The paper concludes by giving a brief review of various types of program effects referred to in the literature of cost-benefit analysis.

109. WEISBROD, BURTON A. "Conceptual Issues in Evaluating Training Programs." *Monthly Labor Review,* Vol. 89, No. 10 (October, 1966), pp. 1091-1097.

Headings: Introduction; Program objectives and outputs; Benefits to trainees; Employment level; Empirical approaches; Third party effects; Distributional effects; The time pattern.

Abstract: The article discusses the form of benefits and costs in the manpower training area and presents some suggestions regarding measurement methods. Specifying program objectives performs two functions: it facilitates consideration of their appropriateness and provides a framework for judging the success of the program. The goals of manpower training programs are increased income and decreased unemployment. If there are no effects on third parties, evaluation of a training program would involve comparing the given individual's income with and without training, other things being equal. This involves making assumptions about what would have happened to the trainees if the program had not been available to them. One of the assumptions underlying any analysis of benefits from training programs concerns the level of aggregate employment in the economy. The author feels that changes in employment and income resulting from the aggregate demand effects of spending on training programs should not be included in benefits, whereas employment and income effects resulting from more productive workers should. Empirical evaluations are often complicated by the effects of changing levels of total demand during training periods. Evaluations using an appropriate control group of non-trainees tend to be relatively insensitive to cyclical changes in aggregate employment. In considering third party effects, while we should recognize that benefits to trainees may come at the expense of non-trainees, we should not overlook the case where training breaks resource bottlenecks and thereby expands employment and income among other workers. The nature of redistributional consequences of training programs should be noted as part of a complete program evaluation. The analyst should use alternative discount rates for calculating present values, thereby showing the sensitivity of results to the discount rate chosen.

110. WEISBROD, BURTON A. "Income Redistribution Effects and Benefit Cost Analysis." In *Problems in Public Expenditure Analysis,* edited by Samuel B. Chase Jr., pp. 177-222. Washington: Brookings Institution, 1968.

Headings: Introduction; Efficiency and equity: a case for their integration; The separate presentation of distributional effects; integrating efficiency and equity; Summary; Comments by Robert H. Haveman and Ruth P. Mack.

Abstract: This paper concentrates on the proper role of distributional considerations in a benefit-cost framework. If "costs" and "benefits" are regarded as synonyms for "advantages" and "disadvantages", then there is no logical basis for the separation of efficiency from equity: the problem is placing a value on distributional effects so that they will be commensurable with other costs and benefits. Concern for distributional effects could be accounted for in the cost-benefit analysis by weighting costs and benefits according to their incidence among various socio-economic groups in society. In this way every expenditure project could be evaluated in terms of "grand efficiency" — both distributional-equity considerations and allocative-efficiency considerations would be evaluated in commensurable terms. One step in this direction would be for economists to supplement evaluations according to economic efficiency with an analysis of the distribution of costs and benefits among the population. To obtain full integration of distributional and allocative efficiency, a social welfare function is required. A model is outlined for deducing the distributional weights (in effect, marginal utilities of income) assigned to various groups in society by the policy maker from comparisons of alternative rankings of projects by efficiency and distributional considerations. The method assumes that government decision-makers are rational and fully informed about the consequences of their actions. An illustrative application of the model is included in the paper.

111. WEISBROD, BURTON A. "Concepts of Costs and Benefits." In *Problems in Public Expenditure Analysis,* edited by Samuel B. Chase Jr., pp. 257-262. Washington: Brookings Institution, 1968.

Headings: External versus internal effects; Real versus pecuniary effects; Employment versus allocative effects; Intangible versus tangible effects; Explicit versus implicit effects.

Abstract: This appendix contains a brief review of various types of program effects. External effects are those accruing to persons not part of the decision-making unit. Both internal and external effects can be "real" or pecuniary. Real effects alter the total production possibilities or the total welfare opportunities for consumers in the economy. Pecuniary effects, on the other hand, involve only redistributive effects. The external pecuniary results of a project are often termed "secondary" effects: these effects reflect only shifts in relative demand patterns which involve redistribution of income. In general, it can be assumed that the alternatives to a given project are public or private expenditures having equivalent effects on total employment. The employment effects of government projects, therefore, can usually be disregarded. Intangible effects are those costs and benefits which cannot be quantified or at least cannot be priced. What is measurable or non-measurable, however, is less a matter of what is abstractly possible than it is of what is pragmatically, and, at reasonable cost, feasible. Implicit costs represent forgone benefits, e.g., the forgone opportunity to earn income while at school, and implicit benefits represent forgone costs, e.g. a reduction in the costs of juvenile delinquency. Implicit effects are more difficult to accommodate than explicit payments and receipts.

112.   WEISBROD, BURTON A. "Benefits of Manpower Programs: Theoretical and Methodological Issues." In *Cost-Benefit Analysis of Manpower Policies, Proceedings of a North American Conference, May 14-15, 1969,* edited by G. G. Somers and W. D. Wood, pp. 3-15. Published jointly by the Industrial Relations Center, Queen's University, Kingston, Ontario, and the Center for Studies in Vocational and Technical Education, The University of Wisconsin, Madison, Wisconsin, 1969.

Headings: Introduction; Program objectives; Economic stability; Allocative efficiency; Are governmental manpower programs likely to be economically efficient; Manpower programs and the equity of income distribution; Summary.

Abstract: The author asks what can be expected of manpower programs in terms of the three main and interrelated objectives of public policy — allocative efficiency (the objective of balanced growth), distributional equity (the goal of reducing poverty), and economic stability (the goal of reducing unemployment and inflation). Manpower programs can promote economic stability through a reduction in unemployment caused by altering the quality and location of labour supply. Are manpower programs as efficient as alternative devices for reducing unemployment? This raises the question of allocative efficiency. The author examines the effects of manpower programs on unemployment, "structural imbalance", inflationary pressure, and long-run economic growth, and asks whether manpower programs are more efficient during periods of low and falling unemployment. While we might concede that manpower programs produce benefits, the issue is whether the benefits exceed the costs. If manpower programs do have efficiency benefits, why does the private sector fail to undertake adequate programs of retraining, relocation, and job-matching? Justification for government manpower programs on efficiency grounds can take three forms: it can be argued that there are external benefits; that there are imperfections in manpower markets; or that there are capital imperfections which prevent the low income worker from financing a training course. The author feels that lack of allocative efficiency in the private sector is not likely to be an adequate justification for governmental support of manpower programs. We should not be surprised if benefit-cost analyses show that these programs are inefficient. It does not follow that an inefficient manpower program is "undesirable". It may have favourable income distribution consequences and it may redistribute income in a manner that is socially preferable to the alternative of transfer payments. We must find some way in our evaluation of manpower programs of weighting income redistribution consequences against possibly unfavourable allocative consequences.

113. WELLISZ, STANISLAW. "On External Diseconomies and the Government-Assisted Invisible Hand." *Economica,* Vol. 31, No. 124 (November, 1964), pp. 345-362.

Headings: The modern-old approach and its limitations; The Pigovian solution to the problem of externalities; Conclusions.

Abstract: The article surveys the attacks by Coase (71) and Buchanan (69) on the Pigovian principle of public intervention to equalize private and social costs. These authors claim that a Pareto optimum can be reached through a market in externalities whereas administrative measures can be costly and may cause divergences from the optimum. The author argues that the private bargaining solution applies only to exceptional cases, and that such cases are of little interest to the policy maker. The Pigovian tax-subsidy approach has been criticized on theoretical grounds by Davis and Whinston (72) who argue that the Pigovian method cannot deal with "non-separable" externalities, i.e. cases where the output of one firm affects the marginal cost of another. The author puts forward a formal proof showing that a Pigovian system of taxes which internalizes the external effects can be designed for the "non-separable" case. On the other hand, he admits that such a system may not be easy to design or administer. This latter point relates to Buchanan's objections to the Pigovian system — that any administrative measure is likely to impose externalities of its own.

114. WENNERGREN, E. BOYD. "Surrogate Pricing of Outdoor Recreation." *Land Economics,* Vol. 43, No. 1 (February, 1967), pp. 112-116.

Headings: Introduction; The theoretical formulation; Sampling and data collection; Results of the study; Conclusion.

Abstract: This discussion is concerned with the question of how a surrogate or substitute price can be estimated for outdoor recreation. The problem is one of deciding which of the recreationist's several money costs is relevant to his decision concerning the consumption of outdoor recreation. Economic theory suggests that the consumer will maximize his satisfaction from the recreation experience at that level of consumption at which the cost of the marginal visit is equal to the value of the utility received. Furthermore, economic theory indicates that short run decisions concerning, for example, the consumption of boating services, are unrelated to the level of either fixed or average costs. Thus, the postulate is that the number of trips taken by an individual during the boating season is a function of the travel and on-site costs per trip. Regression analysis was used to relate various cost items to the number of trips made by a sample of boaters in Utah. Only one cost variable, travel and on-site costs, was statistically significant.

4. INVESTMENT CRITERIA and the SOCIAL DISCOUNT RATE

115. ALCHIAN, ARMEN A. "The Rate of Interest, Fisher's Rate of Return Over Costs and Keynes' Internal Rate of Return." *American Economic Review,* Vol. 45, No. 5 (December, 1955), pp. 938-943.

Headings: Introduction; Keynes' marginal efficiency of capital; Fisher's rate of return over cost; Sources of confusion; Significance of confusion.

Abstract: The author points out that Keynes' marginal efficiency of capital is not identical with Fisher's marginal rate of return over cost. The marginal efficiency of capital is the rate of discount which equates the present worth of the receipt stream to the present worth of the expense stream. The marginal return over cost is the rate of discount which sets the series of differences between two streams of net benefits, given by alternative investment opportunities, equal to zero. Fisher's rate of return over cost does not rank investments once and for all; it merely determines all the rates of interest at which one investment would be preferred to another. Fisher ranked investments by present value at the market rate; his ranking gives the same results as the internal rate of return if we assume that the net receipt stream can always be reinvested in new investment options with the same Keynesian internal rate of return.

116. ARROW, KENNETH J. "The Imperfections of the Private Capital Market." A Discussion Paper prepared for the RFF Seminar on the Discount Rate for Public Investments, March 24, 1965, Washington, D.C. Mimeographed. Washington: Resources for the Future, 8 p.

Headings: Introduction; Risk and rates of return; The consumer's allocation between consumption and saving; Marketability and liquidity.

Abstract: If the private capital market were perfect and if there were no divergencies between social and marginal benefit on it, the discount rate appropriate to public investment would be that found on the market. The view that the capital market is imperfect derives immediately from the observation that many different rates of return appear to be available in our economy. Different forms of investment are imperfect substitutes because they vary in riskiness and marketability. The author argues that optimal allocation through the market would require a set of markets for risk bearing which do not in fact exist. It is suggested that risk aversion should be irrelevant in the choice of public, as opposed to private, investments. While empirical analysis has not been successful in identifying the consumer-time preference, it is probable that market rates of interest have little to do with individual time preference. The author feels that the pure rate of time preference is rather higher than the rate of investment opportunities open to the consumer. These opportunities have a non-monetary utility associated with their liquidity and marketability.

117. ARROW, KENNETH J. "Optimal Public Investment Policy." A Discussion Paper prepared for the RFF Seminar on the Discount Rate for Public Investments, March 24, 1965, Washington, D.C. Mimeographed. Washington: Resources for the Future. 11 p.

Headings: Introduction; The consumption rate of interest; The model; A heuristic discussion; The exact discussion of the model; Disaggregation of the discount conditions; Budgetary constraints; Population changes.

Abstract: The paper seeks to determine the optimal public investment policy in an aggregate model. In this model the economy attempts to maximize a sum of discounted utility of consumption subject to constraints governing private capital formation and consumption. The appropriate discount rate for public investment is found to be the social discount rate or natural rate of interest. The natural rate of interest is determined by time preference, the marginal utility of consumption, and the rate of increase of consumption, and is independent of the rate of return in the private sector. The author points out that his model has circumvented the problem of allowing for different timing patterns of investment projects. He concludes by considering the impact on the model of budgetary constraints and population changes.

118. ARROW, KENNETH J. "Discounting and Public Investment Criteria." In *Water Research,* edited by Allen V. Kneese and Stephen C. Smith, pp. 13-32. Baltimore: Johns Hopkins Press, 1966.

Headings: The setting of the problem; The imperfections of the capital market; Elementary propositions on economic growth; The natural rate of interest;

A simple optimal growth model; Public and private capital with fixed savings ratio and tax financing; The implications of bond financing; Risk and the rate of return; References (37).

Abstract: The discount rate on public investment should be different from that found on the private market only where the private capital market is imperfect. The view that the capital market is imperfect is supported by the many different rates of return which appear to be available. In addition, the fact that observed rates of interest fail to reflect time preference is demonstrated by the general inability to borrow against future earnings at the usual market rates of interest. Public investment policy must be judged in the context of a growing economy; the natural rate of interest is introduced as a counterpart of the natural rate of growth given by the Harrod-type growth model. In the perfectly planned economy, current investment, including reinvestment, is governed by the short term rate of interest which tends over time to the natural rate. In an economy with an imperfect capital market, the optimal tax and public investment policy equates the marginal productivity of public investment to the natural rate of interest; the rate of return on private capital need not equal the national rate. When bond financing is introduced however, the optimal path of capital formation can be achieved by an appropriate policy mix of taxation and bond financing, and the rate of interest applicable to public investment should equal the private rate. The paper concludes by arguing that the government should not display risk aversion in its behaviour.

119. ARROW, KENNETH J. "The Social Discount Rate." In *Cost-Benefit Analysis of Manpower Policies, Proceedings of a North American Conference, May 14-15, 1969,* edited by G. G. Somers and W. D. Wood, pp. 56-75. Published jointly by the Industrial Relations Centre, Queen's University, Kingston, Ontario, and the Center for Studies in Vocational and Technical Education, The University of Wisconsin, Madison, Wisconsin, 1969.

Headings: The basic issues; Economic policy in a mixed economy; Investment policy as optimization over time; The production and valuation assumptions; The publicly optimal policy; Controllability with fixed saving ratio in the private sector; Controllability with perfectly rational consumers; Risk and the rate of return; Some loose ends.

Abstract: Because of capital market imperfections, divergencies between social and private costs, and between social and private values, the market rate of return on capital cannot be used as a measure of its opportunity cost. In a completely centralized economy, an optimum policy could be produced and enforced. In a mixed economy, the government attempts to enforce its policy through the policy instruments open to it. If there exist values of the policy instruments which cause realization of the government policy, then the policy is "controllable": controllability depends upon the number of power of the instruments available. When the instruments are insufficient a second best solution is sought. In order to ascertain whether a policy aimed at simultaneous optimization of present and future investment decisions will be controllable, the author constructs a growth model in which output is a function of labour, private capital, and government capital. The assumptions of the model are such as to give steady-state growth. A utility function is constructed to evaluate alternative policies, and the policy instruments — consumption, government investment, and private investment — are chosen as functions over time in such a way as to maximize the utility function. It is found that optimality requires the marginal net rates of productivity of the two types of capital to be the same, and also to be equal to the consumption rate of interest. The consumption rate of interest is equal to the utility discount rate when the utility function is homogeneous of degree one, but greater than the utility discount rate when there is diminishing marginal utility of consumption. The controllability of the optimal policy depends upon the workings of the private markets and upon the range of instruments open to the government. Assume that the private sector saves a fixed fraction of disposable income. If the government is restricted to one policy instrument only — an income tax — the optimum policy will not, in general, be controllable. A second best solution can be obtained by choosing shadow prices for private and government capital, and choosing a rate of income tax such as to maximize national income in utility terms. In the steady-state growth path which emerges, the long-run rate of return on government capital is the social rate of time preference, even although the return on private capital may be quite different. This is because, indirectly, the returns from government investment include some benefit from private projects. With two policy instruments — taxation of consumption and taxation of saving — the optimum policy will be controllable: optimality will be achieved if the appropriate values of the two policy instruments are chosen. Assume now that the private sector consists of perfectly rational consumers, with full knowledge of future interest rates and wage levels, seeking to maximize the same utility function as the government. In this case optimality can be achieved with two policy instruments — borrowing and a tax. The tax cannot be an income tax because this destroys optimality through the double taxation of saving. A consumption tax or a pool tax would fulfill the requirements of optimality. Risk is not introduced into the analysis: if there is an optimal allocation of risk-bearing, and if the random returns on the government investment are statistically independent of those in the economy before the investment takes place, then generally the uncertain benefits and costs should be evaluated at their expected value and discounted at the rate of return appropriate to riskless investments. Apart from the market imperfections explicitly introduced into the analysis, the paper assumes that the market structure is otherwise perfect. When monopolistic price distortions, excise taxes, or corporate income tax are introduced, the calculation of the social discount rate becomes far more complicated.

120. BAILEY, MARTIN J. "Formal Criteria for Investment Decisions." *Journal of Political Economy,* Vol. 67, No. 5 (October,
1959), pp. 476-488.

Headings: Introduction; Three-period analysis; Multi-period analysis; A
ranking scheme; The opportunity surface; Independent investment opportunities; The rate of return-present value controversy.

Abstract: Hirshleifer's analysis (140) of the investment decison in the two-
period case can be applied only to the simplest cases of multi-period investment. The general solution to the investment decision problem cannot rely
solely on either present-value or rate-of-return reasoning. The author points
out that any three-period investment can be considered as the outcome of
various pairs of two-period investments, where each pair can be obtained by
assuming a rate of return for one period's investment and determining what
the rate of return for the other period's investment must be to produce the
overall results of the three-period investment. The application of this concept
to the case of an investment with a negative third-period receipt makes it clear
why the use of a constant long-term rate of return for judging three-period
investments leads to paradoxes. This result can be extended to multi-period
investments and can be reformulated in terms of a ranking scheme. The author demonstrates that which of any pair of three-period investments is superior may vary according to the values of the two short-term rates of interest;
the ranking of any pair of three-period investments is, therefore, two dimensional. If it is assumed that each investment is independent of any other, a
unique and well-behaved three dimensional opportunity surface can be obtained showing the combination of consumption in the three periods made possible
by all the available investments. The special problems of interindependent
investment opportunities are considered and the paper concludes by showing
how paradoxical results can be obtained by indiscriminate use of the present-
value and rate-of-return criteria.

121. BANKS, ROBERT L. "Discount/Interest Rates in Evaluation
of Public Investment Projects." In *Hearings Before the Subcommittee
on Economy in Government of the Joint Economic Committee, Congress of the United States,* 90th Congress, 1st Session, 1967, pp.
237-242. Washington: Government Printing Office, 1967.

Headings: The role of the discount/interest rate in evaluating the economic
efficiency of government financed transportation projects; Background; The
critical role of discount/interest rates in benefit-cost calculation; An appropriate interest/discount rate; Conclusions; Selected bibliography (8).

Abstract: The author argues that the average rate of interest payable on
long-term marketable securities of the United States is not an appropriate
interest/discount rate for constructing benefit-cost ratios of government investment projects. The benefit-cost ratio varies with the interest/discount

rate used because benefits and costs accrue in different time patterns: in general, the higher the interest/discount rate the lower the benefit-cost ratio. It is clear, therefore, that a benefit-cost calculation is valid only if an appropriate interest rate is used. The social opportunity cost of funds used by the government is not adequately reflected by the interest rate on a selected group of government bonds. The true cost is the cost of *all* the resources used by government, including those diverted by taxation from use in the private sector. Because of the practical problems of measurement, there is a lack of unanimity among economists as to the specific value of this cost, but it is almost certainly above 5 per cent. The Corps of Engineers, on the other hand, using the government bond rate as a guide, has employed a rate of 3⅛ per cent.

122.   BAUMOL, WILLIAM J. "On the Appropriate Discount Rate for Evaluation of Public Projects." In *Hearings Before the Subcommittee on Economy in Government of the Joint Economic Committee, Congress of the United States,* 90th Congress, 1st Session, 1967, pp. 152-159. Washington: Government Printing Office, 1967.

Headings: Significance of the discount rate; The basic criterion: opportunity cost; The opportunity cost of consumer resources; The discount rate on resources from the business sector; Changes in rates on government bonds; Calculation of the rate of return on long-term bonds; Subsidy for the future; Concluding comments: the consensus of professional economists.

Abstract: The correct discount rate for evaluating government projects is the percentage rate of return that the resources utilized would otherwise provide in the private sector. The opportunity cost of consumer resources is, for bondholders, the yield of long-term bonds, and, for non-bond holders, higher than the long-term bond rate; there is, therefore, no justification for using a discount rate lower than 4.75 per cent on resources taken from consumers. The opportunity cost of resources derived from business firms is the *before-tax* rate of return on business investment: this is in the range of 11 to 17 per cent. When the long-run bond rate of return is being calculated for use in project evaluation, the market yield rather than the coupon rate should be estimated, and the term of the bond should be taken as the number of years to maturity rather than the original maturity. If the nation's investment for the future is regarded as inadequate, the appropriate remedy is to institute simultaneous inducements to both private and public capital formation, and not to transfer funds from high to low yielding sectors. The consensus of professional economists is that 4.75 per cent is the lowest discount rate which should be used. If the bulk of a public project's resources is drawn from the corporate sector a discount rate substantially higher than 4.75 per cent is called for.

123. BAUMOL, WILLIAM J. "On the Social Rate of Discount." *American Economic Review,* Vol. 58, No. 4 (September, 1968), pp. 788-802.

Headings: Introduction; The basic model: the role of taxes; Some modifications: the role of risk; Reassessment: total investment and its allocation between the public and private sectors; The role of consumers' subjective time preference; Investment as a public good: the externalities argument; References (16).

Abstract: An incorrect estimate of the value of the social discount rate may result in serious error in the calculation of benefit/cost ratios. The author argues that the appropriate rate of discount for public projects is one which measures correctly the social opportunity cost of the resources involved. Under certain assumptions, the existence of a corporation tax will lead to over-investment in public projects unless adjustments are made to the social discount rate: if the expected rate of return is the same in the public and private sectors, the existence of a 50 per cent corporation tax requires the government to discount public projects at *twice* their expected yield. Private risk has the same kind of effect as the corporation tax since, from the point of view of society, a private project is equally riskless with a public one if there is an equal likelihood of completion. If, for example, corporations employ a 6 per cent risk premium, the corporation tax is 50 per cent, and the expected yield of both public and private projects is 5 per cent, then the social opportunity cost of funds drawn from the private sector is 16 per cent even although their cost to the government is the 5 per cent government bond rate. Because of the corporation tax and private risk, the social discount rate which gives an efficient allocation of resources between the private and the public sectors must be higher than society's time preference rate of discount reflected in the government bond rate. If an arbitrary choice between the social opportunity cost rate and the social time preference rate has to be made, the author would favour the former. He argues that there is no need to redistribute income from present to future generations. This does not, however, imply that the future should in every respect be left to the mercy of the free market: where there are externalities or irreversibilities, public intervention may be necessary. It is possible to envision circumstances in which we would wish to encourage a more general program of investment, although this need not be public investment.

124. BROUSSALIAN, V. L. *On Discounting and Risk in Military Investment Decisions.* Washington: Center for Naval Analyses, August, 1966. i + 12 p.

Headings: Abstract; Introduction; The two senses of discounting; "Discounting" on account of risk.

Abstract: The term "discounting" is often applied indiscriminately to two distinct operations. The first operation attempts to simulate the capital market's evaluation of an investment by discounting the future income stream to give the present value. Since the present value is essentially a market datum, it is meaningless to "Discount", in the first sense of the word, a stream of non-marketable benefits. The second operation consists of a revision of a future benefit or cost stream, usually to take account of time preference. With respect to some goods and at a given instant, however, time preference can be positive or negative and there is no single rate which can be applied. If a discount factor is used to account for risk and uncertainty, it should be such that each term is reduced to its "certainty equivalent". In most cases this would involve deflating the benefit stream and inflating the cost stream.

125. BROUSSALIAN, V.L. "The Present Value Criterion in Military Investments." A paper read at the thirtieth national meeting of the Operations Research Society of America, Durham, N.C., October 17-19, 1966. Mimeographed. 10 p.

Abstract: The author argues that the present value criterion is not appropriate for the non-marketable type of investment. The choice of project in this instance is basically a choice between consumption streams, and the author believes that the present value criterion is not economically meaningful in the case of collective consumption decisions. He points out that it is not possible to alter the time profile of effectiveness of a given defense system by market trading: with non-marketable investments, a decision to invest is simultaneously a decision with respect to the distribution of the benefits and costs over time and over individuals. If the present value of the cost stream of one system is less than that of another system, using the bond rate as the rate of discount, this implies that the decision-maker can improve on a given time profile of taxation by choosing the former system. Since the profile of taxes is not the same as the profile of the decrease in aggregate consumption, which is the true opportunity cost of the investment decision, the decision-maker has no way of knowing which is the optimal payment profile, and there is therefore no present value criterion.

126. DATTA, BHABATOSH. "The Investment Criterion Problem." *Arthaniti,* Vol. 1 No. 2 (May, 1958), pp. 81-92.

Abstract: The author demonstrates that the choice between maximizing current output and maximizing growth potential is really a choice between different time-paths of consumer good production. The problem could also be stated in terms of a choice between alternative time paths of capital goods production. Various time paths of consumer goods output are illustrated: these paths assume a single or composite consumer good, a single or composite capital good, and an unchanging production possibility curve. The planners' maximand may be the height of the consumption curve at the last year of the time-horizon, or alternatively, it may be the total area under the consumption curve up to the last year of the planning period. The author emphasizes that his approach is greatly simplified: there are difficulties inherent in any time-horizon concept; the index number problem stemming from heterogeneous goods has been avoided; and the analysis is carried out in real terms. Nevertheless, even in the basic economics of the criterion problem, one comes face to face with welfare decisions at almost every step.

127. DAVISSON, WILLIAM I. "Public Investment Criteria." *Land Economics,* Vol. 40, No. 2 (May, 1964), pp. 153-162.

Headings: Introduction; Benefit-cost analysis; Cost allocation; Conclusions.

Abstract: This paper outlines the benefit-cost analysis procedure used by the U.S. Department of Agriculture, the Corps of Engineers, and the Bureau of Reclamation. He concludes that benefit-cost ratios are inappropriate as a criterion for evaluation of federal river development projects because the ratios do not give any indication of the net benefits per dollar invested, i.e. the benefit-cost ratios do not take into account the budget constraint. The appropriate criterion is maximization of present worth. Where a project has a number of purposes, it is often important to identify the primary function. Investment in an additional function is justified only if the present value of the resulting benefit stream is at least equal to the separable cost of the function.

128. DENISON, EDWARD F. "Capital Theory and the Rate of Return." *American Economic Review,* Vol. 54, No. 5 (September, 1964), pp. 721-725.

Abstract: This article reviews Solow's *Capital Theory and the Rate of Return* (175). The author has three main criticisms. Firstly, Solow argues that rates of return on investment can be calculated without measuring capital stock: the relevant rates of return however are after depreciation, and the calculation of depreciation involves measurement of capital stock. Secondly, the author does not accept that the conventional calculation of the rate of return in the model with technical progress embodied in capital stock has failed to take account of obsolescence. Thirdly, he feels that Solow's estimates of social rates of return at high employment in the United States are too high on the assumption that all technical progress is embodied, and that the embodied model itself is unreasonable.

129. ECKSTEIN, OTTO. "Interest Rate Policy for the Evaluation of Federal Programs." In *Hearings before the Subcommittee on Economy in Government of the Joint Economic Committee, Congress of the United States,* 90th Congress, 2nd Session, 1968, pp. 50-57. Washington: Government Printing Office, 1968.

Headings: Introduction; The role of the interest rate in a market economy; Imperfections in capital markets; A theoretically correct solution in an imperfect market economy; Some pragmatic considerations; What interest rate for public investments; Conclusion and reconmmendation.

Abstract: The author believes that the imperfections of the U.S. capital market destroy the normative significance of interest rates found in the market. These imperfections give rise to two concepts: the social rate of time preference which is derived from theoretical models of economic growth and postulated functions for the marginal utility of consumption over time; and the opportunity cost of public capital which represents the return which could have been obtained from forgone investment opportunities. A theoretically correct solution to the problem of the choice of an interest rate for public investment planning in an imperfect market economy has been outlined by the author (147). This formulation translates into U.S. Government practice as follows: apply the social time preference rate of interest in the valuation of projects and undertake those projects which have a benefit-cost ratio greater than the benefit-cost ratio of the forgone opportunities. There are two serious difficulties in applying this method: there is no generally agreed upon empirical basis for deriving the rate of social time preference, and, secondly, even if there is a collective desire to redistribute income to the future, it is dubious that public investments are the most desirable method of accomplishing this. Three postulates underlie the author's conclusions about the social discount rate. They are, firstly, that the rate of return on capital in the U.S. is high; secondly, that the competition for budget money will remain stiff; and, thirdly, that the high productivity of capital must be reflected in the interest rate used for evaluating public investments. The borrowing cost for long-term capital for the Federal Government is 5½ per cent while the opportunity cost for tax raised capital is 8 per cent. The latter figure is obtained by adjusting for the current interest rate level an estimate made for 1955 (147). While both these rates are of some pertinence, the heavier weight should be placed on the latter: an interest rate of 7 to 7½ per cent is therefore a proper rate for Federal planning.

130. FELDSTEIN, MARTIN S. "Net Social Benefit Calculation and the Public Investment Decision." *Oxford Economic Papers,* Vol. 16, No. 1 (March, 1964), pp. 114-131.

Headings: Introduction; The social opportunity cost of funds transferred from the private sector to the public sector; Net social benefit calculation; Net social benefit investment algorithms.

Abstract: The author presents an investment decision criterion which takes into account both the social opportunity cost of funds used and society's social time preference. The calculation of the private investment multiplier as a measure of social opportunity cost is illustrated. The private investment multiplier is employed in the estimation of net social benefit. The use of net social benefit values in deciding whether projects are admissible is discussed under various forms of budgeting constraints. The paper abstracts from problems of externalities, the evaluation of inputs and outputs, the normative significance of private sector prices, intangibles and incommensurables, and uncertainty.

131.   FELDSTEIN, MARTIN S. "The Social Time Preference Discount Rate in Cost Benefit Analysis." *Economic Journal,* Vol. 74, No. 294 (June, 1964), pp. 360-379.

Headings: Introduction and references (16); Inapplicability of a "perfect" market interest rate to public policy; Public preference versus the "public good"; The two-period STP function; The STP rate; The STP rate through time; Summary.

Abstract: The author cites the present value of the net addition to consumption created by a project as the most useful measure of the project's worth. He suggests that the social opportunity cost of funds be allowed for by placing a "shadow price" on the funds used in the project, and that all intertemporal comparisons be made with a social time preference (STP) rate. The STP function cannot be derived on the basis of existing market rates but must be administratively determined as a matter of public policy. Indifference curve analysis is used to examine the factors which should affect an administrative determination of an STP function. The effects on the STP rate of changing consumption levels and growth rates, and of changes in pure time preference are examined. It is reasonable to expect the STP rate to rise over time.

132.   FELDSTEIN, MARTIN S. "Opportunity Cost Calculations in Cost-Benefit Analysis." *Public Finance,* Vol. 19, No. 2 (1964), pp. 117-139.

Headings: Introduction; Funds transferred from the private sector; Funds transferred from other projects within the agency; Including STP and SOC; Summary; Résumé: Calcul des coûts d'opportunité dans l'analyse des coûts et bénéfices.

Abstract: The social opportunity cost (SOC) of a public investment project is the value to society of the next best alternative use to which the resources employed in the project could have been put. The SOC is best considered as the alternative consumption time stream discounted at a rate determined by the social time preference (STP). The estimated foregone consumption stream should reflect the source of funds, the productivity of private investment, and the effects of taxation and reinvestment. The author examines the evaluation of public investment projects with and without capital rationing: he pays particular attention to techniques of evaluating water resource development projects. He regards attempts at combining SOC and STP by means of an SOC rate as misdirected, and reaffirms that the SOC is an STP-discounted present value "shadow price".

133.   FELDSTEIN, MARTIN S. "The Derivation of Social Time Preference Rates." *Kyklos,* Vol. 18 (1965), pp. 277-287.

Headings: Introduction; Four basic relations; Case I: constant population, no time preference, and equal distribution; Case II: the general case with equal distribution; Irrelevance of distribution of consumption; Some possible values.

Abstract: The social opportunity cost of funds transferred from private to public investment can be evaluated as the present value of the consumption that would have occurred had the private investment been made, discounted at the social time preference rate, which is a measure of society's marginal rate of substitution between consumption in consecutive years. The social time preference rate is a function of the growth rates of population and consumption and of three policy parameters: the "pure" time preference rate, the elasticity of the utility-consumption function, and a population parameter. Only in Case I is the STP rate equal to the rate of growth. The results require constant but not equal distribution of consumption. The functions are expressed in mathematical form and a table of STP values derived from given values of the two estimable parameters and the three policy parameters is presented.

134. FELDSTEIN, M. S., and J. S. FLEMMING. "The Problem of Time-Stream Evaluation: Present Value Versus Internal Rate of Return Rules." *Bulletin of the Oxford University Institute of Economics and Statistics,* Vol. 26, No. 1 (February, 1964), pp. 79-85.

Headings: Introduction; Two discounting rules for time stream evaluation; Discounting rules under capital rationing; Some complications in the application of the present value rule.

Abstract: The authors discuss and compare the present value and internal rate of return investment rules. The present value rule is preferred for the following reasons: if the net revenue stream changes sign, the value of the internal rate of return need not be unique or even real. Since a valid rule based on the internal rate of return requires the use of Fisher's rate of return over cost, the relevant time streams (which constitute streams of differences between net benefits) are likely to change sign frequently. Secondly, the comparison of any current interest rate with simple or incremental rates of return may be irrelevant if the rate is liable to change over the life of the project: the present value criterion, on the other hand, does not require that the time-preference function be represented as a constant discount rate. Thirdly, the present value rule is simpler to operate. The case for the present value criterion is strengthened if a budget constraint is introduced. The paper concludes with a discussion of the implications for the present value rule of the existence of future investment opportunities associated with a present project.

135. FLEMMING, JOHN S., and MARTIN S. FELDSTEIN. "Present Value Versus Internal Rate of Return: A Comment." *Economic Journal,* Vol. 74, No. 294 (June, 1964), p. 490.

Abstract: The authors agree with Turvey's conclusion (181) that present value calculations are preferable to internal rate of return methods. They point out, however, that the internal rate of return criterion does give less weight to remoter than to nearer costs and revenues where the minimum acceptable rate of return is greater than zero. Where the minimum rate is governed by the size of the budget, it does not reflect a chosen time preference. The authors criticize the omission of Fisher's "rate of return over cost" — the rate which discounts the stream of differences between the net revenues of two projects to zero.

136.   HARBERGER, ARNOLD C. "The Interest Rate in Cost-Benefit Analysis." In *Papers Submitted by Panelists Appearing Before the Subcommittee on Fiscal Policy of the Congress of the United States,* 85th Congress, 1st Session, 1957, pp. 239-241. Washington: Government Printing Office, 1957.

Abstract: The interest rate used in the discounting of benefits and costs is of critical importance in the evaluation of long-term government investments. The author argues that 6 per cent or higher is the appropriate rate for use in evaluating government projects. This compares with a rate of 2.5 per cent most commonly used by the government agencies which undertake cost-benefit analyses. As long as there exist widespread opportunities for investments yielding 6 and 8 per cent and higher, society does itself a disservice by investing at yields of 2.5 or 3.5 per cent. In industry and agriculture it is clear that there do exist many alternative investments yielding 6 per cent and more per year. Government projects do not differ substantially from private projects in their degree of riskiness, and do not, therefore, warrant a substantially lower discount rate. Could the projects actually undertaken pass the test of a higher interest rate? Of twenty-four Bureau of Reclamation projects examined, only two would have been judged acceptable at a 7.5 per cent discount rate when primary benefits only are taken into consideration. Similar results emerged from a study of Corps of Engineers projects.

137.   HARBERGER, ARNOLD C. "On the Opportunity Cost of Public Borrowing." In *Hearings Before the Subcommittee on Economy in Government of the Joint Economic Committee, Congress of the United States,* 90th Congress, 2nd Session, 1968, pp. 57-65. Washington: Government Printing Office, 1968.

Abstract: If one is to use private sector rates of return to obtain the opportunity cost of public funds, what is called for is a weighted average of the rates of return applying in all relevant sectors of the private economy, the weights reflecting the degrees to which investment in each sector is estimated to be displaced by public sector borrowing. When government borrowing displaces private investment, the cost of such borrowing to the economy is better measured by the rate of interest on Government bonds plus the tax loss on the income foregone because of displaced private investment, rather than by the overall yield of the displaced investment. Three categories of displaced investment should be recognized — corporate, non-corporate, and owner- occupied residential housing (because of its peculiar tax status). All taxes foregone because of government borrowing are relevant to social opportunity cost: these include corporation taxes, income taxes, property taxes and sales and excise taxes. The author presents an illustrative calculation of the overall social opportunity cost of capital and arrives at the figure of 10.7 per cent; he feels that further research would not modify this figure by more than 2 percentage points. Eckstein (147) applied a similar methodology to that of the present paper to the raising of funds by taxation rather than by borrowing. This raises three questions: should the opportunity cost of public funds obtained via borrowing be regarded as superior to the opportunity cost of funds raised by taxation as the social discount rate? Since funds came from both sources should the relevant rate be a weighted average? Should not different rates of discount be used depending on how the funds in question are raised? The conclusion is that the social opportunity cost of borrowing is the relevant rate since there is a definable pattern in which government borrowing displaces private investment, but no standard pattern in decisions about changes in tax rates and tax bases.

138. HARBERGER, ARNOLD C. "Professor Arrow on the Social Discount Rate." In *Cost-Benefit Analysis of Manpower Policies, Proceedings of a North American Conference, May 14-15, 1969,* edited by G. G. Somers and W. D. Wood, pp. 76-88. Published jointly by the Industrial Relations Centre, Queen's University, Kingston, Ontario, and the Center for Studies in Vocational and Technical Education, The University of Wisconsin, Madison, Wisconsin, 1969.

Headings: Arrow's approach; Comments on Arrow's approach; An alternative conceptual framework.

Abstract: After summarizing Arrow's approach (119) to the calculation of the social discount rate, the author makes the following points. Arrow's utility function discounts utility at a rate which is described as "a discount factor for utilities". This discount factor appears to be typical of the utility function and not related or responsive to market phenomena; nevertheless it is a basic determinant of the interest rate in Arrow's model. Secondly, if we posited a utility function which generates a constant savings rate under all circumstances, a solution with a positive tax on savings would be non-optimal since the tax on saving, in conjunction with the tax on consumption, would make the marginal rate of substitution between present and future consumption differ from the marginal rate of transformation. Thirdly, where a second-best solution is derived and the discount rate differs from the social yield on additional savings, the analyst must solve the reinvestment problem — what will be the effect of this project on investment at each future point in time?

72

Fourthly, Arrow's analysis leads to a full optimum or at least to a constrained optimum under the assumption of certain distortions. If we accept, however, that distortions will remain, we are not able to pursue any kind of optimum in a strict sense. The kind of question we must ask is simply "does this course of action increase utility?" The only kind of optimization which may prove to be possible is reaching the optimum program design for a specific policy objective. It is possible, therefore, that Arrow's analysis contains so much abstract theory as to preclude its having any practical value. As an alternative, the author suggests that the social discount rate may be obtained as a weighted average of the marginal rates of productivity of capital in the various sectors from which investment is displaced, and of the marginal rates of time preference applicable to the various groups whose saving is stimulated by the additional government borrowing. This weighting method can also be used to calculate the social opportunity cost of an input into a public sector project and the social opportunity cost of foreign exchange. To calculate the social discount rate, assume that the rate of return after such taxes as corporation tax and property tax, but before personal income tax, is equalized in all lines of investment by market forces. Accordingly, the marginal productivity of capital will be different in different lines of activity, and the after tax rate of return for savers will be different for different marginal tax brackets. The weights are, for each tax bracket, the elasticity of supply of savings with respect to their rate of yield, and, for each investment sector, the elasticity of the investment schedule with respect to the cost of capital. This approach has a number of advantages. Firstly, the basic data required for estimating the social discount rate can in principle be obtained from market observations. Secondly, the procedure is consistent with the three basic tenets of cost-benefit analysis; as long as we accept these three principles this procedure is the appropriate one and the reinvestment problem disappears. Thirdly, the approach takes existing distortions into account without, however, building in too great a degree of rigidity. The projected values of the social discount rate may embody any desired set of changes in the pattern of distortions which would almost improve the economy: in other words, this methodology leads to reform of the tax structure directly from economic theory.

139. HENDERSON, P. D. "Notes on Public Investment Criteria in the United Kingdom." *Bulletin of the Oxford University Institute of Economics and Statistics,* Vol. 27, No. 1 (February, 1965), pp. 55-89.

Headings: Introduction; Investment decision formulae; The choice of an interest rate; The problem of capital rationing; The appraisal of public investment projects; a suggested procedure; References (44); Appendix I - A note on the principal sources; Appendix II - Rate of return calculations; Appendix III - British practice in the public sector.

Abstract: The author presents a survey of the questions indicated in the section headings. He examines the discounted cash flow approach in the evaluation of public projects, and the two methods of applying it — the present value rule and the internal rate of return rule. Four possible choices of interest rate are considered: the rate on long term government securities; the social time preference rate; an opportunity cost rate; and a combination of the social time preference rate with a calculation of the social opportunity cost of the public project. The fourth method is theoretically more satisfactory, but there are a number of practical problems associated with determining the cost of a project. In addition, it is conceded that the suggested discount rate of 5 per cent is merely a crude guess at a reasonable figure for the social time preference rate. Appendix II mentions some alternatives to the method of discounted cash flows for evaluating investment projects.

140. HIRSCHLEIFER, J. "On the Theory of Optimal Investment Decision." *Journal of Political Economy,* Vol. 66, No. 4 (August, 1958), pp. 329-352.

Headings: Introduction; Two-period analysis; A brief note on perpetuities; Multiperiod analysis; Concluding comments.

Abstract: The paper begins by examining, through the use of isoquant analysis, and in the light of Fisher's work on interest, the present value and internal rate of return rules of investment behaviour. The present value rule works whenever the internal rate of return rule does, and also correctly discriminates among multiple tangencies when the capital market is perfect. Even the present value rule, however, fails in cases which involve the comparison of multiple tangencies when there is an imperfect capital market. Multiple tangency cases result from non-independent investment opportunities, e.g. where poorer projects are a prerequisite to better ones. The failure of the internal rate of return rule in multiperiod analysis stems from the implicit assumption that all intermediate cash flows are reinvested at the internal rate; in addition, this rule does not allow for varying interperiod preference rates.

141. HIRSCHLEIFER, JACK. "Marginal Efficiency of Capital: Comment." *Economic Journal,* Vol. 69, No. 275 (September, 1959), pp. 592-593.

Abstract: The author points out that Pitchford and Hagger's demonstration (163) that there may not be a unique solution for the marginal efficiency of capital has been preceded by Lorie and Savage (150), Samuelson, and by the author himself (140). The final word on this topic is probably Martin Bailey's article (120). The difficulty with dual or multiple solutions for the marginal efficiency of capital is a symptom of an underlying defect in the concept: investment alternatives cannot in general be evaluated or ranked by a measure derived solely from their constituent cash-flows, but only in comparison with the market or the productive alternative opportunities available.

142. HIRSCHLEIFER, JACK. "Efficient Allocation of Capital in an Uncertain World." *American Economic Review,* Papers and Proceedings, Vol. 54, No. 3 (May, 1964), pp. 77-96.

Headings: Introduction; Multivalued returns — μ, σ preferences; Multivalued returns — time — state preferences; Harmony of market yields; Concluding comment; References (25); Discussion by D. W. Jorgenson, W. Vickrey, T. C. Koopmans, and P. A. Samuelson.

Abstract: The existance of uncertainty leads to multivalued returns being anticipated from an investment. The objects of choice are usually expressed as a mathematical expectation μ and the standard deviation σ of the subjective probability distribution of returns: σ measures the "riskiness" of the investment. The author feels that a more satisfactory method than the approach in terms of μ, σ preferences is a formulation in terms of time-state preferences. For a state-preference at a given time, the Neumann-Morgenstern theorems permit a special formulation of the preference function which cannot be obtained from the μ, σ preferences except by means of arbitrary restrictions upon the subjective probability distributions. The observed pattern of market yields tends to support this theory of choice when convex indifference curves are assumed: this assumption of risk aversion or "conservative behaviour" is supported by empirical observation. If yield divergencies can be explained by the theory of time-state preferences, with the assumption of "conservative behaviour", the rate structure in the capital market will have to be given greater weight in the choice of appropriate discount rate for government projects. This would indicate the use of rates higher than the government's risk-free borrowing rate.

143. HORVAT, BRANKO. "The Optimum Rate of Investment Reconsidered." *Economic Journal,* Vol. 75, No. 299 (September, 1965), pp. 572-576.

Headings: Introduction; The traditional approach; Criticism of the solution suggested in the 1958 paper; The assumptions of an empirically relevant solution; Conclusion.

Abstract: The paper criticizes the traditional utility approach to social discounting. The author's 1958 paper suggested that the optimum rate of investment be determined by zero social marginal efficiency of investment. He defends this view and lists a set of assumptions under which the optimum rate of investment is determined by the point on the investment line where social marginal efficiency of investment with respect to a twenty to twenty-five year period becomes zero.

144. JEAN, WILLIAM H. "On Multiple Rates of Return." *Journal of Finance,* Vol. 23, No. 1 (March, 1968), pp 187-191.

Headings: Multiple rates of return; References (20).

Abstract: This article demonstrates that multiple positive solutions to the equation yielding the internal rate of return are possible only if negative cash inflows occur in the middle of the project's life. There are at least two mathematical theorems that can be used to count the number of positive roots — Budan's theorem and Sturm's theorem. If multiple rates of return are identified, the theory indicated by Wright (184, 185), Silcock (172) and others may be used for capital budgeting analysis.

145.   KAMIEN, MORTON I. "Interest Rate Guidelines for Federal Decision Making." In *Hearings Before the Subcommittee on Economy in Government of the Joint Economic Committee, Congress of the United States,* 90th Congress, 1st Session, 1967, pp. 145-149. Washington: Government Printing Office, 1967.

Abstract: The choice of a rate of interest to be used for discounting future benefits and costs of government projects involves a twofold problem: what portion of society's resources should be devoted to the provision of future benefits and how should that portion be divided between the private and the public sector? What is sought is the interest rate which will maximize the total satisfaction of both present and future generations. In the author's opinion, the appropriate rate of interest to be used in cost-benefit analyses is the rate paid on newly issued long-term government bonds. The maturity of the bond should correspond to the projected lifetime of the project under consideration. Uncertainty regarding future benefits and costs of the project should be reflected in the estimation of benefits and costs, not in the discount rate. No special adjustment is needed to take account of collective preferences regarding present sacrifice for future gain. In cost-benefit studies, adjustments to take account of the present tax structure should be made: both benefits and costs should be calculated *after* taxes. A downward adjustment in the nominal interest rate may be required to make up for anticipated future inflation. The author demonstrates how these conclusions were reached by examining the formation of interest rates, the role of interest rates in the allocation of resources, the kinds of uncertainties which have to be taken into account, and the relationship between collective and individual preferences.

146.   KARMEL, P. H. "The Marginal Efficiency of Capital." *Economic Record,* Vol. 35, No. 72 (December, 1959), pp. 429-434.

Abstract: If an investment project is terminable at any stage during its lifetime, and provided that the scrap value of the asset is always non-negative, the marginal efficiency of the truncated project expected to have the highest marginal efficiency will be a unique value. In cases where projects involve a legal obligation to continue for a certain length of time or have substantial shut-down costs, multiple values of the marginal efficiency may occur if some of the net yields are negative. An example of a project with one of its net yields negative, and with multiple values for its marginal efficiency is constructed; it is found that the marginal efficiency of the project exceeds the rate of interest, but that the present value of the project is less than the supply price. Where the expected rate of earnings on funds (positive or negative) accumulated in the course of the project, but not used for the specific project, is equal to the internal rate of return on the project, the relevant marginal efficiency is the greatest of the multiple values. The paper concludes by pointing out some errors in Soper's article on the marginal efficiency of capital (176).

147. KRUTILLA, JOHN V., and OTTO ECKSTEIN. "The Social Cost of Federal Financing." In *Multiple Purpose River Development,* pp. 78-130. Baltimore: Johns Hopkins Press, 1958.

Headings: Introduction; Saving and investment in the United States; Interest rates in the American economy; Measuring the social cost of public capital: the method of this study; Model A: A tax cut stimulating consumption; Model B: A tax cut stimulating investment; Interpretation of our results; Note to Chapter 4.

Abstract: In considering alternative methods of financing public projects and in evaluating the economic worth of projects, reasonable estimates of the social cost of public funds are essential. Because of the imperfections in the U.S. economy, a market rate of interest cannot be used as the social discount rate. The true social cost of public funds can be measured by determining the incidence of the marginal tax dollars needed to finance a public project, and estimating what value attaches to these funds in their alternative uses. Two models using different sets of assumptions about the potential tax cuts are presented; model A assumes that personal income tax is reduced in a manner most advantageous to low-income families, and that sales taxes are lowered; model B consists of a reduction of the personal income tax with emphasis on upper-income brackets, combined with a reduction of the corporation income tax. Model A gives an estimate of 5.79 per cent for the opporunity cost of public funds, while model B gives 5.44 per cent. The authors believe that, if neither major unemployment nor severe inflation is allowed to develop, the value of the social discount rate is between 5 and 6 per cent. This rate would achieve an efficient allocation of resources. Efficiency is a relative concept dependent on a specific distribution of income. If the community decided to distribute consumption among generations in a manner different from that indicated by the saving behaviour of its members, the opportunity-cost measure of the interest rate would cease to be a proper indicator of social value.

148. KUBINSKI, Z. M., and C. A. WILKINS. "The Marginal Efficiency of Capital and the Effect of the Discounting Period." *Economic Record,* Vol. 36 (August, 1960), pp. 424-425.

Abstract: Wright (184) has pointed out that the length of the accounting period directly influences the number of negative returns. The present note demonstrates that the length of the accounting period can also affect the length of the life of the investment.

149. LIND, ROBERT C. "The Social Rate of Discount and the Optimal Rate of Investment: Further Comment." *Quarterly Journal of Economics,* Vol. 78, No. 2 (May, 1964), pp. 336-345.

Abstract: Marglin (151) assumes that successive generations are completely separated so that there is no market through which individuals can exchange titles to future benefits for present consumption. If it is assumed that a generation is a group of people whose ages lie within a certain age range, a number of generations will normally be living at the same time and transactions between them can be made. It follows that governments may undertake long-term investments in order to maximize the utility of the present generation. Where the members of a society have similar preferences and incomes, an individual's private rate of discount is likely to equal his social rate. For a large population with varying incomes and preferences, on the other hand, interdependence effects will be such that, for a given individual, the social rate of discount may be greater than, equal to, or smaller than the market rate. In these circumstances social agreements are available that will make everyone better off. Thus the presence of interdependence effects necessitates a political solution to the problem of determining the total amount of investment and its distribution among individuals.

150. LORIE, JAMES H., and LEONARD J. SAVAGE. "Three Problems in Rationing Capital." *Journal of Business,* Vol. 28, No. 4 (October, 1955), pp. 229-239.

Headings: Introduction; The three problems; Some comparisons with the rate of return method of capital rationing; Summary.

Abstract: The three problems discussed are: given the cost of capital what group of "independent" investment proposals should the firm accept? given a fixed sum for capital investment, what group of investment proposals should be undertaken? how should a firm select the best among mutually exclusive alternatives? These problems are solved using the criteria of maximizing present value of net worth, and of ranking projects by rate of return. The two criteria do not give the same results in all cases. The rate of return criterion is likely to be misleading, particularly in solving the second problem — that of selecting a group of investment projects under a capital constraint.

151. MARGLIN, STEPHEN A. "The Social Rate of Discount and the Optimal Rate of Investment." *Quarterly Journal of Economics,* Vol. 77, No. 1 (February, 1963), pp. 95-111.

Headings: Introduction; The authoritarian answer; The schizophrenic answer; The interdependence answer; Determining the social rate of discount; Conclusion.

Abstract: The paper argues that individual and collective "savings vs. consumption" decisions must be viewed differently because of the absence of a market through which a generation, as opposed to an individual, can exchange title to future returns for present consumption. The author examines three answers to the question of whether a social rate of discount, distinct from the individual rates of discount applied to unilateral savings decisions, is required. The Pigovian argument for authoritarian rejection of individual time preference maps is inconsistent with the notion that a democratic government reflects only the preferences of present members of society. The schizophrenic answer is that individual market preferences and political preferences are inconsistent: if this is the case there is no way of knowing which set of preference maps provides the better indication of "real" preference. The interdependence answer is that a change in the frame of reference (from private to social decision) involves not a schizophrenic change in preferences but rather a difference between the machinery of the market and political processes for implementing one's preferences. None of us may be willing to invest unilaterally for the benefit of the future generation, but each is prepared to if the coercive power of the state enforces investment by all. If we regard investment as a public good, then the marginal private rate of discount for an individual is the net marginal rate of substitution of future consumption for his own consumption where the trade is a unilateral venture: the marginal social rate of discount is the trade-off where the individual's sacrifice for future generations is accompanied by sacrifices by everyone else. If the social rate is lower than the private rate, then, in a frictionless and competitive model, the State should undertake those investments which are viable according to the social rate but not the market rate. The actual rates of growth, investment and social discount for the community can be estimated iteratively.

152. MARGLIN, STEPHEN A. "The Opportunity Costs of Public Investment." *Quarterly Journal of Economics,* Vol. 77, No. 2 (May, 1963), pp. 274-289.
Headings: Introduction; The formal models; Conclusion.
Abstract: The goal in planning a public investment program should be to avoid displacing "better" investment opportunities in the private sector. The appropriate basis of comparison of alternative private and public investments is the present value of their net benefits to society evaluated at the marginal social rate of discount. Because private investment decisions are made in terms of a marginal time preference different from that governing public investment decisions, an opportunity cost term replaces the money cost of the portion of the resources drawn from the private investment sector. A series of models is presented expressing opportunity cost as a function of displacement, reinvestment, and yield rates. These simplified models illustrate the relationship between public and private investment.

153. MEEK, RONALD, L. "Ideal and Reality in the Choice Between Alternative Techniques." *Oxford Economic Papers,* Vol. 16, No. 3 (November, 1964), pp. 333-354.
Headings: Introduction; "Minimum total annual costs" and "maximum annual rate of profits"; Criteria giving the same results as "minimum total annual

costs"; Criteria equivalent to "maximum annual rate of profits"; Influence of the rate of interest and wages on the investment decision; Implications.

Abstract: The paper examines the nature and effects of a bias against relatively capital-intensive techniques associated with businessmen's use of certain "rate of return" criteria in the choice between individual mutually exclusive investments. The following criteria are demonstrated to be "correct" from the social welfare point of view: present value of stream of costs: capitalized value of stream costs; present worth; rate of return on additional investment; rate of return available for capital charges on additional investment; and justifiable additional investment. In certain circumstances the following criteria may give the "wrong" result: internal rate of return; present worth per unit of investment; and minimum pay-off period. Under exceptional conditions, a rise in the wage rate may induce the businessmen using the "wrong" criterion to make the "correct" choice, but a fall in the interest rate will not.

154. MERRETT, ANTHONY, and ALLEN SYKES. "Calculating the Rate of Return on Capital Projects." *Journal of Industrial Economics,* Vol. 9, No. 1 (November, 1960), pp. 98-115.

Headings: Introduction; The implied rate of return and the rate of return methods; Errors resulting from the use of the rate of return method; Risk; Deficiencies of the IRR; Conclusions; References (4).

Abstract: This paper attempts to reach a definitive conclusion about the relative merits of conventional accounting and academic methods of calculating the rate of return on capital projects. The implied rate of return is considered the most satisfactory academic method: the IRR of a project is that rate of interest which discounts the future net cash flows generated down to the present value which is the cost of the project. The two most common business or accounting methods of assessing capital projects are Payback and the Rate of Return; the limitations of Payback are well known, but the use of the RR method remains widespread. The RR expresses expected profit net of depreciation as a percentage of the initial capital employed. The authors demonstrate that the use of the RR method can lead to the following errors: incorrect ranking of investments, tending to operate against the acceptance of projects with short lives or falling cash flows: systematic underestimation of rates of return; and imperfect comparisons between internal and external investment. The three main dificiencies of the IRR method are that a given capital project may have more than one IRR where there is at least one negative net cash flow; that the IRR is unable to distinguish between mutually exclusive projects that which is the more profitable; and that the marginal cost of capital may change in the future. The authors conclude however, that the IRR is markedly superior to the commonly used accounting methods.

Its three main advantages are its accuracy, its ability to deal with risk, and the comparison it offers with the return on external investments.

155. MILLER, WILLIAM L. "The Magnitude of the Discount Rate for Government Projects." *Southern Economic Journal,* Vol. 28, No. 4 (April, 1962), pp. 348-356.

Headings: Introduction; The discount rate; Inflation; Unemployment; Lagging regions; Summary.

Abstract: This paper surveys Eckstein's work on the discount rate in J. V. Krutilla and O. Eckstein, *Multiple Purpose River Development* Chapter 4 (147). The author explains why an average of rates of return in the private sector is too high a discount rate for Government projects. He chooses a rate of 4-6½ per cent and points out that where the project is financed by inflation severe enough to impose costs on society, the discount rate should be higher. The discount rate appropriate for full employment does not lose its relevance during unemployment, and a low rate of discount may not be the best policy for stimulating the advance of lagging regions such as the U.S. South. Thus, in general, the same range of discount rates will apply to a variety of situations.

156. MILLS, GORDON. "The Marginal Efficiency of Capital and the Present Value Rule." *Yorkshire Bulletin of Economic and Social Research,* Vol. 12, No. 1 (March, 1960), pp. 28-31.

Abstract: The author verifies that the present-value rule and the marginal efficiency criterion for deciding whether or not to invest give the same answer where there are no negative yields. In the case of negative yields, the marginal efficiency criterion may contradict the present-value rule, where the latter is universally valid. The practical importance of this failure of the marginal efficiency criterion may not be very important: there seems to be no reason for the entrepreneur to expect a negative yield when the investment is in full working order and, therefore, no reason to include negative yields in the *ex ante* analysis. A sequence of negative returns at the beginning of the life of an asset is, on the other hand, conceivable. In this case, the author demonstrates, the marginal efficiency criterion *is* valid. When the asset has a sequence of negative returns at the end of its life as well as at the beginning, there are at most two marginal efficiency rates, and the investment will be profitable provided the market rate of interest lies between the two marginal efficiency rates.

157. MISHAN, E. J. "Criteria for Public Investment: Some Simplifying Suggestions." *Journal of Political Economy,* Vol. 75, No. 2 (April, 1967), pp. 139-146.

Headings: Introduction; Social rate of time preference; Public-investment criterion; Criticisms; References (9).

Abstract: The paper makes three criticisms of the public-investment criteria proposed by Marglin (152) and by Feldstein (130). Under the circumstances posited, there should be no distinction made between the different methods used by the government to finance investment projects: the yield in the private-investment sector is the opportunity yield for all public-investment funds no matter how raised. Secondly, the choice of the private-investment yield as the discount rate (instead of the social-discount rate) gives the simple investment criterion that the present value of the public-investment stream of benefits be higher than the stream of returns from the alternative private-investment. Thirdly, the reinvestment of encashable primary benefits of public-investment projects should be undertaken only where the reinvestment opportunities yield more than the private investment yield. In such a case the whole of the primary benefits ought to be reinvested and not just a proportion.

158. MISHAN, E. J. "A Proposed Normalisation Procedure for Public Investment Criteria." *Economic Journal,* Vol. 77, No. 308 (December, 1967), pp. 777-796.

Headings: Introduction; Normalisation procedure; Implications; Admissibility of a single investment project; Comparison of normalised and ordinary criteria; Subsequent outlays and investment criteria; A special case; Appendix: Choosing a set of investment projects subject to a budget constraint; References (23).

Abstract: The paper outlines a normalisation procedure which ensures identical ranking of investment streams irrespective of whether the internal rate of return or present discounted value criterion is used. Under the assumptions common to a number of contributions in this field, the process of normalisation consists of four steps: all magnitudes must be compounded forward to yield a terminal value at a future date; each investment stream must realize maximum reinvestment potential; where the capital sums of the investment projects to be compared are different, the largest costing project is chosen as the common outlay and the other projects are assumed to employ the additional funds as advantageously as possible; the investment streams under comparison must be brought to a common period. The implications of this approach are considered, and a criterion for the admissibility of a single investment project is provided. The results obtained from the conventional criteria are contrasted with the uniquely determined normalised version.

159. NEUBERGER, EGON. "The Yugoslav Investment Auctions." *Quarterly Journal of Economics,* Vol. 73, No. 1 (February, 1959), pp. 88-115.

Headings: Introduction; Yugoslav experience with investment auctions; The theory of investment auctions; Conclusions.

Abstract: The author outlines the auction system of allocating investment funds in Yugoslavia. He describes this system and model of semi-planning

where the authorities determine the level of total investment and the allocation of investment funds among sectors of the economy, while the market
system determines the allocation among firms within a sector, and the technological variants within a firm. For this system to operate, a national price
system and delegation of authority as to investment choice are necessary. The
author concludes that there are certain theoretical and practical justifications
for investment auctions as a policy alternative, particularly in underdeveloped
countries.

160.   NICHOLS, ALAN. "The Opportunity Costs of Public Investment: Comment." *Quarterly Journal of Economics,* Vol. 78, No. 3
(August, 1964), pp. 499-505.

Abstract: The conventional capital rationing problem is one of allocating
a fixed supply of funds. This supply may appear as a flow of appropriations
for which tightness of restraint is constant, as for Eckstein (36) and McKean
(50), or as simply a given stock of funds, as for Steiner (60). Marglin (151),
on the other hand, is concerned with how weak or strong the restraint would
be. It can be demonstrated that, in the conventional capital rationing problem, the "social discount rate" becomes a mere scale term under two main
specifications: firstly, projects must be compared at a common terminal; and
secondly, the rates of return applicable to nonexplicitly considered projects
in the public and private sectors should be used for amortization in their
respective sectors. The value of the internal government opportunity cost
rate (which is the rate on nonexplicitly considered government projects) depends upon the size of appropriation made available through the political
process. Thus the political process giving rise to an operational social discount
rate manifests itself only through the marginal internal rate of return applicable to the government. Marglin's approach is the reverse of this — he wants
to use the discount rate to determine the size of the budget, whereas the
conventional capital rationing problem accepts the budget as given by the
political process.

161.   NISKANEN, WILLIAM A. "A Suggested Treatment of
Time-Distributed Expenditures in Defense Systems Analysis." Internal
Note N-396 (R). Arlington: Institute for Defense Analyses, 1966.
17 p.

Headings: Introduction; Selecting the planning period; Estimating the residual
values; Selecting the interest rate.

Abstract: There are three primary problems of aggregating systems costs.
The first task is to select the planning period over which the costs will be
aggregated: the first year of the planning period should be the first year that
the expenditures for a specific system might be influenced by the analysis;
the last year of the planning period is arbitrary if the value of all assets at
that time can be estimated accurately. The second task is to estimate the

value of assets at the beginning and end of the planning period: the author proposes some simple rules which should be followed in making this calculation. The third problem is the selection of the discount rate. The appropriate rate of interest depends critically on whose interests the government is maximizing, and on the opportunities for exchanging present and future resources. A rate of 10 per cent is suggested for discounting the costs of government defense programs.

162.   PEGELS, C. CARL. "A Comparison of Decision Criteria for Capital Investment Decisions." *Engineering Economist,* Vol. 13, No. 4 (Summer, 1968), pp. 211-220.

Headings: Abstract; Introduction; Review of objective decision criteria; Subjective utility as a decision criterion; Simulation experiment; Subjective utility of short-term discounted cash flow; Conclusion; Appendix: Utility calculations; References (6).

Abstract: This paper reviews six objective and one subjective capital investment decision criteria, consisting of two rate-of-return criteria, two payback criteria, two discounted cash flow criteria, and a subjective utility criterion. Two hypothetical capital investment proposals, A and B, are presented in the form of probability distributions of input variables such as sales rate, sales growth, product price, capital investment required, etc. Simulation runs on a digital computer are used to sample values of the input variables and, from these sampled values, estimators of the output variable distribution parameters μ and σ are calculated. Six of the seven decision criteria favour proposal B over A. Nevertheless, the present value criterion is heavily in favour of A while the other criteria only marginally favour B. The management should, therefore, decide in favour of A. The simulation experiment clearly indicates that investment proposals should be evaluated on the basis of several decision criteria, instead on the basis of one pre-selected criterion.

163.   PITCHFORD, J. D. and A. J. HAGGER. "A Note on the Marginal Efficiency of Capital." *Economic Journal,* Vol. 68, No. 271 (September, 1958), pp. 597-600.

Headings: Introduction; The uniqueness of the rate of return; Consequences of multiple marginal efficiencies for the Keynesian investment function.

Abstract: Keynes's definition of the marginal efficiency of an income-earning capital asset was *"that* rate of discount which would make the present value of the series of annuities given by the returns expected from the capital-asset during its life just equal to its supply price". The authors demonstrate that if one or more of the returns expected from the capital asset is negative, there will be more than one rate of discount which will satisfy Keynes's equation. The Keynesian investment function holds that the level of aggregate investment expenditure is a unique function of the rate of interest. Where there is more than one marginal efficiency corresponding to a given rate of investment in the asset and, consequently, more than one rate of investment which will equate marginal efficiency and the rate of interest, the level of aggregate investment cannot be fixed at that rate of interest. The importance of this conclusion depends upon how prevalent expected negative returns are.

164. REITER, STANLEY. "Choosing an Investment Program among Interdependent Projects." *Review of Economic Studies,* Vol. 30 (February, 1963), pp. 32-36.

Headings: Introduction; The problem; An algorithm; References (2).

Abstract: This paper demonstrates the application of the analytical techniques needed to formulate and solve a class of investment decision problems involving interdependent projects. The essential feature of such problems is that the pay-off to any project may depend on the other projects undertaken with it. In these circumstances, the total pay-off to the joint undertaking of several projects may be analyzed into a sum of contributions made by each pair of projects undertaken. The problem confronting the decision-maker is to choose, out of the possible combinations of projects he might undertake, a program which makes the total pay-off as large as possible. The procedure for finding optimal programs, which is illustrated by a simple numerical example, consists of a sequence of repetitions, with random starting programs, of the algorithm for finding locally maximal programs, together with a stopping rule which tells in what circumstances to end the repetitions. There is a fairly high probability that an optimal program will be found in very few iterations.

165. REUBER, GRANT L. "The Social Discount Rate: Discussion." In *Cost-Benefit Analysis of Manpower Policies, Proceedings of a North American Conference, May 14-15, 1969,* edited by G. G. Somers and W. D. Wood, pp. 88-94. Published jointly by the Industrial Relations Centre, Queen's University, Kingston, Ontario, and the Center for Studies in Vocational and Technical Education, The University of Wisconsin, Madison, Wisconsin, 1969.

Abstract: A critical issue in the determination of the discount rate to be used in the evaluation of public expenditures in mixed economies is the question of how much normative significance can be attributed to market rates of interest. If we assume that the level and allocation of private investment are completely predetermined, we can argue that public projects should be undertaken in the order of their internal rates of return. The cut-off internal rate of return, however, cannot simply be identified with the tax-adjusted rate at which the government borrows since, as Arrow (119) points out, market rates are neither unique nor necessarily consistent with the observed savings behaviour of consumers. If we assume that the total amount of investible resources is predetermined, public investment is undertaken at the expense of private investment. In these circumstances public projects must be evaluated at the pre-tax rate of return in the private sector. This raises two questions:

firstly, what is the rate of return at the margin in the private sector? and secondly, since we want an efficient allocation of consumption over time as well as an efficient allocation of investment between sectors, is the marginal rate of return in the private sector equal to the social discount rate? Arrow suggests that we ask the policy-maker to specify a target rate of growth of consumption so that we can derive the discount rate which will determine a level of public and private investment consistent with the target rate of growth. Where it is possible to impose separate tax rates on consumption and on saving, the marginal rates of return in the public and private sectors can be equated with the social discount rate: the consumption tax ensures the appropriate level of investment and the savings tax ensures the appropriate allocation between the public and private sectors. There are four general remarks to be made about Arrow's approach. In the first place, it is doubtful whether the approach is operational or whether it is likely to lead to greater agreement among economists about the social discount rate. Secondly, the approach is unrealistic in trying to resolve too many issues simultaneously and in a general equilibrium context. At present the author opts for the simple rule that the rate of return on public projects should equal the marginal rate of return calculated by Harberger's method. Thirdly, the fact that there are imperfections in the private capital market does not mean that a direct method of estimation will necessarily lead to a better approximation of the marginal rate of return in the private sector than market rates. This point is illustrated using a Cobb-Douglas aggregate production function. Lastly, if we drop the assumption of a closed economy, optimality might require that the private, public, and consumption rates of interest be equated with the rate at which international capital can be borrowed or lent. Inclusion of the international sector suggests a number of questions which are not normally covered in the cost-benefit literature. If a disparity existed between the cost of borrowing abroad and the rate of return in the private sector, the government might borrow abroad and provide funds to the public and private sectors in accordance with the highest rate of return. Within the Harberger framework, foreign borrowing or lending would be included as one of the areas from which resources are drawn when a project is undertaken.

166. REUBER, G. L., and R. J. WONNACOTT. *The Cost of Capital in Canada — With special reference to Public Development of the Columbia River.* Washington: Resources for the Future Inc., 1961. ix + 101 p.

Headings: Introduction; Approximation of real rates of interest via financial rates; Estimating the opportunity cost of capital in an imperfect market; Cost of capital if funds derived from Canadian sources; Cost of capital if funds derived from U.S. sources; Conclusion; Appendix A: Estimation of capital productivity from national aggregates; Appendix B: Charts showing the structure of Canadian interest rates, March 1950 - June 1959.

Abstract: To make an economic assessment of the proposed development of the Canadian reach of the Columbia River it is necessary to have estimates of construction costs and future benefits. It is also necessary to have a discount rate so that benefits and costs at different points in time can be compared. The authors attempt to estimate the opportunity costs of capital by adjusting the observed financial market rate of interest for various factors which are judged to account for the differences between the "real" rate and this "financial" rate. These factors are expectations of price changes, short-term pressures exerted on interest rates by governmental monetary and fiscal policies, and the absence of a pure and perfect capital market. The first two factors are adjusted for by using the rate on Government of Canada bonds as an upper limit, and the dividend return to common stocks as a lower limit. The third factor presents us with a market in which there are many interest rates: in this case, the correct opportunity cost of capital is its marginal cost at the source from which funds are drawn. The authors feel that the Columbia project is likely to be financed through borrowing rather than taxation. Statistical estimates are presented of the real rates of return in sectors forgoing funds as a result of domestic borrowing to finance Columbia development. These estimates indicate that the opportunity cost of borrowing in Canada by the federal government is around 5.6 per cent, and slightly higher if borrowing is undertaken by the British Columbia government. The authors examine the factors which prevent Canadian interest rates from falling to the level of comparable U.S. rates. If welfare in Canada alone is to be maximized, the opportunity cost of capital borrowed in the U.S. varies from 4.8 to 5.1 per cent depending upon the specific Canadian agency raising the funds. The effective cost of funds to Canada could be reduced to 4.5 per cent if the U.S. government were to borrow in New York and transfer the funds without additional charge. In interpreting the conclusion of the study it should be remembered that the estimates represent real not financial costs, and that they have a tolerance limit of ± ½ per cent.

167. RICHARDSON, G. B. "Ideal and Reality in the Choice of Techniques." *Oxford Economic Papers,* Vol. 17, No. 2 (July, 1965), pp. 291-298.
Abstract: The author rejects the particular divergence between private and social interest identified by R. L. Meek (153). He argues that uncertainty makes it justifiable to discriminate on grounds both of profit and welfare against investments which involve fixed commitments, i.e., capital intensive projects. He points out that rising marginal cost of finance and "capital rationing" tend to promote rather than impede the efficient use of resources.

168. ROBICHEK, ALEXANDER A., and STEWART C. MYERS. "Conceptual Problems in the Use of Risk-Adjusted Discount Rates." *Journal of Finance,* Vol. 21, No. 4 (December, 1966), pp. 727-730.
Headings: Introduction; The risk-adjusted rate versus the certainty equivalent; Implications of the use of the risk-adjusted rate in capital budgeting; The risk-

adjusted rate as a predictor of the rate at which future income is expected to be realized.

Abstract: Since time and risk are logically separate variables, summing their effects in a discount rate requires an assumption about the relationship between the effects of time and risk on present value. The authors demonstrate that a discount rate incorporating risk can be used to assess the present value of a stream of future returns only where the ratio of the certainty equivalent of the return to the expected value of the return is decreasing at a constant rate determined by the spread between the riskless and the "risk-adjusted" discount rates. In other words, if successive returns are considered equally risky, then a unique "risk-adjusted" discount rate will not evaluate all of the individual returns correctly. The "risk-adjusted" rate can be used as a predictor of the rate at which future income is expected to be realized only if uncertainty is expected to be resolved at a constant rate over time.

169. ROBINSON, ROMNEY. "The Rate of Interest, Fisher's Rate of Return Over Costs, and Keynes' Internal Rate of Return: Comment." *American Economic Review,* Vol. 46, No. 5 (December, 1956), pp. 972-973.

Abstract: In his comment on Alchian's paper (115), the author demonstrates that the internal rate of return criterion and the present discounted value criterion can apparently yield conflicting results. The two rules are not in conflict, however, when a sufficient description of the available investment opportunities is supplied. The projects must be compared over a common multiple of the original time spans, and consequently, the terms of renewal of one or both projects must be known. Implicit in the present discounted value criterion is the assumption that the investments could be renewed only at the market rate of interest after the expiry of the stated time periods. The internal rate of return criterion, on the other hand, assumes that the investments can be renewed on the same terms. In a world of uncertainty and imperfect competition, the latter assumption may be preferred.

170. SEN, A. K. "On Optimising the Rate of Saving." *Economic Journal,* Vol. 71, No. 283 (September, 1961), pp. 479-496.

Headings: Introduction; Some traditional methods of intertemporal judgements; Individual preferences and assumed values; Limits of variation of the saving rate; Summary and conclusions; Appendix on Harrod's second essay.

Abstract: The author outlines solutions to the problem of intertemporal allocation of consumption. He finds the use of utility functions an unsatisfactory method of introducing the political element into the choice. Individual preferences are an unreliable guide because of external economy, i.e., the individual is prepared to sacrifice his own pleasures for future generations only if others are prepared to do the same. The limits imposed on the problem by political and technological factors make the range of choice fairly narrow in the short run. These limits govern the nature of the political choice offered. The author declines to accept Harrod's "natural" rate of growth as a "welfare optimum" rate. He points out that the growth rate of technology is not an independent variable.

171. SEN, AMARTYA K. "Isolation, Assurance and the Social Rate of Discount." *Quarterly Journal of Economics,* Vol. 81, No. 1 (February, 1967), pp. 112-124.

Headings: Introduction; The isolation paradox and the assurance problem; Optimum savings; The rate of discount; Rich they, poor us; Conclusions.

Abstract: The author sees the saving problem as an application of the "isolation paradox" — an N-person version of the "prisoners' dilemma". The isolation paradox assumes that, no matter what others do, each individual will prefer not to save an additional unit for the sake of the future community, but that each regards nobody saving as strictly worse than an additional unit of saving by everyone. The outcome is Pareto-inferior unless a collusive solution is adopted and enforced. If, in the special case where everyone else saves for the future, the individual prefers to save also, then the solution will be Pareto optimal as long as each individual has "assurance" that the others are going to save. In this case, enforcement of the collective decision is unnecessary. Both the author's (170) and Marglin's (151) argument for the inoptimality of market savings are based on the isolation paradox as opposed to the "assurance problem". In order to make the isolation paradox hold, it was assumed that individuals do not discriminate between their own heirs and the rest of the future generation. The isolation paradox can be shown to hold under Lind's alternative set of assumptions (149) except where each set of heirs receives all of the results of its progenitor's savings. The paradox will also hold despite any change in the wealth of the future generation vis-à-vis that of the present generation.

172. SILCOCK, T. H. "Complementarity and Future Time: A Note on the Marginal Efficiency of Capital." *Economic Journal,* Vol. 69, No. 276 (December, 1959), pp. 816-819.

Abstract: The author argues that Soper's proof (176) that multiple values for the marginal efficiency of capital cannot prevail under profit-maximizing conditions is fallacious. Negative yields which occur as a consequence of earlier investment cannot be considered as part of a new investment plan: they have become simply a part of the environment. The flexibility rightly postulated at the initial point of an investment process cannot, therefore, be assumed as between two future points of a present plan.

173. SOBIN, BERNARD. "Interest Rate Concepts for Analysis of Government Expenditures." A paper read at the thirtieth national meeting of the Operations Research Society of America, Durham, N.C., October 17-19, 1966. Mimeographed. 14 p.

Headings: Introduction; Interest rate propositions; Selected basic references (7).

Abstract: The paper seeks to clarify interest rate concepts and to state logically demonstrable principles for the use of interest rates in cost-effectiveness studies. It puts forward six propositions each of which narrows the choice of how interest rates should be used and estimated. The six propositions are: firstly, to the extent that a properly calculated interest rate can provide exchange rates between quantities in one time period and quantities of the same kind in another, it can serve to reduce the number of dimensions that the decision-maker need consider; secondly, an interest rate for money costs is applicable to benefits only where the benefits are measured in the same units as the costs; thirdly, the interest rate for money between any two time periods is independent of the use to which the money is put; fourthly, the correct discount rate on money for a class of expenditures is the ratio between the marginal utilities of the two pools of money (different dates) from which the expenditures are made; fifthly, the rate of return on investments by taxpayers in private business exceeds the published, market rates of return to investors; finally, there are three basic alternative approaches to determining what rate of return can be imputed to taxpayer expenditures on household consumption.

174. SOLOMON, EZRA. "The Arithmetic of Capital-Budgeting Decisions." *Journal of Business,* Vol. 29, No. 2 (April, 1956), pp. 124-129.

Headings: Introduction; Mutually exclusive proposals; The problem of "dual rates of return"; Summary.

Abstract: The source of the conflicting results obtained from the use of the present value and internal rate of return investment decision rules in the choice between mutually exclusive (or non-independent) projects is the nature of the implicit assumptions about the reinvestment rate. Correct and consistent ranking of competing proposals can be obtained if the comparison is made not simply between two projects, but between two alternative courses of action, and if the correct reinvestment rates are used. Where the terminal section of a project contains a net cash outflow, the usual rate of return procedure will yield the wrong results: this situation also requires an explicit estimate of the reinvestment rate. Given this estimate, the value of the incremental cash flows can be computed explicitly and compared with the project's outlays to give a correct measure of the rate of return.

175. SOLOW, ROBERT M. *Capital Theory and the Rate of Return.* Amsterdam: North-Holland, 1963. 97 p.

Headings: Introduction; Capital and the rate of return; The rate of return and technical progress; Technical progress; The aggregate production function, and the rate of return; References (9).

Abstract: The author believes that the central concept in capital theory should be the rate of return on investment. He defines in general terms a one-period rate of return where, by sacrificing some consumption in the present, society can earn extra consumption in the next period without altering the time-path of consumption in subsequent periods. This approach provides a theory of capital which is free from problems of measurement of "capital", the definition of the "period of production", and other problems which have occupied so much discussion. How well does this approach to capital theory accomodate technical change? There are three basic problems: in the first place, technical change has to be built into the production function; secondly, the rate of return on investment has to be defined and calculated in the context of technical change; and, thirdly, it has to be determined whether there will be, in this context, a tendency for the private and social rates of return on investment to diverge. There are a number of reasons why private rates of return cannot be considered as approximations of the social rate of return. The author calculates the social rate of return in the U.S.A. and Germany by fitting, for each country, an aggregate production function. In the model, the social rate of return on investment equals the marginal product of effective capital minus an allowance for depreciation and for obsolescence. The analysis yields a number of tentative conclusions: the social profitability of investment appears to have fallen in both countries between 1954 and 1957; differences among advanced countries in the rate of return on investment are slight; and social rates of return are high (in the area of 20 per cent), suggesting that higher rates of investment than at present may be socially desirable.

176. SOPER, C. S. "The Marginal Efficiency of Capital: A Further Note." *Economic Journal,* Vol. 69, No. 273 (March, 1959), pp. 174-177.

Abstract: The author outlines the conditions under which there can be one and only one positive root to the equation which yields the marginal efficiency of capital. If the investor is aiming at a maximum rate of profit on his investment, he will discriminate among different "lengths of life" for the investment, choosing that length which includes the maximum number of consecutive yields which are still consistent with a discounting equation with one, and only one, positive root. The confusion in the Pitchford and Hagger note (163) derives from ignoring the "life" of the potential investment as a possible variable in the maximization process.

177. STOCKFISCH, JACOB A. "The Interest Rate Applicable to Government Investment Projects." In *Hearings Before the Subcommittee on Economy in Government of the Joint Economic Committee, Congress of the United States,* 90th Congress, 1st Session, 1967, pp. 133-143. Washington: Government Printing Office, 1967.

Headings: Introduction; The principle; Estimating the rate of return; Technical notes on tables of assets, earnings, and rates of return.

Abstract: Decision-makers should apply to government investment project an interest rate that equals the opportunity return on investment in the private sector of the economy. The interest rate should be based on the *before-tax* rate of return in the corporate sector. At present this rate is between 10 and 15 per cent. The author outlines two principles which influence economists' views as to the appropriate interest rate. The equalization principle holds that the interest rate used in the public sector should be the same as the return on investment in the private sector. The social time preference school of thought, on the other hand, argues that the government has an obligation to promote the welfare of unborn generations and that, consequently, the social discount rate should be lower than the "myopic" market rate. The author supports the former principle. He attempts to arrive at a measure of the "marginal efficiency of investment" in the private sector before corporate rate and property taxes. Rates of return are estimated for a number of sectors of the private economy. The overall before-tax rate of return in the private sector is around 13.5 per cent. This rate should therefore be applied to government investment projects.

178. STROTZ, R. H. Myopia and Inconsistency in Dynamic Utility Maximization." *Review of Economic Studies,* Vol. 23 (1955-56), pp. 165-180.

Headings: Introduction; The utility of the consumption plan; The optimal plan as seen today; The question of inconsistency; Consistency, inconsistency, and the nature of the discount function; Two strategies in the face of inconsistency; Generalization; The discount function; Consumer sovereignty; Summary.

Abstract: This paper considers an aspect of intertemporal utility maximization. It is argued that even under conditions of certainty the optimal consumption-time curve at a given date may not be the one which the individual will actually follow. This would be the case if the individual does not discount all future pleasures at a constant rate of interest. The author suggests that the individual may adopt a strategy of precommitment or a strategy of consistent planning to prevent continuous repudiation of past plans. It is also suggested that a log linear discount function is substituted for the true function through parental teaching. The implication for the concept of consumer sovereignty is that it has no meaning in the context of dynamic decision-making since the individual over time is an infinity of individuals and interpersonal utility comparisons are not possible.

179. SUNDRUM, R. M. "The Evaluation of Time Streams — An Aspect of the Appraisal of Capital Projects." *Malayan Economic Review,* Vol. 10, No. 2 (October, 1965), pp. 7-34.

Headings: Introduction; The present value function; Mixed projects; The present value criterion; The amounts of investment and of indebtedness; The uniform flow model; Criteria for choice of projects; Choice of investment strategies; Reinvestment patterns; Appendix.

Abstract: Given the time streams of inputs and outputs of a set of capital projects available for implementation at various dates, and certain preferences over possible time-paths of consumption, which projects should be chosen and when should they be implemented? The author distinguishes three kinds of projects — investment, banking, and mixed projects. He examines the conflict between the present value and internal rate of return criteria, and compares the investment strategies based on these criteria.

180. TULLOCK, GORDON. "The Social Rate of Discount and the Optimal Rate of Investment: Comment." *Quarterly Journal of Economics,* Vol. 78, No. 2 (May, 1964), pp. 331-336.

Abstract: Marglin (151) is correct in arguing that transfers by different donors yield interdependent utilities. His use of this argument, however, to support his claim that the individual will have his utility increased by a transfer paid to the entire next generation, depends upon the values selected for the parameters in the utility function. For certain conceivable parameter values, collective disinvestment in order to increase current consumption would be indicated. The author points out that there are four possible forms of sacrifice, each of which enjoys the same advantage of collective provision: the reduction of consumption to increase the incomes of today's poor; the reduction of savings in order to help today's poor; the reduction of consumption in order to make investments which will be used to help the poor of the future; and finally, the reduction of present consumption in order to increase the income of the entire future generation. Since the future generation is likely to have a higher average income than the present, the latter form of sacrifice would require an unusual "altruistic" preference function. Thus, Marglin's explanation of government-directed sacrifice of current consumption is based on the assumption of unlikely values for the parameters of the utility function.

181. TURVEY, RALPH. "Present Value Versus Internal Rate of Return — An Essay in the Theory of the Third Best." *Economic Journal,* Vol. 73, No. 289 (March, 1963), pp. 93-98.

Abstract: The author points out that, while the present value and internal rate of return criteria are equivalent in the Paretian model, this is not so in the non-Paretian world of the applied economics. His paper deals with sub-optimising criteria. Whether or not any investment criterion is correct can be discovered only by examining its consistency with the maximand or minimand and constraints. Where the maximand is the rate of growth of assets — the "Stalinist maximand" — time preference and social discount are irrelevant and the internal rate of return is the appropriate criterion. The conclusion, however, is that the present value criterion is more generally relevant since the policy maker is not indifferent to the relative degree of futurity of costs and revenues.

182.　USHER, DAN. "The Social Rate of Discount and the Optimal Rate of Investment: Comment." *Quarterly Journal of Economics,* Vol. 78, No. 4 (November, 1964), pp. 641-644.

Abstract: Marglin's paper (151) presumes that the optimal rate of investment exceeds the rate which will be chosen when each man decides individually how much he wishes to save for the future. This is because one man's charity has a negligible impact on the community's present or future consumption. We can assume, consequently, that the individual maximizes only the hedonistic portion of his utility function, but that, if he believes the community as a whole to be underinvesting or overinvesting, he has recourse to public action designed to induce more or less saving. This argument indicates that the optimal rate of investment may be greater or less than the rate resulting from individual decisions. Marglin's evidence for future oriented altruism is the general concern for economic growth. However, a man who "wants" economic growth is not necessarily prepared to buy it by reducing present consumption. Thus, neither the theoretical argument nor the empirical evidence establishes that the optimal rate of investment necessarily exceeds the rate chosen by a collection of individual decisions.

183.　USHER, DAN. "On the Social Rate of Discount: Comment." *American Economic Review,* Vol. 59, No. 5, Part II (December, 1969), pp. 925-929.

Abstract: Baumol stated (123) that there is an "unavoidable indeterminacy" in the choice of the rate of interest to be used in discounting projects in the public sector. The choice of the rate cannot, however, be indeterminate if, as Baumol says, it can be obtained as a second best solution. This paper demonstrates how the social discount rate can be chosen using Lipsey and Lancaster's theorem of the second best. It is proved that, under some quite general assumptions, the appropriate interest rate on government projects lies between the rate of time preference and the rate of transformation between present and future consumption in the private sector.

184.　WRIGHT, J. F. "The Marginal Efficiency of Capital." *Economic Journal,* Vol. 69, No. 276 (December, 1959), pp. 813-816.

Abstract: Pitchford and Hagger argued (163) that the economic importance of multi-valued marginal efficiencies depends upon the prevalence of negative expected returns. This note contends that while negative expected returns may often be negative, it is rare for them to be sufficiently negative for the marginal efficiency of an asset to be multi-valued. The Pitchford and Hagger case is rare because the costs of extrication are likely to be relatively small except where they are voluntarily incurred because of offsetting salvage values. The case is not however impossible and might become more common if there were an increase in the extent of legal and social obligations placed on entrepreneurs to compensate their redundant labour forces and to restore the sites they abandon.

185. WRIGHT, J. F. "Notes on the Marginal Efficiency of Capital." *Oxford Economic Papers,* Vol. 15, No. 2 (June, 1963), pp. 124-129.

Abstract: This paper examines the concept of marginal efficiency of capital or internal rate of return, given various types of cash flow. The existence of multiple solutions in cases where the cash flow has three or more "phases" leads to ambiguities in rate of return calculations.

5. SCHOOLING

186. ASHENFELTER, ORLEY, and JOSEPH D. MOONEY. "Graduate Education, Ability and Earnings." *Review of Economics and Statistics,* Vol. 50, No. 1 (February, 1968), pp. 78-86.

Headings: Introduction; The sample, variables, and methods; The additive earnings function; The interactive earnings function; Conclusions.

Abstract: The paper attempts to indicate the relative importance of factors other than years of education on the earnings stream of a cohort of recent, former graduate students. The determinants of present annual salary are analyzed in two different ways: by means of a general additive model, and by means of interactive regression analysis. "Dummy variables" are used to express all but one of the independent variables. The conclusions are: firstly, that applications of "rate of return" analysis to the area of graduate education must control for a number of the independent variables included in this study; secondly, that there are significant interactive effects among these variables; and, finally, where a sample of highly educated people is used, misspecifications caused by the absence of an ability variable seem to be quite small.

187. ASHENFELTER, ORLEY, and JOSEPH D. MOONEY. "Some Evidence on the Private Returns to Graduate Education." *Southern Economic Journal,* Vol. 35, No. 3 (January, 1969), pp. 247-256.

Headings: Introduction; Summary of existing research; The sample; Methodology and findings; Implications and conclusions; References (11).

Abstract: The data for this study came from a sample of recent Woodrow Wilson Fellows. The advantages of this sample for a "returns to education" study are that the group is homogeneous with respect to ability, sex, age, and labour force experience; in addition, detailed information is available on each Fellow. The drawback to the use of this sample for estimating lifetime returns to educational investment is that it contains observations on only the first few years of the lifetime income profile. Two solutions to this problem are described: firstly, income differences at the time of the sample can be extrapolated; secondly, hypothetical lifetime income profiles can be obtained from cross-section data on the incomes of people of different educational levels at various ages. The hypothetical lifetime income profiles are used to calculate incremental present value estimates at age 21 for graduate programs of varying lengths over the B.A. degree. These present value estimates yield estimates of the private internal rates of return: the internal rates vary from 7.1 per cent for a 5-year Ph.D. to 10.8 per cent for a 3-year Ph.D. The estimates of the internal rates of return by Field of Graduate Study and Profession calculated by the authors are not very reliable because of small sample cell sizes. The rates of return presented in this paper fit into the general pattern of educational investment yields suggested by other authors.

188. BECKER, GARY S. "Underinvestment in College Education." *American Economic Review,* Papers and Proceedings, Vol. 50, No. 2 (May, 1960), pp. 346-354.

Headings: Introduction; Private and social returns; Quality of students; Summary.

Abstract: The author divides the economic effects of education into the effect on the incomes of persons receiving education and the effect on the incomes of others. The evidence reveals no significant discrepancy between the direct returns to college education and to business capital. The argument that there is under-investment in college education must therefore be based on external or indirect returns. Since there is little known about the external returns to education, no firm conclusion can be reached. The contribution of college education to progress might be increased by an improvement in the quality of college students.

189. BECKER, GARY S., and CHISWICK, BARRY R. "Education and the Distribution of Earnings." *American Economic Review,* Papers and Proceedings, Vol. 56, No. 2 (May, 1966), pp. 358-369.

Headings: Introduction; Theory; A statistical formulation; Empirical analysis; Summary and conclusions.

Abstract: The paper assumes that the amount invested in human capital results from optimizing behaviour. Ignoring property income, and earnings from "original" human capital, the distribution of earnings is determined by the shape and distribution of the supply and demand function for investment in human capital. The contribution of human capital to the distribution of earnings could be easily calculated if the rates of return and amounts of investment in education were known. The analysis has to be reformulated, however, to utilize what information we do have, namely years of schooling. The authors find that schooling usually explains a not negligible part of the inequality in earnings within a geographical area, and a much larger part of differences in inequality between areas.

190. BLAUG, MARK. "The Rate of Return on Investment in Education in Great Britain." *Manchester School of Economic and Social Studies,* Vol. 33, No. 3 (September, 1965), pp. 205-261.

Headings: Introduction; The rate of return approach; An omnibus of objections; Multiple correlations among the income-determining variables; The psychic returns to education; Current earnings and lifetime earnings; A non-competitive labour market?; The indirect benefits of education; The policy implications of the approach; Appendix — Estimate of the rate of return to education in Great Britain.

Abstract: This paper supports the use of rate of return calculations in evaluating the economic benefits of education. A number of objections to this approach are discussed: the problem of isolating the pure effect of education on earnings; the nonpecuniary attractions of certain occupations and the consumption benefits of education; the projection of future trends from cross-section evidence; the problem of an imperfect labour market; the spill-over benefits which are not adequately reflected in a social rate of return; and the existence of policy goals other than maximization of net national product. The question of the social opportunity cost of education is examined, and there is a discussion of the factors tending to produce biased estimates of the rate of return. The appendix consists of an estimate of the actual rate of return to education, and can be regarded as an illustration of the technique of calculating the rate of return from cross-section data.

191. BLAUG, M. "An Economic Interpretation of the Private Demand for Education." *Economica,* Vol. 33, No. 130 (May, 1966), pp. 166-182.

Abstract: The author discusses the relationship between educational planning and manpower planning. He points out that of the four variables involved — demand and supply in the "education market", and demand and supply in the labour market — only one, supply in the education market, is a direct policy-variable. Demand in the education market is explained by the theory of investment behaviour. Since the education market and the labour market are interdependent, manpower and education policies cannot be discussed separately.

192. BLAUG, MARK. "The Private and the Social Returns on Investment in Education: Some Results for Great Britain." *Journal of Human Resources,* Vol. 2, No. 3 (Summer, 1967), pp. 330-346.

Headings: Abstract; Introduction; The first survey; The second survey; Conclusions.

Abstract: This paper summarizes the results of two recent efforts to estimate rates of return to educational investment in Britain. Because there is no basic source of age-education-income data such as is available in the U.S., the analyses employ data which are by-products of surveys conducted for other reasons and which, consequently, require rather extensive adjustments. The results of the two separate calculations, which are not directly comparable, indicate that, if 8 per cent is accepted as the social opportunity cost of resources invested in education in Britain, there is little evidence of social underinvestment in British higher education. The argument for social underinvestment in higher education must rest almost entirely on "spillover effects". There is, on the other hand, clear indication of social underinvestment in certain types of secondary education. The private rates of return on all forms of higher education exceed the social rates thereby reflecting the considerable subsidies to British higher education. Lastly, it appears to be profitable to acquire the General Certificate of Education at the '0' level, but unprofitable at the 'A' level unless one goes to university or to obtain higher technical certificates.

193. BOWMAN, MARY JEAN. "Social Returns to Education." *International Social Science Journal,* Vol. 14, No. 4 (1962), pp. 647-659.

Headings: Introduction; The aggregative and differential approaches; The quantity of education; The relations among components of social and private returns; A digression on the age incidence of social versus private returns; Empirical measurement of changes in monetary private and social returns over time; Characteristics and determinants of non-private monetary returns; A more dynamic view.

Abstract: This paper focuses on "social" versus "private" returns to education. The total social return may be larger or smaller than the sum of individual returns unless a correction for interactions among the individual components of social return is made. The social returns to education can be separated into monetary and nonmonetary components. The sum of these components will equal the sum of the aggregates of individual monetary and individual nonmonetary returns plus a term to cover interactions among individuals' monetary components and another term to cover interactions among individuals' nonmonetary components. The author outlines the two main approaches to estimating the returns to education. The first approach involves calculating the quantity of education embodied in the labour force and applying estimated internal rates of return to the calculated quantity of education in order to derive an estimate of the contribution of education to national product. The second approach estimates returns to education and technical and organizational changes as that part of economic growth which cannot be explained by changes in other more easily identifiable inputs. The author's method of calculating the monetary returns to education attempts to fuse the two main approaches. It is based upon her equation relating the aggregate of individual returns to social returns.

194. BOWMAN, MARY JEAN. "Converging Concerns of Economists and Educators." *Comparative Education Review,* Vol. 6, No. 2 (October, 1962), pp. 111-119.

Headings: Introduction; The conceptual framework of allocative analysis; Interdisciplinary links and research opportunities.

Abstract: The paper outlines the application of the rate of return approach to economic analysis of investment in education. While the basic proposition and techniques of this approach are indispensable to any rational analysis of investment, opinions differ as to the interpretation of costs and returns, the reliability of empirical rate of return calculations, and the uses to which they are put. Both private and social decision-making frameworks are presented: the latter is divided into "partial social" and "global social" models. The "global social" model incorporates secondary and diffusive effects on national income and also structural changes which cannot be accommodated by marginal analysis. Discrepancies among observed rates of return are caused by a number of factors of which economists are chiefly interested in distortions in measures of private costs and returns and differences among true private rates. It is suggested that these can be explained by "specialized occupational" and "incremental level" comparisons. The article concludes by examining the relation between school drop-out rates and opportunity cost; by attempting to identify the contribution of education to productivity; by examining training in schools and on the job, and innovation and obsolescence in human skills.

195. BRIDGMAN, D. S. "Problems in Estimating the Monetary Value of College Education." *Review of Economics and Statistics,* Vol. 42 (Supplement, 1960), pp. 180-184.

Abstract: A study by Glick and Miller (207) indicates that the differences between the lifetime incomes of high school and college graduates, as well as the amounts of such incomes, were substantially greater in 1956 than in 1949. It should be recognized, however, that college costs have not been deducted from the differences in lifetime income for the two educational levels. In addition, the data used to calculate these differences represent income rather than earnings; this tends to increase significantly the advantage of the college graduates. The difference in income for the two educational levels derived from median lifetime incomes for each, computed from 1956 data, was only 60 per cent of that derived from the means. This suggests that mean lifetime incomes are greatly affected by a number of high incomes, more common among college graduates. The author cites evidence from a study of educational and ability patterns of World War 2 veterans and from two studies of earnings and ability of college graduates to support the view that ability is a major reason for the income differential between high school and college graduates. For these reasons, the author concludes that the monetary return to college education may have been exaggerated.

196. CAMPBELL, ROBERT, and BARRY N. SIEGEL. "The Demand for Higher Education in the United States, 1919-1964." *American Economic Review,* Vol. 57, No. 3 (June, 1967), pp. 482-494.

Headings: Introduction; Theoretical basis of demand estimates; Measurement of demand; Formulation of the empirical demand model; Estimation of the demand function; Two-year college enrollments; Conclusion; References (8); Appendix: Sources and methods of statistical estimates.

Abstract: This paper integrates the investment and consumption approaches to educational demand. The investment approach asserts that an individual will purchase a college education if the present value of the expected stream of benefits resulting from the education exceeds the present cost of the education. The consumption approach implies that the demand for education is sensitive to the money costs of enrollment relative to current consumer goods prices. The study uses the following data to test the model of educational demand: the ratio of enrollments to eligible college population; real disposable income per household; and an index of tuition costs deflated by the consumers' price index. The results of the regression analysis support the hypotheses that the income effect on the enrollment ratio is positive and the price effect is negative. Further research is needed to separate the contribution of investment and consumption elements to the demand for higher education.

197. CARNOY, MARTIN. "Rates of Return to Schooling in Latin America." *Journal of Human Resources,* Vol. 2, No. 3 (Summer, 1967), pp. 359-374.

Headings: Abstract; Introduction; The Mexican case; Comparison of rates of return among Latin American countries and the United States; Conclusions.

Abstract: This paper analyzes rates of return to formal schooling in Latin America. The analysis attempts to draw implications for investment in schooling which are applicable to developing economies. The author describes his calculation of the rates of return to different levels of schooling in Mexico, and compares his results with rates of return to education in the United States, Chile, Columbia, and Venezuela. His findings are as follows: the average level of rates of return is high in all four Latin American countries, relative even to the high rate of return to physical capital in Latin America; the patterns of rates indicate that if an economy grows rapidly at this stage, bottlenecks develop at the higher and primary levels; a high rate of investment in education must be accompanied by a high rate of investment in physical capital in order to generate economic growth; if the pattern of declining equilibrium rates of return with increasing amounts of schooling identified for the United States is considered as the "desired" pattern, the rates in Chile, which had the lowest economic growth rate of the countries studied, are nearest to the "desired" pattern. It is not surprising that the search for the universal rule to allocate resources to education, and "efficiently" within education, yields different rules for different countries.

198. CARTER, C. F. "The Economics of Higher Education." *Manchester School of Economic and Social Studies,* Vol. 33, No. 1 (January, 1965), pp. 1-16.

Abstract: The author discusses the economics of universities in the United Kingdom. He argues that more attention should be given to cost comparisons and efficiency. In addition, there should be an effort to identify the product of university education. In the future, investment in university facilities should be governed by the techniques of cost-effectiveness analysis.

199. CARTER, ALLAN M. "Economics of the University." *American Economic Review,* Papers and Proceedings, Vol. 55, No. 2 (May, 1965), pp. 481-494.

Abstract: The author attempts to assess the quality ranking for leading U.S. graduate programs in economics. He compares the quality rankings based on questionnaire replies with some less subjective indices: the quantity of scholarly publications originating in the various departments; the level of faculty salaries; size of departments; overall size of institution. He concludes that qualitative measures in education offer interesting avenues of study for the economist.

200. CORAZZINI, ARTHUR J., and ERNEST BARTELL. "Problems of Programming an Optimum Choice Between General and Vocational Education." *Kyklos,* Vol. 18, Fasc. 4 (1965), pp. 700-704.

Abstract: This note criticizes Correa's programming model of educational planning (201). The author points out that Correa omitted consideration of nonmeasurable returns, and failed to distinguish between private and social costs, and between private and social yields. They question the availability of data for his variables and parameters and criticize his use of a programming model in this context. Correa's analytic procedures are, it is claimed, deficient in terms both of theoretical economic significance, and operational relevance.

201. CORREA, HECTOR. "Optimum Choice Between General and Vocational Education." *Kyklos,* Vol. 18, Fasc. 1 (1965), pp. 107-115.

Headings: Introduction; Characterization of general and vocational education; Mathematical expression; The model; Comment on the model; Improvement of the model; Conclusion; Summary; Zusammenfassung; Resumé.

Abstract: The essential characteristic of vocational education assumed in the model is that we know its use and its yield. In the case of general education, however, some of the skills which are taught may not be used in the future. Thus the problem, as seen by the author, is to compare a yield that will be obtained with probability one, with another for which the probability is less than one; this can be done using expected values. The expected yields, and the costs of the different types of education programs are incorporated in a linear programming model with the available resources as one of the constraints. The author also shows how non linearities can be introduced into his model.

202. CORREA, HECTOR "Planning the Educational Curriculum." *Kyklos,* Vol. 18, Fasc. 4 (1965), pp. 685-690.

Headings: Introduction; The structure of a curriculum; Mathematical expression; Linear programming; Summary; Zusammenfassung; Resumé.

Abstract: The author suggests that educationists should prepare a matrix of prerequisites for various courses, vectors of cost and benefits, and information as to the quantity of resources available. Armed with this data, economists, mathematicians, and operational researchers can take over the planning of the educational curriculum.

203. DEITCH, KENNETH. "Some Observations on the Allocation of Resources in Higher Education." *Review of Economics and Statistics,* Vol. 42 (Supplement, 1960), pp. 192-198.

Abstract: From the viewpoint of an administrator the purpose of investment theory is to present criteria which will enable him to determine how to allocate his institution's resources. The criteria which have been established in traditional investment theory are the present value criterion and the marginal returns criterion. These criteria are of limited usefulness in the allocation of resources in education since an educational institution has not one but many objectives and its returns may not be calculable in dollar terms. The author feels, nevertheless, that the administrator of education ought to work within the general framework of the traditional criteria. Before the administrator can make his allocation decisions he must rank the objectives of the institution, decide which variables he can control and which are exogenous, and determine where relations exist between changes in the relevant variables and achievement of the desired objectives. The schematic framework for dealing with the problem of the allocation of resources in education is outlined: the optimum allocation occurs when the rate at which two input variables may be substituted for each other, with total costs remaining constant, equals the rate at which the two variables may be substituted for each other while total benefits are held constant. The system's operation is illustrated by a numerical example. The measurement of benefits remains the most problematical issue in the analysis.

204. DENISON, EDWARD F. "Education, Economic Growth, and Gaps in Information." *Journal of Political Economy,* Vol. 70, No. 5, Part 2 (October, 1962, Supplement), pp. 124-128.

Abstract: The author describes his attempt to identify the sources of past growth in the United States. He uses earnings differentials between groups classified by education to represent differences in their contributions to production. Three-fifths of the earnings differentials are assumed to result from differences in education and work experience. Since it will be impossible to maintain the past rate of increase in the quantity of education offered, an improvement in the quality will be necessary to prevent the contribution of education to growth from declining.

205. DODGE, DAVID A. *Returns to Investment in University Training: The Case of Canadian Accountants, Engineers, and Scientists.* Kingston, Ontario: Industrial Relations Centre, Queen's University, forthcoming.

Abstract: The objective of this monograph is to assess the methodology of rate of return analysis applied to higher education, and to estimate the "true" economic return to investment in undergraduate and graduate training for accountants, engineers, and scientists. The first section discusses the theory of earnings differentials: the conclusion is that annual earnings differ from marginal productivity for most individuals, the size of the difference being a function of the degree of imperfection in the product and factor markets, and the stage in the life cycle of the individual. It is also concluded that some part of the earnings differential attributable to formal education is due to the licencing effect of the degree in professions where entry is limited to those with a certain level of education. It is suggested that the effect of education on earnings should be estimated for broad occupational groups, taken individually, rather than for all individuals regardless of occupation: the latter method leads to biased estimates if the labour market is out of long-run equilibrium. The relationship between education and "ability" is examined: a marked correlation is found between ability and education level attained; the level of education attained, however, explains a higher proportion of the variance in earnings than does the ability variable. Finally it is concluded that rate of return analysis, carried out according to the standard methodology, produces estimates of the economic return to investment in education which are biased upwards.

206. GISSER, MICHA. "On Benefit-Cost Analysis of Investment in Schooling in Rural Farm Areas." *American Journal of Agricultural Economics,* Vol. 50, No. 3 (August, 1968), pp. 621-629.

Headings: Introduction; The cost of schooling; Returns to schooling; The benefit-cost ratio of schooling; Conclusion; Appendix: The data; References.

Abstract: The author describes two effects of raising the level of schooling in rural farm areas: the first is the stimulation of outmigration and the second is the raising of productivity on farms. This article focuses on the latter effect. The benefit-cost ratio of schooling in rural farm areas is based on estimates of the cost of schooling and the monetary benefit of schooling. An estimate of the annual direct cost of schooling per pupil is obtained from current and capital expenditure data and enrollment figures. The indirect cost is the income forgone while attending school. The returns to schooling are calculated from a model of farm wage determination. Farm wages are assumed to be a function of capital per farm, nonfarm wages, the level of schooling of males in rural farm areas, and the ratio of whites to total farm employees. Cross-sectional pooled data by states for 1950 and 1960 are used to estimate the regression coefficients of the model. The estimates indicate that, on average, raising the level of schooling of one individual in rural farm areas 10 per cent will lead to an increase in his wage rate of 6.5 per cent. When the wage-schooling elasticity figure is applied to cost and income data for the average farm worker (assuming that he bears all the costs), the benefit-cost ratio of an additional year's schooling is 2.37. It can be inferred from this that more schooling affects favourably the process of agricultural production.

207. GLICK, PAUL C., and HERMAN P. MILLER. "Educational Level and Potential Income." *American Sociological Review,* Vol. 21, No. 3 (June, 1956), pp. 307-312.

Abstract: The authors conclude from their survey of education and income levels, based on data from the 1950 U.S. Census, that the completion of additional increments of education is associated with higher and progressively increasing earning power. This relationship is much less pronounced for non-white than for white men: nonwhites have lower incomes, and their incomes are less responsive to changes in educational attainment. The authors' estimates of lifetime incomes for men with different amounts of education are calculated from cross-sectional data for 1949. They find that the value of a college education is about $100,000 more than that of a high school education. When the additional cost of a college education is taken into account, the return to college education can be shown to be far in excess of the return to a comparable investment in government bonds. The authors conclude by pointing out that they have left unanswered questions about the influence on education and earnings of such factors as intelligence quotient, class rank at high school graduation, and the financial status of parents.

208. GOUNDEN, A. M. NALLA. "Investment in Education in India." *Journal of Human Resources,* Vol. 2, No. 3 (Summer, 1967), pp. 347-358.

Headings: Abstract; Introduction; Rates of return; Net education capital accumulation, 1950-51 to 1960-61; Policy implications; Conclusion.

Abstract: In this paper an effort is made to explore the relationship between the costs and benefits of educational investment in India. In order to estimate the rate of return to investment in education, data on age-earning profiles by level and type of education, and data on costs are needed. With these data, life-cycle cost-earning streams are constructed which show for each type and level of education the flow of costs incurred during the process of education and the subsequent flows of additional income that can be attributed to education. The internal rates of return can be calculated by ascertaining that rate of discount which equates the present value of the cost outlays with the present value of the additional income flow. When the rates of return on education are compared with Harberger's estimates of the rates of return to physical capital in India, it is found that the rates of return to education at all levels except primary are lower than the return to physical capital. The growth of educational capital 1950-51 to 1960-61 is estimated at 48 per cent; the growth of physical capital was 60 to 70 per cent. The general conclusion of the study is that since the rate of return of physical capital is higher than that of education, relatively more emphasis on physical capital formation may accelerate the growth of the economy.

209. HANOCH, GIORA. "An Economic Analysis of Earnings and Schooling." *Journal of Human Resources,* Vol. 2, No. 3 (Summer, 1967), pp. 310-329.

Headings: Abstract; Introduction; Estimates of income-age profiles; Rates of return and the demand for schooling; Conclusions.

Abstract: The author uses 1960 Census data to estimate eight different earnings-age profiles corresponding to eight school levels within each race-region. For each pair of schooling levels the rate of return on the amount of schooling which is the difference between the two levels can be calculated. This is the marginal rate of return where the marginal unit is the difference between the two levels. When the marginal rates of return are plotted against schooling levels, the resulting schedule is the marginal efficiency of investment in schooling when investment is measured in school years. It is, therefore, the demand for schooling. The values computed for internal rates of return are highly sensitive to those elements of the earnings profiles which are the most vulnerable to omissions and biases — measured net earnings at young ages. Among the other important biases inherent in the estimated income profiles are those associated with ability. There is probably a significant positive correlation between ability and the level of schooling achieved. Bearing in mind the drawbacks and limitations of these rates of return, the author asks what factors cause the levels of marginal efficiency of investment to vary among the four major race-region groups. The three major types of factors are quality of schooling, marginal market discrimination, and ability. It is stressed that the analysis refers to private rates of return and private demand for schooling. The application of the analysis to society would require that social costs and benefits be taken into account and a social rate of discount be used to appraise the social rates of return obtained.

210. HANSEN, W. LEE. "The 'Shortage' of Engineers." *The Review of Economics and Statistics,* Vol. 43, No. 3 (August, 1961), pp. 251-256.

Headings: Introduction; Average earnings comparisons; Two types of comparisons; The growing shortage of engineers; Conclusions.

Abstract: This paper examines the approach and findings of Blank and Stigler in *The Demand and Supply of Scientific Personnel* which concluded that there was a "surplus" of engineers. The author warns against comparing shifts in relative earnings positititions when changes have occurred in the composition or quality of one type of labour relative to another. He finds that more recent data indicate a reversal in the long-run deterioration in the relative earnings position of engineers, and, in fact, suggest a growing "shortage".

211. HANSEN, W. LEE. "Total and Private Rates of Return to Investment in Schooling." *Journal of Political Economy,* Vol. 71, No. 2 (April, 1963), pp. 128-140.

Headings: Introduction; Estimation procedures; Internal rate of return estimates; Alternative measures of private economic returns from schooling; Conclusion.

Abstract: The author examines the nature of the data used to estimate the rate of return to investment in education. Despite the limitations of this data, he feels it is worthwhile, from the point of view of resource allocation, to make crude estimates of the rate of return. He argues that the rate of return method gives a better ranking of the returns to investment in schooling than do the value or present value of lifetime income methods. The conclusion is that rates of return to private investment exceed those to total resource investment, and that marginal rates of return vary over the period of schooling.

212. HANSEN, W. LEE. "The Economics of Scientific and Engineering Manpower." *Journal of Human Resources,* Vol. 2, No. 2 (Spring, 1967), pp. 191-220.

Headings: Abstract; ˙Introduction; The participant's views and the issues; Alternative approaches to research; The evidence from the projections; Economic studies; Conclusion; Discussion by David Brown and Claus A. Moser.

Abstract: This paper attempts to define some of the issues in the discussion of shortages of engineering manpower. A suggested definition of a shortage is a situation in which the supply of engineers increases less rapidly than the number demanded at the salaries paid in the recent past. An alternative definition of a shortage uses starting instead of average salaries. These two bases

106

of comparison give different results, and the author puts forward a third measure — the rate of return. A shortage of engineers can be identified by comparing the rate of return to an investment in an engineering training to the average for all college graduates. The discussants favour the rate of return approach and ask whether it can be used for projecting future needs.

213. HANSEN, W. LEE, BURTON A. WEISBROD, and WILLIAM J. SCANLON. "Determinants of Earnings: Does Schooling Really Count?" Mimeographed. Economics of Human Resources Working Paper 5A. Madison: Department of Economics, University of Wisconsin, April 1968. 29 p.

Headings: Introduction; Models of earnings determinants; Empirical application; Regional-color disaggregation; Some extensions of the results; Summary; Appendix A: Correlation coefficients; Appendix B; Means and standard deviations of variables.

Abstract: The authors put forward a model of the determinants of individuals' earnings. The explanatory variables include physical condition, mental capability, learning and experience, psychological characteristics, family environment, and job access. The data used is a sample of 2,500 men who were rejected for military service because of failure to pass the Armed Forces Qualification Test (AFQT). The proxies for the explanatory variables are as follows: total money income less transfer payments, years of educational attainment, the AFQT score, whether or not the individual received training outside of school, age, color, current marital status, divorce of parents, family size during childhood, and region. Formal schooling is not as significant as is often supposed in explaining earnings differentials, and its significance diminished with the introduction of the AFQT score as a measure of learning. In other words, what one learns influences earnings more than does the mere fact of spending time in school. This leads the authors to question the policy of encouraging students to remain in school, even when they are performing quite poorly. The authors utilize their findings to explore the following questions: does there exist a "sheepskin effect"? Can the AFQT be used as a predictor of civilian productivity? And what is the relative payoff of education versus training?

214. HIRSCH, WERNER, Z., and ELBERT W. SEGELHORST. "Incremental Income Benefits of Public Education." *Review of Economics and Statistics,* Vol. 48, No. 4 (November, 1965), pp. 392-399.

Headings: Introduction; Concepts and hypothesis; Description of technique and data; Findings; Incremental lifetime incomes and their present value; Summary.

Abstract: The authors submit sample survey data collected for Clayton Missouri to multivariate analysis in order to estimate incremental lifetime earnings resulting from education. The hypothesis tested is that before-tax income of the household head is a function of race, sex, years of schooling, quality of education in terms of expenditures, occupation, self-employment and supervisory status, informal education as reflected by occupation of father, experience in terms of age, migration from the Deep South, and size of birth place. Three other variables were dropped for lack of data: native ability, motivation, and physical ability. The net regression coefficients revealed a consistent positive effect on income of an additional year of schooling for both primary and secondary education. The stream of future income benefits of a year of public education was estimated and its present value calculated using discount rates of 3½, 5 and 10 per cent. The authors compare their results with those of Denison, Miller (220), and Hansen (211). Using a 5 per cent discount rate and the estimates of incremental student income, the total present value of education provided in the 1959-60 school year to male and female Clayton students is calculated. This figure is compared with the cost of providing education in Clayton for the same period and the rate of return is found to be 34 per cent. A more liberal estimate gives a rate of return of almost 83 per cent.

215. HIRSCH, WERNER Z., and MORTON J. MARCUS. "Some Benefit-Cost Considerations of Universal Junior College Education." *National Tax Journal,* Vol. 19, No. 1 (March, 1966), pp. 48-57. (Reprinted by the Institute of Government and Public Affairs, University of California, Los Angeles, 1966).

Headings: Introduction; Framework for analysis; Some benefit-cost estimates; Some additional considerations; Conclusion.

Abstract: A framework is established for evaluating, by means of benefit-cost analysis, the anticipated consequences, for society as a whole, of a universal junior college program and some of its alternatives. The analytical framework adopts the opportunity-cost concept: costs are defined as direct operating costs, capital costs, and imputed operating costs, such as forgone earnings. Benefits are defined as increased resources available to society; these include incremental output, resources freed through decline in demand for public services (e.g., through reduction in poverty and delinquency), increments in the social product of second parties (e.g., children and co-workers of recipients of education), intangible benefits, and employment effects. Benefit-cost estimates are presented for two years of higher education at present institutions of higher education, at junior colleges, at liberal arts colleges, and at technical institutes. Since the analysis does not point to a clear cut advantage for a universal junior college program, the author suggests a "high school enrichment program" consisting of five integrated summer sessions of eight weeks each. Such a program would provide the equivalent of a year of junior college with larger returns on investment than in a two year junior college program.

216.   HOUTHAKKER, H. S. "Education and Income." *The Review of Economics and Statistics,* Vol. 41, No. 1 (February, 1959), pp. 24-28.

Abstract: This note presents some calculations on the relation between education and income. Using data from the three and a half per cent sample of money incomes of males over age fourteen which forms part of the 1950 U.S. Census of Population, the author estimates income levels before and after tax for various age groups and levels of schooling. Arguments for and against discounting the income streams are discussed: on the one hand, education is an investment but it is difficult to determine the appropriate rate of discount; on the other hand, it might be argued that discounting is implicit in the adjustments for mortality, and that discounting is unnecessary because each individual can expect an upward trend in his own earnings superimposed on the cross-sectional pattern for a particular year. The author uses discount rates of zero, 3, 6, and 8 per cent. He finds that capital values increase uniformly with level of schooling. He concludes that his estimates systematically overstate the specific effects of education on income since no adjustment is made for factors such as ability and family background which are positively correlated with both education and income; Glick and Miller's figure (207) of $100,000, which is generally recognized as the money value of completing college rather than stopping at high school, should be regarded only as an upper bound.

217.   HUNT, SHANE J. "Income Determinants for College Graduates and the Return to Educational Investment." *Yale Economic Essays,* Vol. 3, No. 2 (Fall, 1963), pp. 305-357.

Headings: Introduction; The data; The measurement of labor quality; The measure of other income determinants; Regression computations; Other regression tests; Rates of return on investment in education; Concluding comments.

Abstract: The paper identifies and measures the determinants of income for college graduates. These determinants are related to income through a multiple regression equation. The following variables are in some way determinants of earned income: ability, occupation, years since graduation, whether or not self-employed, size of college, and, for businessmen only, city size and mother's education. An attempt is made to control these variables while measuring the relation between education and income. The rates of return on investment both in graduate education and in improved quality of undergraduate education are assessed, and the sensitivity of the results is indicated.

218.   INNES, JON T., PAUL B. JACOBSON, and ROLAND J. PELLEGRIN. *The Economic Returns to Education: A Survey of the Findings.* Eugene: Center for the Advanced Study of Educational Administration, University of Oregon, 1965. ix + 45 p.

Headings: Introduction; The concept and measurement of human capital; Education and earnings; The rate of return on investment in education; The contribution of education to economic growth; Summary; Bibliography (45).

Abstract: This monograph is a survey of recent literature on the economic returns to education. It is pointed out that education has numerous non-economic benefits, and that a number of factors other than education affect the earnings of the individual. The following factors, each of which contributes to a person's earning power, tend to be positively correlated with formal education: intelligence, number of hours worked, other kinds of education, and restrictions on entry to a profession. It is clear that the entire increase in earning power associated with formal education cannot be cited as the economic benefits of education. The use of the rate of return approach in evaluating investment in education involves a number of assumptions: that private product is a satisfactory representation of social product; that rates of return on physical and educational capital are conceptually similar; that analysis of cross-section data provides useful estimates for projecting trends into the future; and that the associated increase in money income is a satisfactory measure of the private returns to education. Bearing in mind these limitations of the economic analysis of education, the authors survey the findings of a number of economists on the effect of education on earnings, the rate of return on investment in education, and the contribution of education to economic growth.

219. MERRETT, STEPHEN. "The Rate of Return to Education: A Critique." *Oxford Economic Papers,* Vol. 18, No. 3 (November, 1966), pp. 289-303.

Headings: The rate of return on education; Appendix on scarcity of data and estimating procedures; Bibliography (17).

Abstract: The author outlines the method used for calculating the rate of return on education and proceeds to examine the major difficulties involved in calculating costs and benefits. The most complex difficulty on the cost side is that of calculating student opportunity costs. The author argues that income forgone should not include the forgone earnings on part-training. Expenditures on residential accommodation which would have been made in any case should be excluded from the cost estimate as should expenditures on research and consumption activities. On the benefit side, economists seem unable to deal with psychic income, changes in the nature of leisure activities, and the measurement of external economics. These effects, along with the creation of skilled personnel, are the objectives of education. It is mistaken in some societies to assume that factor prices are equal to productivity or opportunity cost. In consequence, large errors will probably be made in deriving the benefit stream as a residual from two income streams predicted from cross-section data. The author discusses the econometric difficulties involved in measuring education's rate of return: derivation of the net contribution of education to income involves multivariate analysis, using a large number of variables, both quantitative and qualitative, heterogeneous in their units, inter-correlated, and holding nonadditive relations. The conclusion of the paper is that research into the rate of return on education should be discontinued.

220. MILLER, HERMAN P. "Annual and Lifetime Income in Relation to Education: 1939-1959." *American Economic Review,* Vol. 50, No. 5 (December, 1960), pp. 962-986.

Headings: Introduction; Annual income in relation to education: 1939-1958; Annual income in relation to age and education: 1939-1958; Lifetime income in relation to education: 1939-1958; Conclusion; References (23).

Abstract: This paper attempts to ascertain whether the increase in the number and proportion of high school and college graduates during the past generation has been associated with a reduction in income differentials for these groups. In the long run, such a reduction could be expected assuming no changes in the demand for more highly educated workers. In the short run period under consideration, the relative increase in the supply of highly educated workers does not appear to have affected their relative income position. It is concluded, therefore, that the demand for more highly educated workers has kept pace with the increased supply. Estimates of lifetime income, based upon cross-section data, support the conclusion that the large increase in the number of college graduates during the postwar period has not adversely affected their relative income position.

221. MILLER, HERMAN P. "Income and Education: Does Education Pay Off? In *Economics of Higher Education,* edited by Selma J. Mushkin, pp. 129-146. Washington: U.S. Department of Health, Education, and Welfare, Office of Education, 1962.

Headings: Introduction; Income and education: differences between whites and nonwhites; Income and education: veteran, nonveteran differences, 1947-1959.

Abstract: Education is only one of the many factors that determine income. The observed relationship between schooling and earnings may be spurious, and what essentially may remain undisclosed are underlying causes both of advanced education and higher earnings, conditions such as superior intelligence, better home environment, and greater opportunities both socially and economically. Analysis of income changes of nonwhites and of veterans raises questions about the extent to which education is primarily responsible for income gains. The association between education and income is closer for whites than for nonwhites. While veterans have considerably higher average incomes than non-veterans, there is only a small difference between the average income of veterans who participated in the educational program under the "GI bill of rights", and those who did not.

111

222. MORGAN, JAMES and MARTIN DAVID. "Education and Income." *Quarterly Journal of Economics,* Vol. 77, No. 3 (August, 1963), pp. 423-437.

Headings: Introduction; The problem of method; Proposed procedures; Statistical method and source of data; Explanatory factors in addition to education; Search for interaction effects and more detail on education; Estimated life-time earnings; Qualifications; Summary.

Abstract: The authors attempt to measure the effect of education upon worker productivity. Productivity is best measured by hourly earnings since annual money earnings indicate not only productivity but also reflect the unwanted unemployment of the less educated and the desired extra leisure that can be afforded by those with more education. Since the data, drawn from a national sample conducted by the Survey Research Center, are used for estimates of life-time earnings, separate education coefficients are derived for each age group in the cross-section sample. Multiple regression analysis, using a separate dummy variable for each class of explanatory factor, is employed to derive estimates of the effects of education on hourly earnings, relatively free from the effects of other factors correlated both with education and with earnings. The analysis does not take account of interaction effects beyond that of age and education; such interactions among explanatory variables do exist but appear to have a negligible effect on estimates of the effects of education and age on hourly earnings. The authors present estimates of hourly earnings (for white, male, nonfarmer heads of spending units who worked in 1959) net of the intercorrelations of education with the other explanatory variables. These estimates of hourly earnings by age and education can be used to calculate present values of life-time earnings estimates, and can be compared with actual earnings to give a measure of the extent to which previous estimates of the value of education may have been exaggerated because of the correlations between education and other factors.

223. MORGAN, JAMES, and CHARLES LININGER. "Education and Income: Comment." *Quarterly Journal of Economics,* Vol. 78, No. 2 (May, 1964), pp. 346-347.

Abstract: Data from four Surveys of Consumer Finance ranging from 1957-1963 were used to calculate income differentials among educational groups. It was found that the 1961-62 average differentials tend to be larger than the 1956-57 average differentials, and larger than the 1959 differential noted by Morgan and David (222). The implication is that the private and social value of investment in education is greater than was previously thought.

224. MORGAN, JAMES, and ISMAIL SIRAGELDIN. "A Note on the Quality Dimension in Education." *Journal of Political Economy,* Vol. 76, No. 5 (October, 1968), pp. 1069-1077.

Headings: Introduction; Removing the effects of other determinants of earnings; Quality of college; Summary; References (14).

Abstract: A test of the hypothesis that the quality of schooling has an effect on hourly earnings must first remove the effects on hourly earnings of other variables such as years of schooling, whether or not the family head grew up on a farm, sex, race, and age. Farmers and self-employed businessmen are excluded in order to avoid including some of the return to capital. Unemployment is also excluded as a variable. The regression analysis indicates that $1.00 more per year per pupil spent on elementary and secondary education in a state means 24 cents an hour more earned by those who went to school there, other things being equal. The authors recognize, however, that the quality of education may be only mildly correlated with expenditures upon schooling. Another type of variation in educational quality has to do with the kind of college attended by the college-educated. The index of quality of college is based upon "the scholastic potential of the student body". After accounting for other variables, a higher quality of education is again associated with higher earnings.

225. PEJOVICH, S. and W. SULLIVAN. *The Role of Technical Schools in Improving the Skills and Earning Capacity of Rural Manpower: A Case Study.* Washington: U.S. Department of Labor, Office of Manpower Policy, Evaluation and Research, September, 1966. i + 19 p.
Headings: Introduction; The model; Sources and uses of data; The results; Conclusions.

Abstract: This study attempts to calculate the private and social rates of return on instructional programs offered by the Winona Area Technical School in Winona, Minnesota. The WATS is a substitute for on-the-job training except that, under the Manpower Development and Training Act of 1962, a part of the general outlay on training is borne by the Community. Direct private costs consist of the after-tax earnings forgone by the trainee. Direct social costs are educational expenditures, capital expenditures, and MDTA subsidies. Indirect social costs consist of forgone earnings *before tax.* The private and social returns are the estimated increases in earnings as a result of training after and before tax respectively. A systematic downward bias was introduced into a number of estimated variables to allow for conceptual and statistical difficulties involved in estimating rates of return on investment in human capital. Private and social rates of return are cited for trainees in a number of age groups and for a number of training programs. The results are generally favourable to investment in WATS: social rates of return tend to be lower than private rates, but higher than average social rates of return.

226. RAYMOND, RICHARD. "Determinants of the Quality of Primary and Secondary Public Education in West Virginia." *Journal of Human Resources,* Vol. 3, No. 4 (Fall, 1968), pp. 450-470.
Headings: Abstract; Introduction; Quality measures; Determinants of the quality of education; Description of empirical results; Summary and conclusion.

Abstract: Inputs into an educational system are often used as a proxy for the quality of output produced by the system. This paper concentrates upon a single aspect of educational output: the adequacy of preparation for higher education. The measures of quality of education are computed from achievement test scores, freshman grade point averages, and high school grade point averages. The quality of education will be influenced by teachers' salaries, the student-teacher ratio, the percentage of teachers teaching in two or more fields, the number of library volumes in excess of standard, and adjusted current expenditures per pupil. Aptitude and motivation of students will also affect the quality of student graduated. Regression analysis was used to determine the significance of these quality variables for a sample of 5,000 West Virginia university students. Teachers' salaries were found to be significant determinants of quality; the other quality variables were not significant. A very large percentage of the variation in quality of education remained unexplained. Another serious problem was that the various school systems probably have different objectives; it would be a misallocation of resources if they all devoted the same amount of effort to preparing students for college. It appears, therefore, that more than one quality index may be needed.

227. RENSHAW, EDWARD F. "Estimating the Returns to Education." *Review of Economics and Statistics,* Vol. 42, No. 3 (August, 1960), pp. 318-324.

Headings: Introduction; Interpretation of the average rate of return; The marginal return to education; Estimating the stock of educational capital.

Abstract: It is pointed out that the use of mean income differentials to estimate the return to education involves imputing to education any return which results from factors which are positively correlated with formal education. Median income differentials are likely to give a better estimate of the return to education, and Census data are typically reported in that way. The author makes an estimate of the stock of educational capital, using median income differentials.

228. SCHULTZ, THEODORE W. "Capital Formation by Education." *Journal of Political Economy,* Vol. 68, No. 6 (December, 1960), pp. 571-583.

Headings: Introduction; Earnings that students forgo; Costs of the services provided by schools; Total costs of education; Concluding observations.

Abstract: This paper presents a set of estimates of the value of the resources which have been entering into education in the U.S. The estimates show that the stream of resources entering into elementary education has increased less than that entering into high school or higher education, but has increased at a faster rate than gross physical capital formation. The resources entering into education consist chiefly of two components — the earnings which students forgo while attending school and the resources used to provide schools. The annual flow of the inputs employed for education consists of the services of teachers, librarians, school administrators, the annual factor costs of maintaining and operating the school plant, and of depreciation and interest. These costs are calculated for the U.S. for a number of years since 1900 and compared with the calculations of forgone earnings: between 1900 and 1956, the total resources committed to education in the U.S. rose three and half times; forgone earnings as a proportion of total costs rose from 26 to 43 per cent. Not only have the streams of resources entering into elementary, high school and higher education increased markedly, but they have changed relative to one another. The author discusses these changes. He concludes by pointing out that several things remain to be done before we can guage the increases in the stock of capital generated by education: the costs of education must be allocated between consumption and investment; and the size of the stock of human capital formed by education and the rate of return to educational capital must be ascertained.

229. SCHULTZ, THEODORE W. *The Economic Value of Education.* New York: Columbia University Press, 1963. xii + 92 p.

Headings: Preface; Economic components of education; Costs of education; Economic value of education; The unfinished search; Selected bibliography (222).

Abstract: The author defines education as consisting of two main components: "schooling" is a concept applied to the educational services rendered by elementary and secondary schools, and by institutions for higher learning, including the effort of students to learn; "education" is applied to those activities of organized education which are not an essential part of the achievement of students, e.g., the advancement of knowledge through research. For purposes of economic analysis, a distinction is drawn between the consumer and producer values of schooling. This distinction yields a threefold classification of the benefits from schooling: present consumption; future consumption (an investment); and future producer capability (an investment). The threefold nature of benefits gives rise to the problem of allocating the costs of schooling between consumption and investment elements: when the rate of return on schooling is being calculated, only the costs of the investment portion of schooling are relevant. An additional problem encountered in the measurement of the rate of return on schooling is that of distinguishing between those benefits which accrue to the student and those which are captured by other individuals. The concept of school expenditures is not appropriate for the purpose of ascertaining all of the costs of schooling. School expenditures do not cover all of the costs not borne by the student, and they cover none of the costs which *are* borne by the student and which, contrary to the common impression, constitute the larger part of the total factor costs of schooling. An important component of the costs borne by the student is the opportunity cost of attending school — forgone earnings. The author concludes by advancing three hypotheses about human capital and by posing a number of questions which remain to be answered. The three hypotheses are: that the inclusion of human capital will show that the ratio of *all* capital to income is not declining; that the structure of wages and salaries is determined in the long-run by investment in schooling, health, on-the-job training, and searching for and acting upon information about job opportunities; and that changes in the investment in human capital are a basic factor in reducing the inequality in the personal distribution of income. The unresolved questions are as follows: are taxes forgone because of special tax treatment for schools part of the costs of schooling? who bears the cost of schooling? are earnings forgone a key explanatory variable of individuals' decisions about schooling? what are the benefits from and what is the rate of return on expenditures on research? what factors determine the growth in demand for individuals with skills associated with schooling? what is the nature and the distribution of the consumption benefits of schooling? what do schooling and the acquisition of knowledge contribute to economic growth? to what extent do tax laws discriminate against the formation of human capital? and how satisfactorily does the capital market function in providing students with funds to invest in their schooling?

230. SCHULTZ, THEODORE W. "The Rate of Return in Allocating Investment Resources to Education." *Journal of Human Resources,* Vol. 2, No. 3 (Summer, 1967), pp. 293-309.

Headings: Introduction; Advantages limited; Earnings from and cost of education; As allocative guides; Conclusions.

Abstract: The author agrees with Solow (175) that the concept of the rate-of-return on investment has a fundamental role in planning economic development. He points out, however, that the rate-of-return approach to planning will remain inefficient until the more important forms of capital are included in the rate-of-return analysis. At present, human capital is one of the major omissions. How real and relevant are rates of return in efficiently allocating investment resources to education? The author feels that education absorbs a large share of resources and, consequently, that misallocations of resources within the education sector and between education and alternative expenditures are potentially very wasteful; secondly, that private educational choices tend to be inefficient and there is not enough information to tell whether they are socially efficient; and thirdly, that there is not enough evidence to tell whether social and private rates of return are proportional in all activities. He argues that the investment horizon which will explain the behaviour of students, schools and even governmental planning agencies is fairly short — mainly because of uncertainty. The short investment horizon is likely to lead to underinvestment in education. The author concludes this paper, which refers to almost fifty studies in the economics of education, by listing ten main conclusions.

231.   SCHULTZ, THEODORE W. "Resources for Higher Education: An Economist's View." *Journal of Political Economy,* Vol. 76, No. 3 (May-June, 1968), pp. 327-347.

Headings: Introduction; From preferences to an agenda of economic problems; From propositions to implications; Searching for solutions; References (19).

Abstract: The author puts forward and discusses the following seven propositions: organized education produces an array of different forms of human capital of varying durability; the three major functions of higher education are discovering talent, instruction, and research; there are few or no gains in the productivity of labour entering into higher education; earnings forgone by students are well over half of the real costs of the human capital formation by higher education; long-term projections of the demand for higher education are beset with all manner of uncertainty; since education is an investment in human capital, the central economic concept in planning and financing it should be the rate of return to investment; and, finally, education changes the distribution of personal income. The author's list of problems that await solution contains two parts: the first part deals with the allocation of resources for higher education in accordance with the test of economic efficiency; the second part pertains to allocations which reduce the inequality in the distribution of personal income.

232.   SHELL, KARL, *et. al.* "The Education Opportunity Bank: An Economic Analysis of a Contingent Repayment Loan Program for Higher Education." *National Tax Journal,* Vol. 21, No. 1 (March, 1968), pp. 2-45.

Headings: Introduction and Summary; The allocation and distributional effects of the Educational Opportunity Bank; Women and the Educational Opportunity Bank; The repayment-tax rate and the rate of return; Fiscal impact of the Educational Opportunity Bank; The size of the program: new loans, outstanding loans, and fiscal impact; Educational opportunity grants for higher education; Suggestions for further research.

Abstract: The U.S. Panel on Educational Innovation suggested that the Educational Opportunity Bank be authorized to borrow money at government rates and to lend it to post-secondary students regardless of the students' resources. The Panel estimated that the Bank could be self-sustaining if it charged one per cent of annual gross income for thirty years for every three thousand dollars borrowed, or at the option of the student, treated his debt as a conventional six per cent interest rate loan. This article provides an analysis of the feasibility and desirability of this proposal. The Educational Opportunity Bank overcomes the two main obstacles to private borrowing to finance investment in education: it circumvents the problem of default by employing taxation powers to ensure that the pledge is fulfilled; and it overcomes the risk attached to individual loans by pooling. The authors advocate a broad definition of "income", for the purposes of the Bank, including wages, salaries, interest, dividends, and capital gains. The definition of "income" for women not participating in the labour force should be family income. The Educational Opportunity Bank which, the authors predict, could have $132 billion of outstanding loans by 1984, would have a significant fiscal impact and taxes would have to be raised to prevent further inflation. The authors present estimates of the rate of the return of the program given various repayment tax rates. They conclude by suggesting the following fields for further research: the impact of the program on the financing of educational institutions; the effect on the allocation of society's resources; the effect on the relative positions of public and private institutions; and the quantitative gain **to society** from the Educational Opportunity Bank.

233. STAGER, DAVID. "Measuring the Output of Educational Institutions." In *The Canadian Labour Market: Readings In Manpower Economics,* edited by Arthur Kruger and Noah M. Meltz, pp. 297-312. Toronto: Centre for Industrial Relations, University of Toronto, 1968.

Headings: Introduction; Aptitude tests; Educational services; Market valuations or earnings differentials; Other output measures; Human capital; Summary and conclusion; Notes and references.

Abstract: Three approaches can be used in the measurement of the output of an educational industry — intellectual development as measured by aptitude tests, the amount of educational services provided, as measured by enrollments, and, thirdly, earnings differentials. The two main objections to the latter approach are that earnings reflect both supply and demand conditions, and that existing wage patterns may be altered by the introduction of new types of institutions. The use of earnings differentials to approximate differences in educational output assumes that differences in employees' marginal value products can be attributed solely to differences in levels and types of education, and that earnings received by employees reflect their marginal value products. The first assumption may not hold because of the influence of factors other than education — on-the-job training, experience, motivation, native ability, and social connections. The second assumption may not hold because of "conspicuous production", "tradition-bound" wage structures, non-monetary attractions of jobs, collective power, and external economies. Other questions relating to the use of earnings differentials data are the use of cross-sectional data for representing expected lifetime earnings, the problem of the discount rate, the question of which earnings data should be used, and the problem of evaluating the education of persons outside the labour force.

234. STAGER, DAVID. "Monetary Returns to Post-Secondary Education in Ontario, 1960-1964." A paper presented to the Société Canadienne de Science Economique, Ottawa, October, 1968. 40 p.

Headings: Introduction; Analytical framework and the assumptions; Data on costs and benefits for post-secondary education in Ontario; Estimated returns

118

to post-secondary education in Ontario; Appendix A — Price indexes for institutional expenditures; Appendix B — Categories and weights for determining basic expenditure unit.

Abstract: This paper estimates the monetary returns to higher education in terms of net present values, benefit-cost ratios, and internal rates of return: from a social and private point of view; both before and after taxes; for males and females separately; and for different degrees and certificates of post-secondary education. From society's point of view, the costs of post-secondary education include the direct expenditures upon salaries, books, supplies, and equipment, the indirect costs of depreciation, imputed interest, and tax exemptions, as well as students' expenditures upon books, supplies, and travel, and the value of output forgone because students are not in the labour force. For the individual, the costs of education include fees, expenditures upon books, supplies, and travel, and forgone earnings. The study includes only the direct monetary returns to society and to individuals resulting from further education. Earnings differentials have to be adjusted to account for factors other than education which cause differences in earnings among individuals. The method of obtaining the costs and benefits estimates is described in detail. While the results indicate that there is a substantial net monetary return to investment in post-secondary education in Ontario, they also exhibit a strong sensitivity to the evaluation method and assumptions used. There appears to be a wide range of both social and private returns to investment in the different faculties and institutions. This suggests market imperfections: the author feels that the imperfections are mainly on the supply side for the higher income occupations and on the demand side for the lower income occupations.

235. SWIFT, WILLIAM J., and BURTON A. WEISBROD. "On the Monetary Value of Education's Intergeneration Effects." *Journal of Political Economy,* Vol. 73, No. 6 (December, 1965), pp. 643-649.

Headings: Introduction; The concept; The model and its empirical application; interpreting the findings.

Abstract: A study in 1960 by Brazer and David [in S. J. Mushkin (ed.) *Economics of Higher Education*] indicated that the spending unit head's education was the most important factor influencing the education level of the children. Incremental amounts of education received by the household head can be related to additional years of education for the child, and hence additional yearly income. The return on the extra education can be calculated as an indirect return on the investment in the household head's education. While the authors admit that their results are tentative because of the difficulty of controlling for variables which may vary systematically with educational attainment, and because of the nature of the assumptions made, their main concern is to establish the concept of a measurable intergeneration return from investment in education, a return which is relevant for efficient resource-allocation decisions.

236. VAIZEY, JOHN. *The Economics of Education.* London: Faber and Faber, 1962. 165 p.

Headings: Introduction; What some economists said about education; Education as consumption or investment; The returns to education; Expenditure on education; The finance of education; The productivity of education; Manpower; Teachers and their salaries; The economist and the schools; Education in economic growth, I; Education in economic growth, II; Conclusion; Select bibliography of the economics of education (119).

Abstract: Education is both a private and a public good, and an investment as well as consumption: hence publicly financed education is a legitimate end of public activity. If education is an investment, to whom does the return accrue and how is it measured? Four methods of measuring the returns to education are put forward: education as the residual factor in economic growth; the additional earnings of the educated over the uneducated; cost-benefit ratios; and the calculation of human capital. The author examines the development of educational expenditures in the U.K., U.S., and France: there is an increasing proportion of national income going to education, and an increasing proportion of education expenditure going to secondary and higher education. The two main sources of finance are public funds and the parents of children educated. The production of education is becoming more capital intensive and relatively less (although absolutely more) labour intensive. The author raises the question of how we can measure the productivity of the inputs involved. Education is a major source of skills and trained talent. The planning of education might proceed as follows: on the basis of projections of economic growth, projections of manpower requirements can be obtained; education can be planned so as to fill these requirements. Manpower planning is examined in the USSR, Italy, and the U.K. The position of women in the U.S. labour market, and the "shortage" of scientists and engineers are also examined in this context. Relative changes in professional skills, competence, and status among teachers in different grades in the U.S. and U.K. are described. The author discusses what we know about intelligence — the "raw material" on which education works. In view of the rapidity of change in the economy, the curriculum should be broad at first, followed by specialization and continuous opportunity throughout life to acquire new skills. The place of education in economic growth is examined and schemes to develop education in Nigeria and Pakistan are described. The book concludes with a triple choice: either education is to be conceived as a formal part of a society which is itself an educative process, or it is to be conceived of as a process of developing a saving remnant — a cultural super-ego, or it is to be conceived of as teaching tricks of the trade. The issue of the role of education in the economy must rest on some such discussion of the issues of its social purpose.

237. WATTS, HAROLD W., and DAVID L. HORNER. "The Educational Benefits of Head Start: A Quantitative Analysis." Discussion Paper Series, No. 14. Mimeographed. Madison: Institute for Research on Poverty, The University of Wisconsin, 1968. 31 p.

Headings: Preface; Purpose of the investigation; Tests and variables; Data and sample; The basic regressions; Supplementary regressions; Costs and benefits; Conclusion; Appendix: Four supplementary regressions.

Abstract: The paper attempts to find out by how much a child's educational and social readiness for primary school improves as the number of weeks in Head Start increases, given control of age and other characteristics. Educational and social readiness was measured by the Peabody Picture Vocabulary Test and the Vineland Social Maturity Scale. The control variables can be classified into four groups: attributes of the child; family attributes; family income and consumption patterns; and location. Regression analysis indicated an imprecisely estimated effect of Head Start in improving PPVT scores, and a fairly reliable estimated beneficial effect on VSMS scores. On the cost side, it is estimated that the average gap in PPVT scores between disadvantaged children and the general population of five year olds could be closed by a two year program costing about $2,250 per child. This would provide an advantage in terms of VSMS scores. A complete evaluation of Head Start would compare the costs and benefits of the non-educational aspects of the program, and also the costs and benefits of alternative programs designed to help underprivileged preschool children.

238. WEISBROD, BURTON A. "Education and Investment in Human Capital." *Journal of Political Economy,* Vol. 70, No. 5, Part 2 (October, 1962, Supplement), pp. 106-123.

Headings: Introduction; Benefits to the student; Benefits external to the student; Summary; Appendix: Costs of education.

Abstract: The paper is mainly concerned with identifying the benefits from education. These include benefits which the individual receives in the form of market opportunities and in other ways, and those benefits which accrue to other persons. The author considers that the education-tax system should recognize the existence of particular groups of beneficiaries. He argues for a stricter application of the benefit-principle of taxation on the grounds that a similar distribution of tax burdens and education benefits is conducive to allocative efficiency as far as total expenditure on education is concerned. He discusses the problem of estimating the opportunity cost of education.

239. WEISBROD, BURTON A. "Preventing High School Dropouts." In *Measuring Benefits of Government Investments,* edited by Robert Dorfman, pp. 117-171. Washington: The Brookings Institution, 1965.

Headings: Introduction; The nature of the dropout problem; Returns from dropout prevention; External returns; Costs and benefits of dropout prevention: a case study; Comments: Fritz Machlup, Michael S. March, Herman P. Miller; Author's concluding statement.

Abstract: The present values of income differentials are used to estimate the benefits of preventing dropouts in various groupings — male and female, white and nonwhite, and South and non-South. It is suggested that earnings differentials would provide a better measure, and that the results should be adjusted for differences in ability. The question of whether dropping out results from incomplete information or from consumption and time preference patterns is discussed. Such private preferences may be overruled if there are significant external benefits from education. The estimate of the social value of dropout prevention, however, tends to be biased upwards by the assumption that the marginal income prospects of an additional graduate equal the average income for current graduates. The case study finding is that the St. Louis Public Schools prevention program is unprofitable if **measured** costs and benefits only are taken into account.

240. WEISBROD, BURTON A., and PETER KARPOFF. "Monetary Returns to College Education, Student Ability and College Quality." *Review of Economics and Statistics,* Vol. 50, No. 4 (November, 1968), pp. 491-497.

Headings: Introduction; Earnings, college quality, and class rank; The return from college education; The effect of schooling and non-schooling variables on earnings; Summary.

Abstract: The paper distinguishes between two classes of variables relevant to the determination of earnings — "schooling variables" describing the quantity and quality of education received by an individual, and "non-schooling variables" describing those personal characteristics which influence earnings. In the analysis presented, school quality is judged subjectively while non-schooling variables are measured by rank in graduating class. The data (a sample of male college graduate employees of the American Telephone and Telegraph Company) indicate that, holding age distribution constant, earnings increase consistently with increases in class rank and college quality. In order to investigate the return from college education, holding student ability and motivation constant, the authors estimate the proportion of the gross returns to college education which can be achieved by a person with college education but with only a high school level of the non-schooling variables. This figure turns out to be three-fourths; in other words, only a quarter of the difference between the mean earnings of college graduates and the mean earnings of high school graduates is a return to the higher level of non-schooling variables possessed by college graduates generally. Do differences in non-schooling variables and in the quality of education exert a once-and-for-all effect on earnings or do they continue to operate through the years? The authors found a tendency for the rate of increase of earnings over time to be larger for graduates with higher class rank. The effect of varying college quality is harder to isolate since similarly ranked graduates at dissimilar quality colleges differ in many important respects.

241. WELCH, FINIS. "Measurement of the Quality of Schooling." *American Economic Review,* Papers and Proceedings, Vol. 56, No. 2 (May, 1966), pp. 379-392.

Headings: Introduction; The general framework; The empirical framework; The empirical results; Summary.

Abstract: This paper reports the results of a cross-sectional analysis of the determinants of the return to schooling. A variant of the multiple regression technique is used to derive an estimate of the return to schooling from income data. The return to education is defined as the number of units of schooling multiplied by the product of quality of schooling and the value of the marginal product of education. The marginal product of education is determined by a production function: it is assumed that production is a function of the number of persons employed, the quantity of education used in production, and an aggregation of nonlabor inputs. From the assumed production function (of the Cobb-Douglas type) a basic estimating equation for the return to one unit of schooling is obtained. This equation is fitted by least squares technique to the author's income and schooling data in order to isolate the more important variables which contribute to the quality of schooling. The most important determinants of differences in the quality of schooling appear to be teacher quality as reflected in salaries and the size of the secondary school; there seem to be great economies of scale associated with school consolidation.

242. WILKINSON, BRUCE W. "Present Values of Lifetime Earnings for Different Occupations." *Journal of Political Economy,* Vol. 74, No. 6 (December, 1966), pp. 556-572.

Headings: Introduction; Present values; The data; Discounted returns for different levels of education and various occupations; Changes in discounted returns to teachers and engineers in relation to changes in college enrolments; References.

Abstract: The paper examines the hypothesis that individuals implicitly consider disparities in present values of lifetime incomes when choosing among occupations or when selecting the amount of education to obtain prior to entering a given occupation. The data, obtained from the 1961 Canadian Census, cover incomes at the Census date for individuals of each age group at a given educational level. It is assumed that these cross-section figures can be used to approximate the lifetime income profile expected by an individual entering a given occupation with a given level of educational attainment. Present values of expected lifetime earnings (after tax) are calculated at age fourteen for different levels of education, using discount rates of 5, 8, and 10 per cent. If a sufficiently high discount rate were used, the discounted returns to university education would be no greater than returns to elementary schooling. This suggests that individuals who achieve a low level of education tend to have high marginal rates of time preference. Adjustments on the supply side are probably the most important influence on the similarity of net present values of earnings for different education levels within the same occupation. Discrepancies in net present values between occupations are mainly caused by variations in ability: occupational choice, formal education, and on-the-job training all tend to be correlated with ability. An examination of changes in returns to teachers and engineers in relation to changes in college enrolments in these disciplines indicates a tendency for people to move into occupations with a high net present value.

243. WISEMAN, J. "The Economics of Education." *Scottish Journal of Political Economy,* Vol. 6, No. 1 (February, 1959), pp. 48-58.

Headings: Introduction; Education and economic freedom; A "free" education system; An outline policy.

Abstract: The author points out that statistics as to the share of GNP taken by education provide us with information but with no understanding. The trend towards state activity has carried with it a tendency to regard the present size and character of such activities as broadly unchangeable, and to concentrate attention on marginal changes in present arrangements. The author feels that the general conceptions also merit attention. In a society which takes the freedom of the individual as a prime social aim, there are three groups of possible reasons for government intervention in the provision of education: true freedom of choice may not be possible because of market imperfections; freedom implies responsibility and children cannot be expected to behave responsibly; and parents who make the education decision on behalf of their children are paying for the external benefit to society as well as for the direct benefit to the children themselves. The last point provides the best case for state intervention in the provision of education. Since the argument for state education rests mainly on the existence of externalities, the argument for state provision of vocational training, which adds directly to the economic value of the student, is not as strong as that for general education. As far as general education is concerned, the state should confine itself to the twofold policy of legislation compelling education up to some minimum age, and subsidization to reflect the additional value of such education to the community. The paper concludes by examining the steps that might be taken to move towards this kind of system in present-day Britain. In their comment on Wiseman's paper, Horobin and Smyth (SJPE 1960) attack the conclusion that a curtailment of government intervention in education is desirable. They argue that state provision of education in a democratic society helps promote freedom and greater equality of opportunity. In his rejoinder Wiseman claims that his aim was simply to consider the implications of parental freedom of choice in the provision of education.

244. WISEMAN, JACK. "Cost-Benefit Analysis in Education." *Southern Economic Journal*, Vol. 32, No. 1, Part 2 (July, 1965, Supplement), pp. 1-14.

Headings: Introduction; Some problems of benefit-cost studies; Economic and other "values"; The returns to individuals from education; Social returns from education; Conclusions and suggestions; The bearing of benefit-cost analysis on policymaking; The education "market"; Comment by T. W. Schultz.

Abstract: The author examines problems to be faced in applying cost-benefit analysis to education. In particular he studies the problems of noneconomic values, and of valuing such goods as leisure and the consumption aspects of education. He argues that value judgements which affect the calculation of costs and returns must be made explicit. Empirical studies in this field, however, cannot easily be separated from the general social and educational environment. We should attempt to improve our methods of assessing returns to investment in education, and at the same time direct some of our attention to the methods of providing education and to the structure of the "education market".

245. WOLFLE, DAEL, and JOSEPH G. SMITH. "The Occupational Value of Education for Superior High-School Graduates." *Journal of Higher Education*, Vol. 27 (April, 1956), pp. 201-212, 232.

Headings: Introduction; Education after high-school related to rank in high-school graduation class; Education after high-school related to intelligence; Education after high-school related to father's occupation; Summary; Appendix—Sampling procedure.

Abstract: This paper presents information about the way in which the U.S. utilizes its intellectual resources. Many high-school graduates, whose school marks and intelligence identify them as potentially good college students, do not go on to college because of lack of money or of motivation. The authors discuss income differentials associated with different amounts of education and conclude that a college degree is a profitable investment.

6. TRAINING, RETRAINING, and MOBILITY

246. BACHMURA, FRANK T. "The Manpower Development and Training Act of 1962 — Its Significance for Rural Areas." *Journal of Farm Economics*, Vol. 45, No. 1 (February, 1963), pp. 61-72.

Headings: Introduction; Opportunities for rural individuals; The underemployment concept; Magnitude of farm underemployment; The opportunity for organized rural effort; Relationship to other programs.

Abstract: This paper considers the repercussion of the Manpower Development and Training Act for the U.S. agricultural sector. In particular it examines the concept of underemployment introduced by the MDTA, and attempts to estimate the extent of underemployment. The geographic impact of the Act, and the interrelationship of the Act with existing programs is discussed.

247. BARKIN, SOLOMON. "The Economic Costs and Benefits and Human Gains and Disadvantages of International Migration." *Journal of Human Resources,* Vol. 2, No. 4 (Fall, 1967), pp. 495-516.

Headings: Abstract; Introduction; Characteristics of past and present movements; Scheme for analysis; Individual migrant; The enterprise calculations; National cost-benefit analysis; Integration of calculations.

Abstract: The author examines the post-war European manpower movements which were primarily a response to job vacancies in the developed European countries. Three units for cost-benefit analysis are considered — the individual, the enterprise, and the national economy. The analysis of the individual's position reflects the temporary nature of these migrations: four sets of circumstances are considered — the individual's position before emigration, during his stay abroad, at the time of return, and after return when the possibility of further emigration exists. Analysis in terms of the three decision- or policy-making units may reveal the effect on decisions of a shift in costs from one unit to another. Economic cost and benefit analysis must be supplemented by analysis of human gains and disadvantages. This kind of analysis requires the establishment of units of measurement of human values.

248. BATEMAN, WORTH. "An Application of Cost-Benefit Analysis to the Work-Experience Program." *American Economic Review,* Papers and Proceedings, Vol. 57, No. 2 (May, 1967), pp. 80-90.

Headings: Introduction; Measures of benefit; Measures of costs; "Break-even" analysis.

Abstract: The Work-Experience and Training Program seeks to increase the employment and earnings potential of family heads who are recipients of public assistance. Thus the exclusive concern of this program is with the "specially disadvantaged". This paper aims at developing an analytical framework for evaluating the work-experience component of the program, and at estimating its potential effectiveness in improving the capability for self-support. The effects of the program upon earnings can be classified as a "wage effect", an "employment effect", and an "interaction effect" resulting from a simultaneous change in the wage and the number of hours worked. The social value of the marginal product of the program enrollee may diverge from the wage cost: the estimate of the economic benefits of the program should be adjusted accordingly. The estimate of costs used is the additional cost of an individual participant which is incurred by the government. These costs are primarily additional administrative costs, work-related expenses, and public assistance payments. Because of the dual nature of the objectives of the program, both redistributional and efficiency considerations being relevant, incremental costs are calculated both with and without public assistance costs, which are transfer payments. Since it was not possible to estimate the factor by which the economic benefits of the program to the individual should be adjusted to yield social values, "break-even" analysis is employed: the ratio of the incremental costs and the estimated present value of the future earnings of an additional enrollee provides an indication of how much earnings would have to rise for the program to break even. The implication of the results is that only a small percentage increase in future earning would be necessary. The author suggests that the program could be made more effective by enlarging its training component.

249. BODENHOFER, HANS-JOACHIM. "The Mobility of Labor and the Theory of Human Capital." *Journal of Human Resources,* Vol. 2, No. 4 (Fall, 1967), pp. 431-448.

Headings: Abstract; Introduction: The development of human capital theory; The human capital approach to labor mobility; Some aspects of labor mobility and potentials for growth; Conclusions.

Abstract: The article begins by surveying the development of the concept of human capital. The author suggests that labour mobility can be fitted into a simple investment framework of costs and future returns. However the close correlations between education, on-the-job training, and labour mobility increase the difficulty of isolating the productivity gains from reallocating manpower. The influences of risk, age of employees, and labour market information are discussed. The human capital approach to mobility has implications for regional and national growth rates. More empirical work in this area is recommended.

250. BORUS, MICHAEL E. "A Benefit-Cost Analysis of the Economic Effectiveness of Retraining the Unemployed." *Yale Economic Essays,* Vol. 4, No. 2 (Fall, 1964), pp. 371-427.

Headings: An introduction to the problem and the study; The benefits of retraining for the individual worker; The benefits of retraining to the economy and to the government; The cost of retraining; A comparison of the benefits and costs of retraining; The sponsorship of retraining; Summary of findings and recommendations; Appendix.

Abstract: The study is based on the experience of a sample of workers involved in state and federal retraining courses in Connecticut. Multiple regression techniques are used to isolate the effects of retraining. The costs of retraining and the benefits (apart from the psychological and sociological effects) are calculated for the individual, the government, and the economy. The average benefit/cost ratio for the government was found to be many times that for the individual, and the average ratio for the economy many times that for the government. This indicates the presence of marked external effects, and, consequently, the author argues that training costs should not fall only on the worker or the firm. He points out that a retraining program should be supported by appropriate aggregate and labour market policies.

251. BORUS, MICHAEL E. "The Cost of Retraining the Hard-Core Unemployed: An Economic Evaluation of the 1963 and 1965 Amendments to the Manpower Development and Training Act." *Labor Law Journal*, Vol. 16, No. 9 (September, 1965), pp. 574-583.

Headings: Introduction; The interrelationship of the objectives and an outline of the study; The costs of retraining the hard-core unemployed; The benefits of retraining the hard-core unemployed; A summary of findings and their implications.

Abstract: The 1963 and 1965 amendments to the MDTA were designed to attract the hard-core unemployed into the retraining programs. The redirection of the MDTA to encompass this group will influence the economic effectiveness of the whole program. Increased retraining allowances, literacy training, and the reduced utilization record of the hard-core unemployed along with the greater number of nonmotivated retrainees will increase the average cost of successfully retraining a worker. The hard-core unemployed will probably benefit from retraining to a greater degree than other possible retrainees, but society gains to the same degree regardless of who is retrained for a given job. If there is a "vacuum effect" society may derive smaller benefits in that the retraining of a hard-core unemployed worker may be for a lower skill level than that of a "cream of the crop" worker. Thus, in terms of alternatives forgone, the economic cost of retraining the hard-core unemployed is fairly high. This analysis, however, does not consider non-economic benefits, and it is possible to envisage situations in which retraining the hard-core unemployed would be economically valuable.

252. BORUS, MICHAEL E. *The Economic Effectiveness of Retraining the Unemployed*. Research Report to the Federal Reserve Bank of Boston, No. 35, July, 1966. 219 p.

Headings: An introduction to the problem and the study; The benefits of retraining for the individual worker; The benefits of retraining to the economy and to the government; The costs of retraining; A comparison of the benefits and costs of retraining; The sponsorship of retraining; Summary of findings and recommendations; Appendices; Bibliography (29).

Abstract: This study weighs the benefits and costs of the Connecticut retraining programs to determine if retraining is a sound investment for the individual worker, the government, and the economy. The analysis is limited to the economic variables. The increase in income of workers who utilized training was primarily due to a five-week reduction in their expected annual unemployment. A number of factors reduced the benefit for the worker — increased taxes, reduced transfer payments, discounting for time preference, and a tendency for retrainees to leave the retraining occupation. Not all of the workers who entered the courses made use of the skills they had been taught. Aggregate benefits of retraining were greater than the sum of individual benefits because the value of the workers' production (the individual benefits) was increased by secondary effects, and the social rate of time preference was assumed to be lower than the individual's rate. The 1963 amendments to the MDTA are likely to reduce the benefits to the government and the economy by admitting less able and motivated workers to retraining courses. Since the retraining allowance exceeded normal unemployment benefits, it was in the financial interest of the workers to enter the courses whether or not they planned to use the skills. The costs of retraining to the economy were the same as those to the government except for the retraining allowances which were merely transfers. For the worker who had an opportunity cost of undertaking retraining of $80 per week, the benefit-cost ratio was between 3.2 and 6.2 The government's benefit-cost ratio was 'between 11.4 and 42.4 depending on worker characteristics and the program chosen. The economy's ratio was considerably higher than the government's, indicating that there were marked external effects involved in retraining. For this reason, it is necessary for the government to assume the costs of the program. On the basis of his findings the author makes the following recommendations: aggregate demand must be maintained at a level which provides sufficient job vacancies; alternative methods of improving the labour market should be used in conjunction with retraining; the retraining program should be expanded to meet the needs of the labour market, and should be carried out with the maximum possible efficiency; finally, special attention should be given to groups for whom retraining will not be feasible, subject to the least-cost constraint.

253. BORUS, MICHAEL E. "Response Error in Survey Reports of Earnings Information." *Journal of the American Statistical Association,* Vol. 61, No. 315 (September, 1966), pp. 729-738.

Headings: Introduction; The data; The validity of the responses; Summary; References (8).

Abstract: This study examines the reported and actual earnings of a sample to determine whether misreporting of earnings data regresses significantly upon any characteristic of the sample or of the jobs they held. The sample consisted of individuals who were interviewed in the course of the author's evaluation of the economic effectiveness of retraining programs for the unemployed (252). The interview records were matched with the employer's unemployment compensation records in order to establish response error. The pattern of response error was found to be similar to that of samples used in earlier studies. Two linear multiple regressions were used to determine whether a change in the composition of the sample would affect the magnitude of the response error. Response error in earnings data was found to regress significantly upon sex, age, education, training status (motivation to respond incorrectly), magnitude of reported earnings, interviewer familiarity with the schedule, and the number of hours employed on a job. The direction and approximate magnitude of the bias is indicated for certain demographic and job characteristics. These values are limited by the nature of the sample involved, and cannot be applied directly to other surveys.

254. BORUS, MICHAEL E. "Time Trends in the Benefits from Retraining in Connecticut." In *The Development and Use of Manpower, Proceedings of the Twentieth Annual Winter Meeting,* Washington, D.C., December 28-29, 1967, pp. 36-46. Madison: Industrial Relations Research Association, 1967.

Headings: Introduction; The data; The sample; The method; Summary.

Abstract: This study attempts to discover the actual trend in average retraining benefits, and also to determine whether this trend differs significantly depending upon the characteristics of the trainees. The data presented cover the period 1962-1966. They appear to justify the extrapolation of the benefits observed in the immediate post-training period: the gains from "vestibule retraining" in Connecticut were substantial in each of the five years after training. The average gain from retraining over the five year period was not influenced by the sex, race, marital status, education, number of dependents, and prior earnings of the trainees. The age of the trainee, however, had emerged as a statistically significant factor by the third year following training.

255. BOWMAN, MARY JEAN and ROBERT G. MYERS. "Schooling, Experience, and Gains and Losses in Human Capital through Migration." *Proceedings of the American Statistical Association,* 1966, pp. 210-225.

Headings: Introduction; Recent applications of human investment models to migration; Alternative earnings streams and one-way migration; Migration and re-migration; In conclusion; References (19).

Abstract: The authors survey recent treatments of human capital in migration by Sjaastad (324), Weisbrod (107), Grubel and Scott (293), and Fein (280). Estimates of the relevant income streams in private or social assessments of migration tend to be governed by the availability of data. Applications of human investment models to migration have suffered from insufficient disaggregation of the population of migrants: it is obvious that within-each-region disaggregation by age, sex, race, educational attainment, and income is needed; in addition, information is also required about ability, motivation, quality of schooling, environmental experiences as a youth, job experience, and labour market imperfections in order to distinguish migrants and their earnings in a meaningful way. Differences in school-quality and experience, and the segmentation of markets are examined in detail. Disregard of remigration, which is shown to be quantitatively important, leads to serious misinterpretations of gross migration flows. Human investment models which incorporate remigration sequences can help a developing country chose between sending individuals abroad for study and importing outside experts on a temporary basis. This kind of choice can be placed in a cost-benefit framework. The authors emphasize the need for census tapes with data for samples large enough to permit refined breakdowns.

256.   BRAZZIEL, WILLIAM F. "Effects of General Education in Manpower Programs." *Journal of Human Resources,* Vol. 1, No. 1 (Summer, 1966), pp. 39-44.

Headings: Purpose; Methods; Findings; Bibliography (5).

Abstract: This paper outlines an attempt to identify, in the post-training performances of two groups of graduates of MDTA training programs, differences which were attributable to basic education experiences. Two groups, in Norfolk, Virginia, were selected: one group had completed a combination curriculum of basic and technical training, while the other had been given technical training alone. The study indicates that the combination curriculum contributed to greater technical competency, a higher incidence of employment, and a greater earning power. In addition, it may have contributed to an intangible set of factors including self-esteem, ambition, and initiative.

257.   CAIN, GLEN G. "Benefit/Cost Estimates for Job Corps." Discussion Paper Series, No. 9 Mimeographed. Madison: Institute for Research on Poverty, The University of Wisconsin, 1967. 51 p.

Headings: Preface; The role of benefit/cost in evaluating job corps; A summary of the results; Technical detail of the analysis; Appendix: An explanation for excluding transfer payments from net costs; References (12).

Abstract: This study attempts to assess investment in Job Corps in terms of economic efficiency. The impact of the Job Corps on increasing the earnings of the Corpsmen above what their earnings would have been in the absence of the program is the sole measure of benefit used. Two alternative measures of earnings improvement for ex-Corpsmen who participated in the program for a period of five months or more are put forward: firstly, present value of the expected improvement in lifetime earnings resulting from increased education; and secondly, the present value of the current earnings differential between ex-Corpsmen and a sample of successful applicants who did not participate. Discount rates of 3 and 5 per cent are employed: these figures represent conventional discount factors less the percentage growth rate of future earnings. The costs considered are center operating costs, capital costs, administrative costs, and earnings forgone. Transfer costs are not included since they do not represent real resource costs, and the appraised value of the work projects performed by the Corps is subtracted from the cost figure. The benefit-cost ratios obtained from the study compare favourably with ratios calculated for water-resource projects where much more generous treatment is given to indirect benefits.

258. CAIN, GLEN G., and ROBINSON G. HOLLISTER. "Evaluating Manpower Programs for the Disadvantaged." In *Cost-Benefit Analysis of Manpower Policies, Proceedings of a North American Conference May 14-15, 1969,* edited by G. G. Somers and W.D. Wood, pp. 119-151. Published jointly by the Industrial Relations Center, Queen's University, Kingston, Ontario, and the Center for Studies in Vocational and Technical Education, The University of Wisconsin, Madison, Wisconsin, 1969.

Headings: Introduction; Types of evaluation; Problems of the design of the evaluation; Intentional experiments — a suggested strategy; The acceptability of evaluation results.

Abstract: The authors define two types of evaluation — process evaluation, which is mainly administrative monitoring, and outcome evaluation or cost-benefit analysis. Cost-benefit evaluations can be *a priori* or *ex post*: the latter and more stringent technique is often used in the area of social action programs. In general the measures of program outputs should be tangible changes such as income, employment and education. Often the objectives may have to be identified by observation; the processes of evaluation and of definition of objectives are simultaneous. Once we have identified the objectives we require a control group in order to find out what difference the program makes. The two main alternatives are "before and after" techniques, and "with and without" techniques where the control group does not participate in the program. Evaluations should be made of those projects which are replicable, with respect to both techniques and participants, on a large scale, and should focus upon characteristics of the project which are within the ability of the decision-makers to control. The theoretical framework of an evaluation of a social action program will be drawn from a number of sources: traditional disciplines such as education, demography, and medicine may provide the selection of variables and their functional form. Investment theory makes commensurable the inputs and outputs which are spaced over time. Welfare economics analyzes the distinctions between financial and real cost, between direct effects and externalities, and between efficiency criteria and equity criteria. The authors advocate a total societal perspective in measuring program inputs and outputs. On the outcome side, the problems of measurement may be serious: outcome is often measured in terms of behavioural changes which may or may not be permanent. Follow-up studies can serve

132

as a check on the link between short run effects and longer run goals, but it is often difficult to locate people who have passed through the program. A program evaluation should take place once the program has settled down to normal operations but before fundamental changes start to be made. The design of the evaluation should provide for a wide range of variability of the treatment variables so that it will not become irrelevant once the emphasis of the program is shifted. Large scale programs with heterogeneous projects create "natural experiments" which can help in the process of evaluation. If the projects are non-replicable these "experiments" will be of little value, but there may be scope for intentional experiments. If we do not know which program concept is likely to be most efficacious, we can mount a program with a built-in experimental design. This should help us determine *why* a particular program failed as well as *that* it failed. Few decisions about social action programs have been made on the basis of cost-benefit evaluations because of an inadequate taste for rigor on the part of administrators and an excessive taste for purely scientific standards on the part of academics. It should be recognized that cost-benefit studies will not be the final arbiters of the worth of social action programs. Since, however, it is difficult to demonstrate positive findings we should shift the burden of proof and require clear-cut negative findings instead of an absence of positive results to condemn a program. Finally, we should recognize that the words "success" and "failure" oversimplify the assessment of the typical program: the result of analysis will generally be modification of the program rather than approbation or rejection.

259.   CAIN, GLEN, and GERALD SOMERS. "Retraining the Disadvantaged Worker." In *Proceedings of a Conference on Research in Vocational & Technical Education, June 10 and 11, 1966*, pp. 27-44. Madison: Center for Studies in Vocational and Technical Education, The University of Wisconsin, 1967.

Headings: General discussion; Evaluation procedures; Two case studies; Conclusion; Appendix: Estimated cost calculations of the Job Corps program at Camp Kilmer.

Abstract: The authors feel that the training programs aimed at the hard-core, disadvantaged groups can be analyzed by means of the same benefit-cost procedures as those applied to the regular MDTA programs. There are, however, a number of special problems associated with the new programs: the nature of the benefits is likely to be more complex; the use of customary measures of changes in employment and earnings leads to low performance scores; and data problems tend to be acute. The paper includes studies of two programs aimed at the disadvantaged — the retraining of unemployed Negroes in West Virginia, and the retraining of welfare recipients in Milwaukee. While the results of these studies are highly tentative because of the nature of the measures and data used, they indicate a positive benefit accruing to the trainees.

260. CAIN, GLEN G., and ERNST W. STROMSDORFER. "An Economic Evaluation of Government Retraining Programs in West Virginia." In *Retraining the Unemployed,* edited by Gerald G. Somers, pp. 299-335. Madison: University of Wisconsin Press, 1968.

Headings: Introduction and Summary; A description of the data and a discussion of concepts; The tabulations of costs and earnings; The training program as an investment; Conclusions; Appendix: Can retraining create jobs and reduce unemployment?

Abstract: This paper consists of an economic evaluation of government sponsored training programs in West Virginia in 1961 and 1962. As a basis for weighing the benefits of the program against its costs, the experience of a study group of workers who completed courses of training is compared with the experience of a control group which had no contact with the courses. The factors of time and area were the same for both groups and factors such as race, sex, age, and broad educational level were controlled. The benefits consisted of the additional wages earned by the trainees over and above the earnings of the control group. Costs were quite easily measured. The computed rates of return and present values showed training programs to be a sound investment. The results may, however, be questioned because of the quality of the data and because of market imperfections. The authors emphasize that the worth of retraining programs does not depend solely on efficiency grounds.

261. CARROLL, ADGER B., and LOREN A. IHNEN. "Costs and Returns for Two Years of Postsecondary Technical Schooling: A Pilot Study." *Journal of Political Economy,* Vol. 75, No. 6 (December, 1967), pp. 862-873.

Headings: Introduction; The sample and the variables; Cost of technical edution; Regression analysis; Fringe benefits; The discount rate; Externalities; Conclusion; References (11).

Abstract: Estimation of the costs and returns for investment in technical schooling is hampered by four obstacles: how to obtain a measure of personal income which excludes the earnings of physical capital and public or private transfer payments; how to standardize personal incomes for individual characteristics and economic conditions; how to estimate nonmonetary costs and returns; and how to deal with external effects. Regression analysis is used to control some of these variables in estimating the income advantage of students from Gaston Technical Institute, North Carolina, over high school graduates. The study discusses fringe benefits, the appropriate discount rate, and the use of taxes and subsidies to counterbalance externalities. Rates of return estimated for schooling at Gaston Tech. are higher than rates estimated for college education [Hansen (211), Becker (4)], but the special characteristics of this study tend to reduce its comparability with previous research efforts.

262. CHESLER, HERBERT A. "The Retraining Decision in Massachusetts: Theory and Practice." In *Retraining the Unemployed,*
edited by Gerald G. Somers, pp. 149-169. Madison: University of
Wisconsin Press, 1968.

Headings: Introduction; The institutional setting; The decision rule; Hypotheses and findings; Conclusion; Appendix — Note on methodology.

Abstract: The individual's decision to accept or reject an offer of training
can be regarded as a function of cost and net discounted value of the future
income stream attributable to the training knowledge. Data collected by two
Massachussetts Employment Service Offices in the course of selecting suitable
candidates for A.R.A. retraining separate those eligible for training into two
groups — those interested and those not interested in training. The author
uses the information collected about these two groups to test the significance
of the following variables in the individual's training decision: age; education;
marital status; attitude toward governmental programs and subsidies; employment status at the moment of decision; and employment and unemployment over a relatively recent period of time prior to the retraining offer. It
is suggested that those who refused the retraining offer did so for one of the
following reasons: lack of interest in the skill to be taught; a belief that participation in the program would not increase wages and employment; an aversion to uncertainty; a conviction that the course would be difficult; and a
failure on the part of the individual to perceive a real need for a change in
his present labour market situation.

263. CONLEY, RONALD W. *The Economics of Vocational Rehabilitation.* Baltimore: Johns Hopkins Press, 1965. xii + 177 p.

Headings: Introduction; The extent, characteristics, and costs of disability;
Vocational rehabilitation in the United States; An economic evaluation of the
program; Factors influencing the success of rehabilitation; Should more persons be rehabilitated?

Abstract: The author argues that a knowledge of the material results of rehabilitation is important. If measured returns exceed costs, rehabilitation can
be justified on material grounds alone; if costs exceed material returns the
difference against which human values must be weighed should be made explicit. In addition, data on measured costs and returns are essential aids in
the allocation of the available funds. The benefits conferred upon society as
a result of the vocational rehabilitation program would be measured ideally
by comparing the levels of output, the amounts of housekeeping services, and
the costs of special medical, nursing, and custodial care for the disabled with
those values had rehabilitation not taken place. Similarly, the incremental
social costs of rehabilitation are the value of the resources which would have
been available for other uses had rehabilitation not occurred. These data are
not available, but proxies for the relevant variables indicate that the present
value of the long-run gain to taxpayers of the rehabilitation program in the

United States is between one and five times its costs. The author concludes that, while the optimum size of the rehabilitation program cannot be predicted, the program should be helping more disabled persons into gainful activity than it actually does. Other important conclusions are: that the returns per dollar spent on rehabilitation may be as great for the less productive as for the more productive rehabilitants who have more potential in the absence of rehabilitation and who generally have higher costs of rehabilitation; and that rehabilitation is hindered not only by the unemployability of a person due to disability, age, and the lack of education, but also by the attitudes of the disabled towards work and of employers towards the disabled.

264. CONLEY, RONALD W. "A Benefit-Cost Analysis of the Vocational Rehabilitation Program." *Journal of Human Resources,* Vol. 4, No. 2 (Spring, 1969), pp. 226-252.

Headings: Introduction; The vocational rehabilitation program; Some preliminary observations; Data and procedure; Benefits of vocational rehabilitation; Value of rehabilitation to taxpayers; Factors influencing success; Summary.

Abstract: Vocational rehabilitation is the process of assisting disabled persons to obtain or retain productive employment or to locate more productive employment. This study concentrates on estimating only the increase in marketable output that can be attributed to vocational rehabilitation. There are three objections to using the change in earnings between acceptance and closure of the rehabilitant's case for this purpose: firstly, this measure ignores external income effects; secondly, it tends to underestimate earnings in the absence of rehabilitation; and thirdly, earnings may change after closure. Under certain assumptions, total increased output attributable to rehabilitants will equal the average number of years worked by rehabilitants still employed five years after closure multiplied by the increase in earnings between acceptance and closure. An estimate of the social costs of rehabilitation is obtained by making adjustments to program costs: the major adjustments allow for "repeaters" earnings forgone by rehabilitation clients, and the costs of previous research, training, and construction. Using discount rates of 4 and 8 per cent, the author calculates benefit-cost ratios which indicate that expenditures on vocational rehabilitation are, on average, repaid many times over in increased output. This high average return does not necessarily imply a high marginal return; decisions to expand the program, therefore, must rely primarily on estimates of "unmet needs". The major material benefits of the rehabilitation program to taxpayers are a decrease in transfer payments and an increase in taxes paid by the rehabilitants. These benefits can be contrasted with the part of the social costs of rehabilitation actually borne by taxpayers. This calculation demonstrates that the rehabilitation program is a worth-while project for nonrehabilitants. An analysis of the factors influencing individual success in rehabilitation demonstrates that increased earnings per case service dollar are relatively stable among both high and low productivity rehabilitants. This leads to the conclusion that from the standpoint of an efficient allocation of resources it may be as desirable to assist the uneducated, middle-aged, severely disabled, nonwhite, unmarried and other low productivity groups as their more vocationally successful counterparts.

265. CORAZZINI, A. J. *Vocational Education: A Study of Benefits and Costs (A Case Study of Worcester Mass.).* Princeton: Industrial Relations Section, Princeton University, 1966. iii + 126 p.

Headings: Introduction; The institutional setting; The costs; The benefit-cost considerations; Further considerations of the Vocational program in Worcester, Massachusetts; Summary; Appendices; Bibliography (19).

Abstract: This study assumes that educational administrators receive a limited amount of funds from higher governmental authorities and seek to allocate these funds so that the total return on their investment is maximized. The total return on the educational investment is maximized by measuring the costs and benefits of the alternative allocations and attempting to maximize the net benefit per dollar expended. Costs and benefits can be divided into three main categories; measurable costs and benefits to the individual; measurable costs and benefits to society as a whole; and nonmeasurable costs and benefits to individuals and to society. Costs can be further divided into three subcategories: direct, implicit, and opportunity costs. Benefits can be subdivided into direct and external benefits. The study describes the institutional setting in Worcester, Massachusetts and the procedure followed in this attempt to evaluate vocational education. The cost ratios of regular high school education to vocational education are compared with the starting wage differentials between vocational and regular high school graduates. It was found that, if differentials remain constant or decrease, vocational education for boys may not be as profitable a venture as regular high school education. The study did not, however, attempt to evaluate vocational education as a method of decreasing unemployment among noncollege-bound teenagers. Vocational education for girls is harder to justify than vocational education for boys. Public decision-makers could provide two years of post-high school vocational education in addition to the four years of regular high school for the same cost to society as the four year vocational program. Again the starting wage differentials provide no evidence that post-high school vocational education would be profitable when private costs are taken into account. The study concludes with an examination of the impact of the vocational school on dropout prevention and on geographic and intergenerational mobility. The study questions the economic value of vocational education in the particular high school system under investigation.

266. CORAZZINI, A. J. "When Should Vocational Education Begin?" *Journal of Human Resources,* Vol. 2, No. 1 (Winter, 1967), pp. 41-50.

Headings: Abstract; Introduction; The benefits; The costs; An evaluation.

Abstract: The author points out that, in spite of studies which indicate a high rate of return to education, the decision of whether or not to allocate more resources to public education remains a difficult one. The decision is even more difficult when the mix of an extra amount of education has to be resolved. The present paper examines the choice between vocational high school and vocational post-high school education in Worcester, Massachusetts. The average premium paid to a post-high school graduate over a vocational high school graduate, for his two extra years of training is 8 cents per hour if he takes a course which is also offered to high school students, and 19 cents per hour if his course is one which is only offered to high school graduates. Both the social and private costs of post-high school vocational training are higher than those of vocational high school. The author argues that the 8 cent premium paid to graduates of the post-high school course who train in the same areas as vocational high school students represents a premium for having the ability to graduate from regular high school. Given the uncertain nature of an individual's labour market experience, the best criterion for choosing among programs is the minimum pay-back period. At a 5 per cent discount rate, the 19 cent differential would have to remain for almost 22 years before the additional cost of post-high school technical training is recouped; the 8 cent differential cannot recoup the costs of training within the working life of the trainee. The author's conclusion is that able students should begin a two-year accelerated training program in their eleventh grade; less able students should take the ordinary four-year program.

267. CORAZZINI, ARTHUR J. "The Decision to Invest in Vocational Education: An Analysis of Costs and Benefits." *Journal of Human Resources,* Vol. 3, Supplement (1968), pp. 88-120.

Headings: Abstract; Introduction; Public investment in vocational education; The private decision to invest in vocational education; An empirical evaluation; The dropout problem; Joint returns; Geographic mobility; Summary.

Abstract: The paper attempts to answer two questions. Is vocational education as profitable socially as general high school education? And is investment in high school vocational education profitable when viewed as a dropout-prevention program? The data used is supplied by the public school system of Worcester, Massachusetts. The main source of differences in current costs between the vocational and regular high school programs is the higher per pupil expenditure on teachers' salaries in the vocational program. This is explained by a lower pupil/teacher ratio and higher opportunity costs for the vocational teacher. Schultz's work (228) is used as the theoretical model for the estimates of implicit public costs. Private direct and indirect costs are added to the public cost estimates to give an estimate of total resource costs. The author calculates for a range of starting wage differentials the number of years it would take for the present value of the extra cost of vocational education to equal the present value of the extra returns. The attractiveness of vocational education depends on the time horizon and the discount rate used. Starting differentials are a very imperfect measure of the difference between two lifetime income profiles. When the vocational program is evaluated as a dropout-prevention program, it is credited with the difference in dropout rates between it and the commercial program. For its benefit-cost ratio to be greater than unity, however, it would have to be credited with saving every student who graduated and found a job from dropping out. When a joint return is computed for the vocational school, the benefit-cost ratios are greater than unity again only under favourable assumptions. The data do not, however, permit an estimate of the economic value to local industry of the cooperation of the vocational school. This external benefit, claims the author, could easily make vocational education profitable from the point of view of the local community.

268. CORNELSEN, LEROY A. "The Economics of Training the Unemployed." *School Life,* Vol. 47, No. 1 (October, 1964), pp. 17-18.

Abstract: The article summarizes a study made by the Office of Education using a sample of MDTA trainees. One third of the sample was eligible to receive unemployment benefits, and a small percentage was receiving public assistance. Under the MDTA, these persons were trained for work in high demand in their States. The costs of training include instructional costs, training allowances, and transportation and subsistance allowances. The measure of training costs is based on the complete sample of trainees, while the measure of monetary returns is based on the earnings of those who went to work immediately. It is estimated that the break-even point for the investment was reached after the latter group had been employed for only twenty-four weeks. The trainee can be expected to repay the cost of his training in Federal income tax over a five year period. In addition to proving a sound investment the trainees were removed from the relief roles.

269. DAVIE, BRUCE F. "Cost-Benefit Analysis of Vocational Education: A Survey." A paper prepared for the Conference on Vocational-Technical Education, The Stanford Research Institute, April, 1967. Mimeographed. 32 p.

Headings: Introduction; The elements of cost-benefit analysis; Equity as a criterion in evaluation; Review of three studies; Conclusions; Bibliography (13).

Abstract: The author divides the literature dealing with the application of cost-benefit analysis to vocational education and to training programs into two categories: theoretical-methodological, and empirical. In the former category, the issues of benefits, costs, time horizon, risk, and discount rates are listed both from the societal and individual viewpoint. In most cases the ratio of benefits to costs is preferred (as the appropriate investment criterion) to the present value of net benefits and to the rate of return. The three empirical studies reviewed are by Max Eninger, Carroll and Ihnen (261), and A. J. Corazzini (265). Cost-benefit and cost effectiveness analysis can make a significant improvement in the planning and evaluation of vocational-technical education provided that budgetary, legal, societal, and individual constraints are recognized.

270. DIEHL, WILLIAM D. "Farm-Nonfarm Migration in the Southeast: A Cost-Returns Analysis." *Journal of Farm Economics,* Vol. 48, No. 1 (February, 1966), pp. 1-11.

Headings: Introduction; An economic theory of farm-nonfarm migration; Rate of migration as a function of farm income, capital gains, and nonfarm income earned locally by farm people; The location hypothesis and farm-nonfarm migration in the Southeast; Summary and qualifications; References (6).

Abstract: The rate of farm-nonfarm migration is hypothesized to be a function of potential returns and potential costs. Two age and two education variables, a skill variable, and a race variable are considered, and multiple regressions are run on migration and income data. Farm income is consistently and negatively related to migration from farm regions. The variable expressing age is significant and positively related to the rate of migration, while capital gains are found to be a significant deterrent to farm-nonfarm migration. The hypothesis that the rate of migration varies inversely with the distance from nonfarm income opportunities was not substantiated. This may be the result of the omission of nonfarm sources of income to farm people from the farm-income concept used.

271. DROUET, PIERRE. "Economic Criteria Governing the Choice of Vocational Training Systems." *International Labour Review,* Vol. 98, No. 3 (September, 1968), pp. 193-223.

Headings: Purpose and scope of the article; Definition of systems and criteria; Experimental application of the criteria to the different systems; Vocational training policy in an industrialising economy: attempt to apply the method of analysis; Conclusion; Appendix: Summary of order of preference for training systems according to certain selection criteria, expressed by two employers.

Abstract: The article illustrates the use of various criteria in choosing the most effective type of training in given circumstances. The analysis is confined to the training of skilled workers in the metal trades. For such workers there are six main types of training employed in Western Europe: full-time vocational training at a school; day release courses; block release courses; sandwich courses; evening classes; and vocational training of adults. The economic criteria which are applied to each of these training methods in turn are as follows: economy in scarce resources; economies of scale; flexibility; methods of financing; acceptability; admission standards; and duration or speed of training. Full-time training in a school is suitable for economies which can make long-term plans for their manpower needs. Day-release courses are cheap but at the expense of quality and breadth of training. Sandwich or block-release courses tend to be specific in their purpose and are well suited to the part-time instruction of young people who are anxious to earn money. Attendance at evening classes is steadily declining because of competition from more expensive but more efficient forms of training. What should be the vocational training policy of an industrializing economy? The background against which the choice of training system must be made is assumed to be as follows: scarcity of resources; existence of a large traditional sector; many opportunities for production and investment; imports of foreign capital and the likelihood of a good deal of wastage of training. The criteria of choice selected by the author for circumstances such as these are: economy in scarce resources; speed of training; acceptability of training to employers and workers; and admission standards. Given these criteria, the formula of part-time courses would appear to be the most logical choice: day-release and sandwich courses economize on scarce resources; and accelerated training of adults meets the criteria of speed and acceptability.

272. DRUMMOND, IAN. "Labour Markets and Educational Planning." In *The Canadian Labour Market: Readings in Manpower Economics,* edited by Arthur Kruger and Noah M. Meltz, pp. 243-295. Toronto: Centre for Industrial Relations, University of Toronto, 1968.

Headings: Introduction: the educational system and labour markets; How education raises output; Changing labour markets: the record; Cost-benefit calculations in educational planning; An example of benefit-cost calculation; Conclusion: The place of cost-benefit studies and manpower forecasting in educational planning; Appendix; Notes and references.

Abstract: Because education affects the relative supplies of various kinds of labour, and because it raises potential output in a number of ways, educational plans must take the economy into account, and the data for educational planning must come from the economy. The two main techniques in educational planning are manpower planning and cost-benefit analysis. Some general methodological problems of cost-benefit analysis are examined — the problems of changing income differentials, external and consumption benefits, innate ability, market imperfection, and the social discount rate. There are three classes of items in the costs and benefits equations: nonmeasurable items; items stemming from decisions about the scope of the educational scheme in question; and items which are observable or forecastable on the basis of market relationships. Benefit-cost analyses are carried out for twenty different types of professional training under different assumptions about the rate of discount and true social costs. Most kinds of formal education have yielded economic benefits considerably in excess of costs. It is possible that the incorporation of manpower forecasts into the cost-benefit analysis could take account of future income differentials and reveal the implications of various assumptions.

141

273.   DYMOND, WILLIAM R. "The Role of Benefit/Cost Analysis in Formulating Manpower Policy." In *Cost-Benefit Analysis of Manpower Policies, Proceedings of a North American Conference, May 14-15, 1969*, edited by G. G. Somers and W. D. Wood, pp. 42-55. Published jointly by the Industrial Relations Centre, Queen's University, Kingston, Ontario, and the Center for Studies in Vocational and Technical Education, The University of Wisconsin, Madison, Wisconsin, 1969.

Abstract: Increased emphasis upon investment in human capital has focussed attention on rates of return on expenditures on education and on other areas of human resource development. Pressure for cost-benefit analysis of alternative resource uses has come from government treasuries. Since this type of analysis treats non-economic variables as exogenous, some program administrators have feared that too narrow an interpretation of benefits and costs might undermine and distort program objectives and endanger the case for program expansion. The exclusion of non-economic variables imposes constraints upon the use of these models in a decision-making context. For example, if the non-economic benefits of a program are significant they may offset low or negative ratios for the economic measures of a program's benefits. Nevertheless there seems to be ample evidence that the purely economic returns from programs directed at increasing the productivity of manpower resources are high. This is not surprising when one considers the malfunctioning of the capital market in the manpower field. Since not all our values are economic, funds will be channelled into programs which are associated with "merit wants": benefit-cost analysis helps us to calculate the cost of satisfying these. Benefit-cost analysis may not be as useful as some of its proponents have suggested in comparing the allocation of resources between programs: in the first place the objectives and clientele served by one program are seldom truly substitutable for another, and choice then becomes a question of income distribution; secondly, it is difficult to attain a reasonable consistency in the assumptions and techniques used in comparing one program with another. Benefit-cost models are more useful for improving the effectiveness of a single program than for making comparisons between programs. Benefit-cost analysis imposes discipline on the thought and decision-making processes of administrators and policy makers. It requires a clear articulation of objectives and a precise methodology for determining exactly how these objectives are being met. The use of benefit-cost models as program monitors requires a continuous flow of incremental data on each program. For example, the Department of Manpower and Immigration's Manpower Mobility Program has provision for a continuous feedback of information through systematic follow-up questionnaires. The model of the Occupational Training for Adults Program provides benefit-cost analyses of its separate components so that it is possible to see which courses have the highest return. The same kind of analysis can help determine the type of program candidate in whom it is most profitable to invest. Applications of what the author calls "micro-benefit-cost analysis" have led to considerable alteration of selection criteria. The information provided by benefit-cost models should provide an indication of the various levels of expenditure on manpower programs appropriate at different stages of the business cycle.

274. ECKAUS, R. S. "Economic Criteria for Education and Training." *Review of Economics and Statistics,* Vol. 46, No. 2 (May, 1964), pp. 181-190.

Headings: Introduction; The criteria of the price system: the measurement of "human capital" and its rate of return; An alternative approach: computing educational requirements; Education and manpower planning.

Abstract: The paper criticizes the use of rate of return criteria for education on the grounds that there is reason to suppose that prices in the relevant markets will not reflect the relative scarcities of the factors involved. An alternative approach is to estimate educational requirements directly. The data requirements consist of an occupational census giving sectoral employment information by job categories, and a description of the educational requirements for each type of job. The author applies this method to the U.S. economy and gets an estimate of requirements for general education and vocational preparation in various industrial sectors. He feels that this kind of research should be the basis of education and manpower planning.

275. EDGERTON, HAROLD A. "The Prediction of Outcomes of MDTA Programs." In *Proceedings of a Conference on Research in Vocational & Technical Education, June 10 and 11, 1966,* pp. 17-26. Madison: Center for Studies in Vocational and Technical Education, The University of Wisconsin, 1967.

Headings: The problem; The sample; Data collection; Statistical evidence; A summary.

Abstract: This paper attempts to predict, on the basis of certain identifiable characteristics of the MDTA training programs and their participants, the percentage of the trainees who will complete the program and the percentage who will get jobs in the occupation for which they were trained. If this kind of prediction can be made there may be considerable gains in trainee satisfaction, in training effectiveness, and in the amount of training per dollar. Data

143

were obtained from OMPER follow-up data for each MDTA program, and from a questionnaire answered by program directors. Only institutional programs were included. The statistical evidence is of two kinds: correlations of each of the 93 independent variables with the retention and placement criteria; and the combination of independent or predictor variables to produce the best possible prediction of each criterion. If trainees were selected to show a high retention rate, they would have education at the twelfth-grade level or higher, would not be receiving public assistance, would have marketable skills, and would have been employed within the three months preceding the training program. These are not the people for whom the MDTA programs were primarily designed. The real problem is that of making the programs fit the trainees rather than trying to select trainees to fit the training. The author lists twelve aspects of program organization and management which, if altered, would, according to the analysis, improve retention and/or placement rates.

276. ERICKSON, EDSEL L., ALBERT RITSEMA, WILBUR B. BROOKOVER, and LEE M. JOINER. "Differences Between Economically Disadvantaged Students Who Volunteer and Do Not Volunteer for Economic Opportunity Programs." *Journal of Human Resources,* Vol. 4, No. 1 (Winter, 1969), pp. 76-83.

Headings: Abstract; Introduction; Procedures; Findings; Conclusions.

Abstract: The Work Training Programs examined by the authors are designed to provide useful work experience opportunities for unemployed young men and women. It was generally assumed that the "life chances" of volunteers were likely to be better than the "life chances" of nonvolunteers, as indicated by achievement levels, aspirations, self-conceptions, and the perceived academic expectations of others. In addition, it was hypothesized that disadvantaged students who volunteer for economic assistance programs do not differ appreciably, in terms of IQ, from disadvantaged students who do not volunteer. It was found, in fact, that both groups of disadvantaged students have a similar mean IQ level, about ten points lower than that of the economically advantaged population. On the other hand, it was apparent that Work Training Program volunteers had lower achievement levels at school, lower levels of educational aspiration, lower occupational plans, and lower self-concepts of academic ability. The study indicated, therefore, that, among the economically disadvantaged, those who sought economic and academic assistance were those who had the poorest "life chances", the ones who most needed this type of involvement.

277. FEDERAL RESERVE BANK OF BOSTON. "Retraining the Unemployed: Part 1, The New England Experience." *New England Business Review,* August, 1962, pp. 1-4.

Headings: Introduction; Connecticut retraining; Massachusetts retraining; Improved annual income.

Abstract: The article examines two pioneering programs in retraining the unemployed — the Connecticut Community Action Program and the Massachusetts Retraining Program. In Connecticut assurances were obtained from employers that trainees graduated from the course would be employed. Initial placement is only one test of the effectiveness of retraining. A survey of Massachusetts retrainees indicated that individuals who had been laid off, took vocational training, and returned to the labour force had increased their yearly income by 35 per cent, compared with a 10 per cent increase experienced by the control group. Most of the improvement in the trainee's annual income came from steadier employment rather than from an increase in weekly wage. Although there were more than 72 types of training courses offered, it was possible to compare meaningfully the results of the various types of training for only a few categories because most of the courses had only a small number of trainees. The article concludes by citing some of the many favourable comments made by the trainees. The following points were raised: receiving unemployment compensation while learning provides strong motivation for self-improvement; many workers were motivated by the desire to obtain steady employment; and the person who elects to take advantage of the program is significantly younger and better educated than the unemployed taken as a whole.

278. FEDERAL RESERVE BANK OF BOSTON. "Retraining the Unemployed: Part 2, Interest in Training." *New England Business Review,* September, 1962, pp. 1-4.

Headings: Introduction; Willing to train; Eager for training; Background education; Successful stitchers; No panacea; Geographic mobility; Adaptability needed.

Abstract: The article is based on a questionnaire designed to find out how the Massachusetts unemployed felt towards retraining. The principal reasons given for not considering retraining were advanced age, lack of education, and satisfaction with present employment despite seasonal or sporadic layoff. Many of the unemployed felt that they could take training only if it were free and available near their homes. They did not expect very high salaries after retraining, but the prospect of steady employment was an important motivating force. Of the vocations for which training courses were offered, electronic technician and machinist apprentice were the most popular for men while women preferred the computer equipment worker's course. Respondents indicated a wide diversity of other vocations which might be offered. Many of the unemployed realized that they lacked the basic education essential for most vocational courses and were willing to take a course to improve their skills in reading or writing. Elementary courses such as food handling or the running of a sewing machine can be very effective in placing unemployed workers in jobs after a short training period. Retraining should not be thought of as a panacea because of the magnitude of the structural problem, but it can help fill the needs of some occupations. Employers will bear most of the cost of upgrading the skills of the labour force but government subsidies, improved formal education, and increased mobility and adaptability on the part of workers themselves will also be necessary.

279. FEDERAL RESERVE BANK OF BOSTON. "Retraining the Unemployed: Part 3, Retraining — A Good Investment." *New England Business Review*, April, 1963, pp. 1-4.

Headings: Introduction; Savings through retraining; Programs in New England; Slow start; Obstacles to expansion; Needed — a broader approach.

Abstract: This article uses a survey of workers who had been unemployed prior to entering the Massachusetts State training program, in an attempt to evaluate the retraining investment. Comparison with a control group indicated that the cost of retraining could be recovered in five years through reduced unemployment compensation payments. In spite of the apparent effectiveness of retraining in restoring the unemployed to productive activity, the MDTA program, initiated in 1962, made a very slow start. The obstacles to expansion of the program are physical facilities, staff, and the response of the unemployed to offers of vocational education. In addition, many of the unemployed interested in retraining are not qualified for traditional vocational education under current standards of eligibility. Before the problem of the hard-core unemployed can be solved, a broader spectrum of training courses, and preliminary courses dealing with basic skills, will have to be offered. Unless relocation is encouraged, training will be most fully developed in areas of low unemployment and retraining efforts in depressed areas will be handicapped. Efforts to increase aggregate demand should support government re-training programs.

280. FEIN, RASHI. "Educational Patterns in Southern Migration." *Southern Economic Journal*, Vol. 32, No. 1, Part 2 (July, 1965), pp. 106-128.

Headings: Introduction; Migration data; Outmigration; Inmigration; Net migration; Educational selectivity; The Southern region; Some economic dimensions; Summary and conclusion; Comment by William N. Parker.

Abstract: The author uses Census data to establish gross 1955-1960 migration streams for males. Focusing on the South and its sub-regions he computes net inflows and outflows for each age-race-education category. Net outmigration from the South is quite low, but net outmigration of nonwhites is higher than that of whites. The net result of migration is to shift the educational distribution of whites favourably (at the extreme educational levels) and that of nonwhites unfavourably. To get estimates of net human capital gains or losses associated with migration, the author multiplies net flows by the present value (at a 5 per cent discount rate) of the Southern income streams associated with each age-race-education category. These sub-aggregates are summed to give the overall net gain or loss to the region. The evidence indicates that the Southern economy is not being held back materially because of an exodus of human capital.

146

TRAINING, RETRAINING, AND MOBILITY

281. FISHER, FRANKLIN M., and ANTON S. MORTON. "Re-enlistments in the U.S. Navy: A Cost Effectiveness Study." *American Economic Review*, Papers and Proceedings, Vol. 57, No. 2 (May, 1967), pp. 32-38.

Headings: Incentives and reenlistment; Costs and benefits of changing the reenlistment rate; A utility function for the Navy: marginal rates of substitution among experience classes; Incentive cost: a dynamic programming problem; Results; References (4).

Abstract: Men entering the U.S. Navy typically enlist for four years. The reenlistment rate; A utility function for the Navy: Marginal rates of substitu- — representing a training investment per man of six to twelve months. The study estimates the effects of possible incentives to increase the first term reenlistment rate (FTRR): active duty pay; retirement pay; educational bene-fits; assignment, housing, and other policies; other fringe benefits; and pro-motion opportunities. It was assumed that these incentives would not affect reenlistment rates other than first term. The costs of a given incentive system can be separated into two parts; direct costs associated with each man in the Navy, and costs involved in the effect the system has on the FTRR. The bene-fits of the system arise from substituting experienced for inexperienced men. A utility function for four experience classes of enlisted men is derived from interviews with supervisors to determine the marginal rates of substitution of men in one experience class for men in another. The objective is to mini-mize cost for official Navy personnel requirements for the next thirty years, translated into utility values by means of the utility function. Subject to con-straints set by official policy, therefore, that incentive is sought which mini-mizes the present value of future costs. It is found that, for every incentive, an increase in FTRR results in an increase in costs for a given effectiveness pattern. The present incentive system ranks better than every other incentive except one: this incentive is an option to retire after ten rather than twenty years of Naval service. The fact that the early retirement incentive reduces costs slightly suggests that rates of pay and other benefits rise with seniority in a manner not matched by rises in marginal products. The conclusion of the study is that a rise in the reenlistment rate means a substitution of fewer but more costly experienced men for a greater number of cheaper inexperienc-ed men. Such substitution, in the range of data and parameters studied, is cost increasing. The conclusion is illustrated by an example.

282. FISHER, FRANKLIN M., and ANTON S. MORTON. "The Costs and Effectiveness of Reenlistment Incentives in the Navy." *Operations Research*, Vol. 15, No. 3 (May-June, 1967), pp. 373-387.

Headings: Introduction; Problem and approach; Model inputs and outputs —

147

overview; The inputs in detail; Operational usefulness in terms of experience class; The model in detail; Methodological results; References (6).

Abstract: In order to measure the operational effectiveness of the Navy, the authors identified empirically four experience classes of personnel with substitution on a constant man-for-man basis within each class. A Cobb-Douglas utility function is used to exemplify the trade-off between experience classes. This function allows ordinal comparison of hypothetical Navies in terms of operational usefulness. Costs per Navy longevity year were determined with present incentives and reenlistment rates, and survey responses were used to estimate the effects of additional incentives. To the model is added the constraint that the Navy must achieve that level of operational usefulness associated with official personnel requirements. An iterative procedure is used to derive for each incentive situation the pattern of annual recruit inputs that would achieve effectiveness goals at minimal present discounted cost. The incentive situation which achieves the effectiveness requirements at least cost can be identified.

283.   FORRESTER, D. A. R. "The Costs and Benefits of Industrial Training." *Technical Education and Industrial Training,* Vol. 9, No. 2 (February, 1967), pp. 60-65.

Headings: National costs and benefits; Growth of expenditure; Manpower forecasts; Individual choice and vocation; Open markets; Effects of sandwiching; Industrial decisions; Administration; Basis of levy; Grant systems; Grant system benefits; Cost control; "Off-the-job" training; Comparative analysis; Change of attitude; LSE manpower report; References.

Abstract: The author points out that it is difficult to forecast manpower requirements unless we know the benefits from having a given number of trained persons and the costs involved in training them. Public expenditure decisions are often ill-considered, while private decisions by individuals and companies to invest in industrial training are taken without considering that proportion of costs which is met by firms or by the state. Because the incidence of costs differs from the incidence of benefits, it is not clear that a free market in qualified labour will promote an optimal amount of investment in training. In the U.K. the government has introduced a levy/grant system: levies on companies in an industry finance government training of apprentices through Industrial Training Boards while grants are made to firms which train their own apprentices through "on-the-job" or "off-the-job" training. In the long-run companies should attempt a benefit-cost analysis for industrial training: they should attempt to maximize benefits plus the grant less the levy and the training expenditure. Some of the important questions to be asked in evaluating benefits from training are listed.

284.   FREEDMAN, AUDREY. "Labor Mobility Projects for the Unemployed." *Monthly Labor Review,* Vol. 91, No. 6 (June, 1968), pp. 56-62.

Headings: Introduction; Employment status of participants; Income before relocation; Occupation before relocation; Other characteristics; The relocation process; Supportive counselling; Types of moves; Jobs and wages after relocation; A broad approach.

Abstract: The experimental labour mobility projects carried out by the U.S. Department of Labor since 1965 have three purposes: to find out if relocating workers is effective in reducing unemployment; to determine whether a broader relocation program is desirable; and to evaluate policies and techniques which might be incorporated in such a broader program. The relocation process involved providing information on jobs in other areas and, in most projects, financial assistance for the move. Financial assistance is a major factor in a family's decision to relocate but counselling and a specific job offer is important. Most workers were relocated to jobs in industrial production work. Relocation seems to have shifted workers from low-paying employment (prior to the spell of unemployment preceding relocation) to moderate-wage jobs. Success is difficult to measure because of problems of definition: some workers returned to their original area and obtained jobs while some remained in their new area but changed their job. In addition to the difficulty of relating labour market status to the mobility program, there is the problem of nonrespondents to the follow-up questionnaire. Mobility assistance is essentially a preventative manpower tool: it prevents an unemployed worker with little or no funds arriving at a city where it may take him some time to find a job. The services necessary to create a planned move for him will differ according to his education, experience, family size and age, and cultural background.

285. GALLAWAY, LOWELL E. "The Effect of Geographic Labor Mobility on Income: A Brief Comment." *Journal of Human Resources,* Vol. 4, No. 1 (Winter, 1969), pp. 103-109.

Headings: Introduction; The data source; The nature of interindustry mobility; Variations in earnings levels of mobile workers; Income levels of mobility females; Conclusions.

Abstract: Lansing and Morgan's position (304) that it is necessary to compare income levels of comparable groups of workers when evaluating the impact of geographic mobility on income implies that there are substantial differences in the relative numbers of certain subgroups which are found among geographically mobile and nonmobile workers. In particular, there exist substantial differences in the relative amounts of interindustry job-changing among geographically mobile and nonmobile workers. Workers who are mobile among industries in the U.S. typically have markedly lower levels of annual earnings than do workers who do not change industry of job. This has been interpreted as reflecting the impact of involuntary mobility, a phenomenon which is undoubtedly correlated with some of the personal characteristics which Lansing and Morgan employ to help explain the relative income levels of geographically mobile and nonmobile workers. The author looks at earnings levels of mobile and nonmobile males for nine broad Census regions in the U.S. according to whether they changed industry of job between 1957 and 1960. The device of classifying male workers according to whether they changed industry of job enables the author to infer that, among males with similar labour market qualifications, those who are mobile have higher levels of earnings than nonmobile workers in both the regions from which and into which they move.

286. GIBBARD, HAROLD A. "Retraining in the South: Factors Affecting Retraining in West Virginia." *Labor Law Journal,* Vol. 15, No. 7 (July, 1964), pp. 424-430.

Headings: Introduction; General conditions; Unequal participation in retraining factors affecting scope and effectiveness; Conclusions.

Abstract: This paper outlines three sets of factors which affect the scope and outcome of retraining in West Virginia: the social and economic conditions which characterize the state; local factors contributing to county-by-county variations in retraining; and factors inherent in the retraining programs themselves. The author points out that the success of retraining rests on whether it helps the unemployed to get jobs. The state of the labour market is, therefore, of obvious importance: the population of West Virginia is predominantly rural and nonfarm with a relatively high precentage of unemployed, and some sections of the state have a one-industry economic base. West Virginia has a relatively low participation of women in the labour force, its education levels are below average for the U.S., but its population tends to be willing to move and to undertake retraining. The variables which determine that scope of an area's retraining effort appear to be the extent of local promotion, the prospect for local employment, and the availability of physical facilities for retraining. The training programs are governed by rules which regulate them consistently with the goals for retraining and the need to allocate retraining funds. Programs are authorized only if there is a reasonable expectation of employment, and candidates are screened in such a way that the bulk of the hard-core unemployed is excluded. While the author supports a policy of retraining those who stand the best chance of getting a job afterwards, he points out that relocation can supply many more job opportunities for retrainees.

287. GIBBARD, HAROLD A., and GERALD G. SOMERS. "Government Retraining of the Unemployed in West Virginia." In *Retraining the Unemployed,* edited by Gerald G. Somers, pp. 17-124. Madison: University of Wisconsin Press, 1968.

Headings: Introduction: the West Virginia economy and the retraining programs; The research design; Administrative arrangements for the establishment of training programs; The recipients of retraining; Retraining: perceptions and attitudes; Retraining and employment; Retraining and relocation;

Employers' views of training and trainees; A concluding balance sheet: the gains and costs of retraining; Appendix: regression analysis of variables influencing employment success.

Abstract: This paper provides a comprehensive description of retraining programs in five sample counties in West Virginia. The authors' findings support the hypothesis that the West Virginia trainees are the least disadvantaged members of the labour force: this hypothesis was tested for age, race, education, and regular occupation. The attitudes of individuals towards retraining both affect and reflect its successes: the authors' survey indicated a favourable outlook on training. Those who have been in retraining classes have subsequently had higher employment rates than those who have not: this impression is substantiated by the appendix regression analysis which controls for the intervening influence of thirteen secondary variables. Cost-benefit analysis of the sample programs gives results which are favourable for government-sponsored training of the unemployed.

288. GILMAN, HARRY J. "Military Manpower Utilization." In *Defense Management,* edited by Stephen Enke, pp. 246-266. Englewood Cliffs: Prentice-Hall, 1967.

Headings: Introduction; Allocation of funds between capital and labor; Allocation of resources among and within military services; Allocation of resources among different kinds of labor; Summary and conclusions; Bibliography (11).

Abstract: There are two main reasons for inefficient allocation of funds between capital and labour in defense: the first is excessive compartmentalization in the budgeting process which does not reveal adequately the possibilities of substitution of one input for another; the second is the draft which understates the real cost of military personnel to society. There is no evidence that the distribution of manpower among the sources is made on the basis of either the relative productivity or relative costs of labour in the various defense activities. The compensation system in the U.S. forces is described as "paternalistic and egalitarian": the absence of rational skill differentials prevents the compensation system from achieving its real objective which is the retention of sufficient numbers of qualified personnel beyond their initial service obligation.

289. GINSBURG, WOODROW, EDWARD A. ROBIE, and DAVID P. TAYLOR. "Manpower and Its Education and Training: Discussion." In *The Development and Use of Manpower, Proceedings of the Twentieth Annual Winter Meeting,* Washington, D.C. December 28-29,1967, pp. 47-59. Madison: Industrial Relations Research Association, 1967.

Abstract: This discussion covers papers by Horowitz and Herrnstadt (298), Somers and McKechnie (334), and Borus (254) on various aspects of retraining. Among the methodological criticisms of the papers are the questions of forming control groups and of eliminating biases such as placement services, unemployment levels, race and prior education. A privately run program for the employment of high school dropouts is described and evaluated.

290. GISSER, MICHA. "Schooling and the Farm Problem." *Econometrica,* Vol. 33, No. 3 (July, 1965), pp. 582-592.

Headings: Introduction; The model; The data; Summary and conclusions.

Abstract: The purpose of this paper is to show that a higher level of schooling will stimulate farm outmigration and that this will dominate the effect of higher productivity on farms. The author constructs a model of the demand for and the supply of farm labour, and uses regression analysis to estimate the structural parameters. The variables included in the model were farm wages, labour input per farm, capital services and current expenditures per farm, the level of schooling, nonfarm wages, and race. The study shows that increasing the level of schooling in rural farm areas by 10 per cent will induce a 6-7 per cent farm outmigration and will raise the farm wage rate 5 per cent. For policy-making purposes, these findings must be related to the cost of raising the level of schooling in rural farm areas, and the author provides some cost estimates.

291. GOLDWASSER, BETTI. "An Approach to Cost-Effectiveness Studies in Manpower Programs." Mimeographed. Washington: U.S. Department of Labor, Office of Manpower Policy, Evaluation, and Research, June, 1966. 8 p.

Headings: Statement of national needs; Analysis; Planning objectives; Legislation; Future analysis.

Abstract: The author lists a number of cost-benefit studies of manpower training programs under the Manpower Development and Training Act. These studies point to the need for more systematic cost-benefit analyses, cast within a framework of all manpower programs, and providing comparisons of program alternatives. The major goals of manpower programs can be translated into the following systems analysis: policies designed to influence the supply of and demand for labour; activities designed to maximize the coincidence of supply and demand; and substitute activities where the first two programs fail. This framework is subject to a great number of assumptions and constraints. The development of a methodology and the choice of subjects for analysis will give an indication of data requirements. Problem areas in acquiring data are in the field of sample design, control groups, and follow-up reports.

292. GORDON, MARGARET S. "Retraining Programs — At Home and Abroad." In *Proceedings of the Seventeenth Annual Meeting,* Chicago, Illinois, December 28-29, 1964, pp. 128-138. Madison: Industrial Relations Research Association, 1965.

Headings: Introduction; Postwar development of European retraining; A permanent retraining program; The role of retraining in industry; The relative role of retraining; Efficiency versus broader social objectives; Other aspects of retraining; Conclusions.

Abstract: Despite the contrasting U.S. and European labour market settings, the U.S. can learn from European experience with retraining. The most important lesson is that government retraining programs should be a permanent instrument of manpower policy. Some European programs emphasize efficiency while others cater for broader social objectives. A balance between the two sets of objectives may be achieved through application of various techniques of cost-benefit analysis. The European experience also sheds light on some of the occupational, geographical, and financial aspects of retraining. It is suggested that MDTA and ARA training allowances are inadequate by European standards.

293. GRUBEL, HERBERT G., and ANTHONY D. SCOTT. "The Cost of U.S. College Student Exchange Programs." *Journal of Human Resources,* Vol. 1, No. 2 (Fall, 1966), pp. 81-98.

Headings: Abstract; Introduction; The U.S. cost of investment in foreign students; Value of services absorbed by U.S. students abroad; The value of non-returning foreign students; The final balance and conclusions.

Abstract: The author feels that any rational process of deciding on the size of the U.S. foreign student exchange must take into account both costs and benefits, and strike an appropriate balance between them. This paper attempts to estimate the social resource cost to the U.S. of its participation in the program. The costs incurred by the U.S. through support for foreign students are set against the increasing value of resources absorbed by U.S. students abroad, and against the value of nonreturning foreign students. Two alternative estimates of the latter figure are presented. Depending on which estimate is used, the U.S. either incurs a very small resource cost through the program, or derives a very small net benefit. The conclusion is that the exchange program should be expanded.

294. HARDIN, EINAR, and MICHAEL E. BORUS. "An Economic Evaluation of the Retraining Program in Michigan: Methodological Problems of Research." *Proceedings of the American Statistical Association,* 1966, pp. 133-137.

Headings: Introduction; Estimating the social product gains; control group design; Quality of earnings data; Measuring the marginal social cost of re-training; Conclusions.

Abstract: This paper outlines four methodological problems which have arisen in the evaluation of the Michigan retraining program and which may be common to a variety of benefit-cost studies of human resource programs. Firstly, it deals with the problem of estimating social product gains: there are four main difficulties — the use of inference from marginal productivity theory to measure the contribution of retraining courses to national output, nonmarket externalities, and the displacement and vacuum effects. Secondly, the investigator faces the problem of constructing control groups since comparisons of before- and after-training income are not acceptable. Thirdly, the quality of the earnings data may be unreliable, and the data often exclude fringe benefits. Lastly, it is difficult to get an estimate of the time value of resources devoted to the retraining program. The authors suggest some ways of improving the evaluation of such programs.

295. HARDIN, EINAR. "Benefit-Cost Analyses of Occupational Training Programs: A Comparison of Recent Studies." In *Cost-Benefit Analysis of Manpower Policies, Proceedings of a North American Conference, May 14-15, 1969*, edited by G. G. Somers and W. D. Wood, pp. 97-118. Published jointly by the Industrial Relations Centre, Queen's University, Kingston, Ontario, and the Center for Studies in Vocational and Technical Education, The University of Wisconsin, Madison, Wisconsin, 1969.

Headings: Introduction; Studies covered by the comparison; Concepts of social economic benefits and costs; Concepts of private economic benefits and costs; Concepts of government economic benefits and costs; Control groups; Estimating the differential effects of training; Observation period and time trends; Statistical methods and data; Findings; Conclusions.

Abstract: All the studies covered by this comparison focus on occupationally oriented, institutional training of adult workers, usually unemployed. Benefit-cost analysis of occupational training may be undertaken from three main points of view — society, the individual, and government. As far as society is concerned it is usually supposed that the impact of training upon national product can be inferred from the impact of training upon earnings. The connection between earnings and output, however, is loosened by a number of factors: wages and employee compensation may not be the same, and there may be external, vacuum, displacement, and multiplier effects. In addition, there is some question as to whether we want to measure the impact on production or on productive capacity. A number of different concepts of benefits and costs for the individual have been put forward. One of the main points at issue is whether we should attempt to measure the impact of training upon the "welfare" of the trainee or whether we should focus upon disposable income: this issue is reflected in the treatment of voluntary leisure by the

154

various analysts. The estimation of costs and benefits for the government involves looking at changes in aggregate tax collections and social transfers, and at the cost of government outlays on instruction and administration. From this kind of information we can get an estimate of the net transfer of funds between trainees and government: this can be seen as an aspect of redistribution between trainees and the rest of society. The author outlines a number of different approaches in defining experimental groups of persons who are trained and control groups of persons who are not trained: this variability in the use of comparison groups affects the comparability of the estimates of training effects in the various studies. Some comments on criteria for the choice of comparison groups are offered. The relation between benefits and costs is not necessarily the same for all kinds of courses, occupations, labour markets, or trainees. Estimates of the effects of these various characteristics may be particularly valuable. The length of the follow-up period should be the same for trainees and non-trainees alike and should be long enough to spot permanent effects. The studies examined have follow-up periods ranging from 6 to 27 months. Since there is evidence that benefits may be of a long-term nature, these periods are probably too brief. The collection of follow-up data is the most difficult data problem: they can be obtained from questionnaires, direct interviews, or in some cases, from government agencies. Multivariate regression analysis in which training status is one of the independent variables is the most feasible statistical approach in studies of the differential effect of training unless very large numbers of observations are available. This type of analysis involves problems of unequal disturbance variance, interdependence in the causation of the dependent variables, and limitations on the dependent variable. The author's findings are as follows: shorter training courses tend to be more profitable than longer ones; enrollment in a training class appears to be financially attractive for the average trainee; and the inverse relation of net benefits to course duration appears to apply also to the returns to government. It is not clear whether the government recovers the funds it spends on training courses. The conclusions as to research method are as follows: we need a clearer definition of social effects, output effects, external effects, private benefits and costs, and the economic effects on the government. More emphasis should be placed on variations in the benefit-cost ratio with various types of clients and types and degrees of training. Strict random sampling should be employed, and studies should be conducted in those areas in which adequate government data are available to the analyst. The use of nonlinear estimation and simultaneous equation methods for estimating the impact of training should be explored.

296. HODGSON, JAMES D., and MARSHALL H. BRENNER. "Successful Experience: Training Hard-Core Unemployed." *Harvard Business Review*, September-October, 1968, pp. 148-156.

Headings: Introduction; Lockheed's experience; Why the programs succeeded; What Lockheed learned; Expansion and change; Concluding note.

Abstract: The article describes two experimental training programs established by the Lockheed Aircraft Corporation before the launching of the National Alliance of Businessmen's program. The Lockheed-Georgia Company ran a sheet-metalwork training program while the Lockheed Missile and Space Company, located in California, ran a program for three kinds of jobs. Both programs concentrated on "hard-core" unemployed: more than half the trainees in each program were from a racial or national minority, more than half were from families on welfare, and less than a quarter had previous industrial work history. Statistics, observation, and opinion all testify to the success of these two programs. The following factors were important: training was closely related to the jobs for which the trainees knew they were being prepared; the students were prepared for skill levels slightly higher than their entry jobs and there were opportunities for advancement beyond entry level; the method of training and the personnel involved were highly effective. Lockheed learned that trainees need a considerable amount of counselling, that psychological tests are not always good predictors of success, and that special education is required for managers and supervisors who will be working with hard-core unemployed. Lockheed is acting upon the lessons it has learned from the two experimental programs. As well as expanding the two initial programs, the corporation has established another program in San Antonio. Despite government aid, these programs cost more than the usual company sponsored training program. This cost, however, represents an investment which should bring returns to society many times over.

297. HOLTMANN, A. G. "Teacher Salaries and the Economic Benefits of Search." *Journal of Human Resources,* Vol. 4, No. 1 (Winter, 1969), pp. 99-103.

Headings: Introduction; Measuring the benefits from search; A case study.

Abstract: The paper uses Stigler's expression (337) for the maximum amount of gain one can make by searching for a better job to measure the benefits from search in a local market for teachers. Economists have shown that teachers' salaries exhibit remarkably little variation compared with those in other occupations. Since it is the dispersion of wages that makes searching for a higher wage worthwhile, we would expect the benefits from search for teachers' salaries exhibit remarkably little variation compared with those in ing 1958 to individuals in 98 metropolitan school districts. The results indicate that the marginal annual gain from search is rather small. Since there are likely to be costs as well as benefits connected with search, it is probably efficient for a beginning teacher not to be concerned with the wage, but to accept any position that offers other important attributes.

298. HOROWITZ, MORRIS A., and IRWIN L. HERRNSTADT. "The Training and Education of Tool and Die Makers." In *The Development and Use of Manpower, Proceedings of the Twentieth Annual Winter Meeting,* Washington, D. C., December 28-29, 1967, pp. 15-24. Madison: Industrial Relations Research Association, 1967.

Headings: Objectives on methodology; Findings; Conclusions and implications.

Abstract: The authors attempt to evaluate the effectiveness of the various alternative paths of skill acquisition in tool and die making. Their approach is to learn how the men in the sample group were trained; then to learn how well they performed on the job; and finally to examine the relationship between training and performance. The effectiveness of training is measured in three ways: the ability ratings of workers; the length of time spent in training; and the amount of time workers estimated they needed to become all-around craftsmen. The conclusion, which is subject to the limitations mentioned by the authors, is that training paths which include vocational high school should be encouraged.

299. HU, TEH-WEI, MAW LIN LEE, ERNST W. STROMSDOR-FER, and JACOB J. KAUFMAN. *A Cost-Effectiveness Study of Vocational Education.* University Park: Institute for Research on Human Resources, Pennsylvania State University, March, 1969. xiii + 301 p.

Headings: Introduction — The objectives of the study; Theory of public expenditures for education; Economic analysis and its relations to education; Special problems in the economic analysis of education; Data needs and problems; Description of the data; Statistical analysis of costs; Statistical analysis of benefits; Vocational-Technical education as an investment; Vocational education and the dropout; Analysis of non-monetary and non-economic benefits and performance; Vocational education and the employer; Summary, conclusions, and implications; Appendices.

Abstract: This study was designed to develop an appropriate methodology for the economic evaluation of vocational and technical education programs, and, secondly, to obtain the data necessary to carry out such an evaluation. Previous studies of this type are examined and it is concluded that vocational programs can best be evaluated by a slightly modified version of cost-benefit analysis known as cost-effectiveness analysis. The effectiveness of vocational programs can be studied by examining their effects on the earnings and employment of an individual, the supply of and the demand for vocational education, or the supply and demand for specific types of skilled workers. All costs must be considered as opportunity costs: they represent the forgone benefits of opportunities which cannot be pursued because a given line of economic activity is followed. While it is generally agreed that in conceptual terms benefits are more difficult to measure than costs, for the indices of benefit and cost chosen in this study, benefit measures pose fewer shortcomings than cost measures. The stream of benefits and costs must be discounted: the authors place the value of the social opportunity cost rate of investment funds in the 6 to 10 per cent range. The authors describe the data collected

157

and point out the inadequacy of some of the data available. They suggest that educational administrators should develop data which permit an appropriate evaluation of their activities. The conclusion of the study is that there is a pay-off to vocational education when compared to nonvocational education. Two further issues considered are the relationship of the vocational education curriculum to the school dropout problem, and the influence of vocational training on the training costs incurred by employers.

300.   JENNESS, ROBERT A. "Manpower Mobility Programs." In *Cost-Benefit Analysis of Manpower Policies, Proceedings of a North American Conference, May 14-15, 1969,* edited by G. G. Somers and W. D. Wood, pp. 184-220. Published jointly by the Industrial Relations Centre, Queen's University, Kingston, Ontario, and the Center for Studies in Vocational and Technical Education, The University of Wisconsin, Madison, Wisconsin, 1969.

Headings: Introduction; Recent studies of geographic mobility; Some general comments on applying benefit-cost analysis to mobility programs; Manpower mobility benefit-cost model; Summary and conclusion; Appendix.

Abstract: The author argues that "one-shot" benefit-cost studies are not sufficient for the purpose of efficiently allocating public services in the manpower field. The Canadian Manpower Mobility Model is a monitoring instrument: it yields a steady flow of incremental and aggregate results, telling administrators which clients have the best likelihood of success, what destination jobs or areas seem riskiest, and where the program appears to be inefficiently administered. The objectives of the Mobility Program are to contribute to increased GNP and accelerated economic growth by allocating more efficiently the economy's stock of human resources to areas of higher productivity. The family is the immediate unit for which benefit is measured. It is assumed that what is good for the worker and his family is normally of net benefit to the economy as a whole. Virtually all secondary, social, and psychic benefits are ignored, and no attempt is made to measure spill-over or multiplier effects, or to estimate the program's impact upon the aggregate trade-off between unemployment and inflation. The calculation of benefit-cost ratios for the Manpower Mobility Program is described in detail. It involves aggregating the differential benefits of: the worker in his first job in the destination area; the worker in subsequent jobs; his wife during the same time period; and other dependents during a calculated time period. These benefits are reduced by a factor to allow for the possibility that the worker might have moved independently of the Mobility Program, and the resulting estimate is related to the mobility grant and overhead costs associated with the worker's move to give the benefit/cost ratio. In order to demonstrate that the model works and yields reasonable results, an example is run through.

301. JOHNSON, HARRY G. "The Economics of the 'Brain Drain': The Canadian Case." *Minerva*, Vol. 3, No. 3 (Spring, 1965), pp. 299-311.

Headings: Introduction; The semantics of the term; The costs and benefits of the migration of the highly educated; Does a "brain drain" really exist?; The "brain drain" in Great Britain.

Abstract: It is pointed out that the Canadian situation differs from the situation in the U.K. where government policy has kept salaries and work-related expenditures from rising in response to growing world demand for professional skills. The author mentions the social and private costs and benefits of migration of skilled persons. He concludes that Canada has been a substantial beneficiary of the international exchange of professional people in the post-war period, and does not suffer from a "brain drain".

302. JOHNSON, PAUL R., and RICHARD D. ROBBINS. *An Evaluation of the Labor Mobility Demonstration Project of the North Carolina Fund.* Mimeographed. Raleigh: Department of Economics, North Carolina State University, 1967. i + 61 p.

Headings: Introduction; The problem; Effect of variables on the decision to return home; Costs and returns to migration; Summary and conclusions; List of references (13).

Abstract: The North Carolina Fund pilot mobility project was intended to relocate the rural poor of Eastern North Carolina. This paper reports on the progress made, and on the problems encountered: a mobility program for the rural poor involves more difficulties than a program aimed at assisting the spatial mobility of industrial workers. Regression analysis is used to determine how different family and socio-economic characteristics were related to the decision by a large proportion of the relocatees to return home. The paper examines the costs incurred and the returns to migration of low income workers at public expense. The rates of return were found by the internal rate of return and present value/cost ratio procedures. There does appear to be a payoff to a mobility program, but it is pointed out that the current study does not consider distributive and aggregative effects and only briefly takes account of ancillary services.

303. KREPS, JUANITA M., SELMA MUSHKIN, and BENSON SOFFER. "Manpower and Welfare Programs: Benefit-Cost Analysis: Discussion." In *Proceedings of the Seventeenth Annual Meeting, Chicago, Illinois, December 28-29, 1964*, pp. 203-214. Madison: Industrial Relations Research Association, 1965.

Abstract: The authors discuss papers by Somers and Stromsdorfer (335), Mac-Donald (380), and Burns in this issue of the IRRA Proceedings. The papers concern the evaluation of manpower retraining, social welfare, and housing programs. The discussion emphasizes the limitations of the data and examines the problem of establishing criteria which take into account economic growth and human welfare objectives.

304. LANSING, JOHN B., and JAMES N. MORGAN. "The Effect of Geographic Mobility on Income." *Journal of Human Resources,* Vol. 2, No. 4 (Fall, 1967), pp. 449-460.

Headings: Abstract; Introduction; Multivariate analysis of hourly earnings in 1959; Analysis of earned income of family heads who worked in 1964; Conclusion.

Abstract: People move from one area to another typically for economic reasons. Comparison of the incomes of migrants with nonmigrants in a cross-section of the population, however, show that the incomes of migrants tend to be lower, not higher, than those of nonmigrants. Using multivariate regression analysis, the authors demonstrate that two of the main migration movements in recent economic history, the movement out of the South and the movement to the urban centres, seem to be associated with higher earning rates. Although they tend to improve their economic position, people who move from a poorer part of the country to a richer part are at a competitive disadvantage in the labour market. One important reason for this disadvantage is the difference in quality of education received by individuals in different areas. For this reason it is misleading to estimate the effect of moving by comparing the incomes of those who have moved into an area and those who have always lived there. Such a comparison confuses the effects of mobility with the effects of disadvantages which, as the present analysis indicates, mobility reduced but could not eliminate.

305. LEVINE, ABRAHAM S. "Cost-Benefit Analysis of the Work Experience Program: Research Strategy." *Welfare in Review,* Vol. 4, No. 7 (August-September, 1966), pp. 1-9.

Headings: Introduction; Computer simulation; Field research; Use of the two methods in concert; Conclusions; References (10).

Abstract: This article outlines a research plan for a cost-benefit analysis of the Aid to Families with Dependent Children program, with emphasis on the work experience and training components associated with that program. There are two major approaches to evaluation research: the field study and simulation. An example of the former type of approach is Borus's study (250) of an MDTA program in Connecticut. A similar kind of evaluation of AFDC would require sampling a wide range of different types of projects in different regions because, viewed as a whole, the AFDC comprises virtually the entire spectrum of social services. An alternative possibility is computer simulation of the program before it has been tried out even on a pilot basis. Simulation consists of taking all of the relevant variables with presumed values based on the best available knowledge and feeding them into a computer where all of the calculable consequences of a proposed program are played out. There are four distinct stages in conducting simulation of welfare services: the development of a data base; construction of the model; simulation; and evaluating the results of the simulation. Computer simulation offers the researcher a great amount of control over alternative conditions and experiments. It is consequently a useful tool for generating program designs. Field research is essential in providing both the necessary data base for a simulation model and the proving ground for the results of computer simulation. It would appear, therefore, that an optimal research strategy should incorporate both field studies and computer simulations.

306. LEVITAN, SAR A., NEIL W. CHAMBERLAIN, JOHN T. DUNLOP, and JACOB J. KAUFMAN. "Occupational Data Requirements for Education Planning." *Journal of Human Resources,* Vol. 1, No. 1 (Summer, 1966), pp. 54-66.

Abstract: This article is composed of extracts from remarks made by four participants in the Conference on Occupational Data Requirements for Educational Planning, held at the University of Wisconsin, June 1965. Levitan favours occupational projections and feels that BLS data would be adequate, given some refinements. Chamberlain feels that general education should be divorced from occupational needs, although the knowledge which underlies occupational changes might be an integral part of the educational process. Dunlop supports regular manpower projections from large private enterprises, and more attention to retraining for occupational shifts. Kaufman opposes occupational projection but favours training for occupational clusters.

307. LOTT, O. C. "Evaluating to Reduce Training Costs: Valid Shorter Courses Can Stretch Training Dollars." *Training and Development Journal,* January, 1967.

Headings: Introduction; Instructional time elimination; Effective evaluation rarely made; Training is expensive; A typical case; Evaluation is expensive, too!; Summary.

Abstract: Evaluation should be an investment which produces, overall, a favourable cost/benefit ratio. The value of the reactions of students and supervisors to a training course is limited for the purposes of evaluation: students and supervisors lack objectivity and the necessary set of standards against which judgements should be made. In view of the rising costs of education and training, the savings from improving and speeding up the learning process and eliminating improductive digressions can be expected to increase in value. The evaluation and reconstruction of training courses is expensive, however, since it requires competent specialists in job analysis. If evaluations are used as means of shortening courses rather than improving their quality and effectiveness, we can expect investment in course evaluation to have a favourable cost/benefit ratio.

161

308. MADDOX, JAMES G. "Private and Social Costs of the Movement of People Out of Agriculture." *American Economic Review, Papers and Proceedings*, Vol. 50 (May, 1960), pp. 392-402.

Headings: Introduction; Costs to farm people who move out of agriculture; Costs in areas from which farm people move; Costs in areas to which farm people move; Conclusions.

Abstract: The generally lower returns to farm labour compared with nonfarm labour suggest that despite the recent rapid movement of people out of agriculture, the incomes of many farm people and the productive efficiency of the national economy could be improved by a still greater shift of population away from farms. Population shifts, however, result in costs as well as benefits. The present study attempts to identify the costs of off-farm migration. People who move out of agriculture are faced with the costs of transporting themselves and their possessions to their new places of abode, the costs of additional outlays for food and lodging during the period of transition, the opportunity cost of farm income during that period, and psychic costs. The areas from which farm people move bear a heavy share of the total costs: farm families produce human capital from which they receive few financial returns; and, where outmigration occurs on a large scale, total income declines and the capital value of fixed assets falls, while the cost of maintaining community services for the remaining residents rises. When immigration from rural areas is high, the receiving areas are subject to increasing public expenditures and social costs. There is a need for careful balancing of the costs and benefits of off-farm migration as they are manifested among different groups. In particular, public action is needed to ameliorate the adverse benefit/cost ratio for the areas from which people move.

309. MAIN, EARL D. "A Nationwide Evaluation of MDTA Institutional Job Training." *Journal of Human Resources*, Vol. 3, No. 2 (Spring, 1968), pp. 159-170.

Headings: Introduction; Method; Comparisons before training; Opinions of training; Training and income; Training and employment; Conclusion; Note on variable definitions.

Abstract: About 1,200 former MDTA trainees were interviewed more than a year after their job training to learn their opinions of the program and the nature of their subsequent employment experiences. To measure the effects of the MDTA program, a control group of people who were unemployed around the same time as the trainees was formed by means of a partial matching process. Even though a majority of the trainees enjoyed their courses and claimed to have learned something, the basic goal of the MDTA program has not been met unless earning power has actually been improved. Multiple regression analysis was used to determine the net effect of MDTA training. Training appears to have had no effect on weekly wages but may have had an effect on family income. The author concluded from this that MDTA training helped trainees to obtain steadier employment rather than higher wages. Regression analysis supports this conclusion: the net effect of training on full time employment appears to be between 11 and 22 per cent of the period after training. Thus the MDTA program does increase employment, even if it does not lead to better paying jobs.

310. MANGUM, GARTH L. *Contributions and Costs of Manpower Development and Training.* Policy Papers in Human Resources and Industrial Relations, No. 5. Ann Arbor: Institute of Labor and Industrial Relations, University of Michigan-Wayne State University, and the National Manpower Policy Task Force, 1967. 85 p.

Headings: Summary; Evaluating social programs; The objectives of manpower development and training; The costs of MDTA; MDTA issues.

Abstract: The author presents an independent general evaluation of the MDTA training program. At present the two main techniques for the evaluation of public programs are PPBS and cost-benefit analysis: each has greater potential than current value as an evaluation technique. Current manpower programs do not have reporting systems capable of producing data of the kind and quality needed for evaluation. In addition, many of the benefits and some of the costs of social programs are nonquantifiable. The generally accepted approach to program evaluation is to identify the program's objectives and then assess the degree, the efficiency and the costs at which those objectives have been accomplished. The contribution of MDTA to its six objectives is examined. These objectives are facilitating employment of the unemployed, reducing poverty, lessening inflationary pressures, meeting labour shortages, upgrading the labour force, and revamping traditional institutions. The financial accounting system of MDTA is structured in such a way as to make the determination of the program's costs in relation to its benefits extraordinarily difficult. With rudimentary data and techniques, all cost-benefit conclusions should be treated with restrained skepticism. Nevertheless the consistency of the findings of the studies examined indicates that the benefits of MDTA have exceeded its costs by substantial margins. There are four major policy decisions which have to be made. Should the program's objectives emphasize upgrading the labour force or rehabilitating the disadvantaged? What should be the balance between institutional training and OJT? What should be the relative federal and state roles in policy and operation? Is a permanent program needed, and what should be its nature and size?

311. MATHUR, GAUTAM. "The Valuation of Human Capital for Manpower Planning." *Applied Economic Papers,* Vol. 4, No. 2 (September, 1964), pp. 14-35.

Headings: Introduction; The educational sector; The linked sectors in steady growth; Manpower-valuation system in a free society; The valuation of manpower in relation to the wage; The balance of payments of the educational sector; The effects of the non-valuation of human capital.

163

Abstract: This paper devises a means of measuring the value of trained workers in a state of steady economic growth, in such a way that the measure can be useful for planning manpower training and allocation. The educational sector is represented as an input-output system. It is interlinked with a simplified industrial sector and the economy as a whole is then observed in steady growth, and its rate of growth, rate of profit, allocation of investment among industries, and distribution of labour of different skill levels among various activities are ascertained. This indicates the prices of capital goods and of skilled personnel which will rule under conditions of perfect competition or steady-growth planning. The determination of these prices leads to conclusions which are at variance with some of the traditional thinking on the subject of valuation of capital in relation to manpower planning. The paper concludes by examining the effects of non-valuation of human capital in the modern capitalist system: if manpower capital is not counted as part of input or output, the rate of profit appears higher than it is; entrepreneurs who do not consider the valuation of human capital will select techniques which are more capital intensive than the optimum; and, thirdly, the failure to value human capital will result in the educational sector being starved of funds.

312. McKECHNIE, GRAEME H. "Manpower Mobility Programs: Discussion." In *Cost-Benefit Analysis of Manpower Policies, Proceedings of a North American Conference, May 14-15, 1969,* edited by G. G. Somers and W. D. Wood, pp. 224-229. Published jointly by the Industrial Relations Centre, Queen's University, Kingston, Ontario, and the Center for Studies in Vocational and Technical Education, The University of Wisconsin, Madison, Wisconsin, 1969.

Headings: The manpower mobility program; The model; The sub-model; Data problems.

Abstract: The criteria of both the U.S. and Canadian mobility programs indicate that they are aimed at structural unemployment. While it is true that freedom from stringent administrative constraints is an important feature of the Canadian program (300, 318), the worker's movement is constrained in that the government must have designated areas which it considers as surplus areas and others where the demand for labour is greater than the supply. The use of the family as the appropriate unit of analysis is a good feature of the model, but secondary, social and psychic benefits are mostly excluded and there is no attempt to guage spill-over and multiplier effects. This kind of program faces a number of problems arising from the nonmonetary variables, problems which should perhaps be tackled by psychologists and sociologists. Jenness's analysis is in terms of a "before and after" rather than a "with and without" comparison. The latter technique, using a control group, is more accurate; problems in the use of control groups are not as serious as those arising from the alternative method which relies on averages, imputed averages, expected wages, and profitabilities computed from averages. The model uses a personality coefficient to help predict the degree of success or failure an individual wiil experience in the destination area, but the variables used and the results of the analysis do not appear to provide this information. The analysis did not utilize many mobility determinants: of the three considered — age, education, and marital status — only marital status was significant. The best use of the mobility coefficient would seem to be as a screening device for selecting candidates for assistance. Once we have identified those individuals who need the mobility program, we can calculate cost-benefit ratios to determine the effectiveness of the program. The use of "imputed" and "expected" averages, however, should make us wary of the results. In conclusion, lack of data is the principal limitation.

313. MINCER, JACOB. "On-The-Job Training: Costs, Returns, and Some Implications." *Journal of Political Economy,* Vol. 70, No. 5, Part 2 (October, 1962, Supplement), pp. 50-79.

Headings: Introduction; Estimates of costs of on-the-job training; Estimates of rates of return; On-the-job training as a factor in income and employment behaviour; Summary; Appendix tables.

Abstract: The paper views on-the-job training as a process of capital formation in people. The economic theory of investment in people is used to bring the process of on-the-job training under the measuring rod of money. Investment in on-the-job training amounts to more than half of the total expenditure on school education. According to the author's calculations, the rate of return on investment in on-the-job training is similar to that in formal training, but the rate of return on private costs appears to be lower. The "investment hypothesis" is used to analyse the causes of male/female and white/nonwhite wage differentials, and multiple regression analysis is used to relate stability of employment to education and training. The results indicate that human capital is a significant factor in explaining wage differentials and employment patterns.

314. ODIORNE, GEORGE S. "The Need for an Economic Approach to Training: A Case for Capital Budgeting for Investment in Human Capital." *Training Directors Journal,* Vol. 18, No. 3 (March, 1964), pp. 3-12.

Headings: Introduction; Is training an economic function?; The future demand for training is high; Investment in human capital as a base point; Capital budgeting for investment in human capital; Conclusions; References (12).

Abstract: The paper points out that little can be learned about the effectiveness of a training course from questioning the participants. Evaluation requires statistical analysis of the behaviour of an experimental group, which is trained, and a control group, which is not. The training director should identify the major segments of training costs and allocate them among the following economic categories: profit improvement, human working capital, and investment in human capital. This classification raises some problems in handling the long range human investment portion of the firm's budgets. The training director should be prepared to forecast long range human capital requirements and to identify sources of funds for this investment. If corporations were allowed tax allowances to cover depreciation of the vast investments they make in human capital, investment in human resources would accelerate and the amount of public money required for this purpose would be reduced. The training director should also handle the rationing of training expenses among various skills and the timing of training expenditures. If a training program cannot be classified in one of the economic categories, the training director should ask himself if it should be conducted at all. The paper concludes with seven guides for today's industrial educator.

315. OI, WALTER Y. "The Economic Cost of the Draft." *American Economic Review*, Papers and Proceedings, Vol. 57, No. 2 (May, 1967), pp. 39-62.

Headings: Introduction; Force strengths and military manpower requirements; The financial cost of the armed forces; The full economic cost of the draft.

Abstract: This paper attempts to compare the financial and economic costs of two hypothetical U.S. armies with the same active duty strength of 2.65 million men: one a purely voluntary force and the other a mixed force composed of conscripts, true and reluctant volunteers. The age and educational composition of a mixed force of the assumed strength for 1970-75 is projected. The cost and composition of an all volunteer force is estimated by assuming that the draft is abolished and that the entire pay profile is shifted upwards in order to maintain the same strength as the mixed force. The pay-roll costs of the mixed force in FY 1965 are estimated at just over $12 billion; the estimated pay-roll costs of the voluntary force in the same year are just over $16 billion. The opportunity cost of the armed forces to the economy is the value of civilian goods and services that could otherwise have been produced by them. The opportunity costs of the mixed and volunteer forces are estimated at $13 billion and over $14 billion respectively. A measure of the full economic cost of the draft would include equalizing income differentials in the opportunity cost of acquiring men for military service. The difference between the minimum supply price at which a draftee could be induced to become a true volunteer and current first term pay is an implicit tax. The annual tax on the reluctant service participants plus the loss of rents to true volunteers is estimated at $5.4 billion.

316. PAGE, DAVID A. "Retraining Under the Manpower Development Act: A Cost-Benefit Analysis." *Public Policy*, Vol. 9 (1964), pp. 257-267.

Headings: Introduction; Objectives of the Manpower Development Act; Costs and benefits of retraining; Conclusions.

Abstract: This analysis uses data from a statistical summary of a population of trainees in Massachusetts. The training program took place under Massachusetts law, but the experience can probably be extended to the Manpower Development and Training Act. The objective of the MDTA is primarily an "efficiency" objective — the training of underemployed and unemployed workers so that they can become more gainfully employed citizens, and make a greater contribution to the national economy. The author assesses costs and benefits in terms of this criterion. He uses a fairly high discount rate, and concludes that under the circumstances and assumptions of his study, retraining is worth while.

317. PARNES, HERBERT S. "Manpower Mobility Programs: Discussion." In *Cost-Benefit Analysis of Manpower Policies, Proceedings of a North American Conference, May 14-15, 1969,* edited by G. G. Somers and W. D. Wood, pp. 221-223. Published jointly by the Industrial Relations Centre, Queen's University, Kingston, Ontario, and the Center for Studies in Vocational and Technical Education, The University of Wisconsin, Madison, Wisconsin, 1969.

Abstract: The author expects that the model of the Canadian Mobility Program (300) will yield data which will be useful for evaluating several aspects of the program. In addition to its general usefulness, the model has some ingenious approaches to some of the problems encountered in measuring program benefits: for example, to avoid overstating benefits, the model calculates the probability that the worker would have moved irrespective of the program; the model also attempts to predict the length of time the migrant will stay in his first job in the new area and to estimate his earnings in subsequent jobs, although there is no attempt to take account of inter-industry differences in lay-off rates and quit rates. Despite the ingenuity of certain aspects of the model, the author has reservations about using the benefit-cost ratios it yields as a basis for evaluating the Canadian Mobility Program, reservations which stem from a basic limitation which he believes to be inherent in the benefit-cost approach — namely the impossibility of measuring accurately all of the benefits and costs. The model explicitly omits a host of secondary or indirect benefits and costs, and the estimates for some of the factors which are included are necessarily extremely crude. The author feels that the chief contribution of benefit-cost analysis to sound policy decisions lies in the comprehensive view of the issue that it engenders: it compels the researcher to consider systematically all the factors which are relevant to a decision. Since the nature of the problem precludes precise quantification of the benefit-cost ratio we should perhaps not strain so hard to produce one: the danger is not so much in wasting effort, but rather that the expenditure of so much effort will make us want to use the result.

318. POLIANSKI, ALEX. "Manpower Mobility Program — A Pilot Project in the Method of Evaluation of Government Programs." In *Proceedings of North American Conference on Labor Statistics, June 12-16, 1967,* Toronto, Ontario, pp. 175-194. Washington: Bureau of Labor Statistics, Department of Labor, 1968.

Headings: Introduction; The evaluation of the Manpower Mobility Program

— general remarks; The evaluation of the Manpower Mobility Program — specific descriptive studies; Cost/benefit analysis of the Manpower Mobility Program; The findings; Some evaluations of the findings; Appendix A: Appropriation Acts — Manpower Mobility Regulations, P.C. 1965-2215; Appendix B: Sample application form for loan or grant; Appendix C: Appropriation Acts — Manpower Mobility Regulations, P.C. 1967-584.

Abstract: The objectives and main features of the Canadian Manpower Mobility Program are outlined. Evaluation of this program along the established principles of existing labour supply and geographic mobility studies is descriptive and informal in nature. Cost-benefit analysis, on the other hand, is based quite rigorously on a formal model, and is an important part of the evaluation process of government programs. The cost-benefit ratios computed for the Mobility Program indicate the ratios which must be secured in other activities for those activities to be deemed preferable on grounds of technical efficiency to the Manpower Mobility Program, given that certain non-technical criteria are also met. It is necessary to carry out cost-benefit studies at three levels — for individuals, the government, and the economy as a whole. Benefits are conceived as gains in the family's income after a move; they have to be adjusted in various ways depending upon whether benefits to individuals, government, or the economy are being measured. They are also reduced, by means of a discount rate, to present values, and, for the government and the economy as a whole, adjusted by a multiplier. Benefit-cost ratios were computed on the basis of 792 applicants for assistance to move. Because of the multiplier effect and the use of different discount rates, the benefit/cost ratios are higher for the government and the economy than for individuals. We should, therefore, be careful not to extrapolate for policy decisions from individuals to aggregates. In all instances the ratios indicate that outlays can be expanded many times under the program before the benefit-cost ratios fall to the cut-off level of unity. Different benefit-cost ratios for different types of candidates for assistance, however, indicate changes in the allocation of the present budget which would increase technical efficiency. The author concludes by listing a number of drawbacks to the present analysis.

319.   REDER, MELVIN W. "Criteria for Judging the Effectiveness of Training Programs." Mimeographed. Stanford: Department of Economics, Stanford University, Unpublished. 21 p.

Headings: Evaluating training programs; Practical difficulties of valuing benefits; Costs of training; Training and alternatives: the quantitative problem; Costs and returns of retraining; Alternative viewpoints from which to appraise programs.

168

Abstract: The technical effectiveness of a training program can be judged by ascertaining the difference in ability to perform a specific task or tasks that can be attributed to participation in the training program. Economic effectiveness, with which this paper is mainly concerned, can be guaged by measuring the economic benefits, positive and negative, that arise from the program. In evaluating a training program, we can assume that the higher the rate of return the better the program. The benefits of a training program will be an increase in the trainee's hourly wage over a future time period, and a reduction in involuntary unemployment. When a training program produces workers able to fill previously unfilled vacancies, it confers a social benefit greater than that which is measured by the increase in the earnings of the trainees. The author feels that Somers and his co-workers (329, 335) have not given adequate attention to two questionable assumptions they make: that the number of jobs available to those outside the training program is not reduced by the enhanced job-getting ability of the trainees; and that the employment and earnings history of the trainees would, in the absence of the training program, have been the same as that of the unemployed in the same community who did not participate. The market values of resources used in training programs have to be adjusted to give figures for social costs. The author warns against training individuals who are severely handicapped in the labour market and who, as a result, will not be employed after training. In deciding whether a program's rate of return is high enough to justify undertaking it, the administrator should consider alternative methods of aiding the unemployed, for example, direct transfers, wage subsidies, investment subsidies, and resettlement allowances. The implications of subjecting training programs to requirements that there be certain allocations to particular geographical areas, age groups, and ethnic groups are discussed.

320. SEWELL, DAVID O. "A Critique of Cost-Benefit Analyses of Training." *Monthly Labor Review*, Vol. 90, No. 9 (September, 1967), pp. 45-51.

Headings: Introduction; Alternative Incomes; Classification of the "poor"; Other characteristics of participants; Selection in versus selection out; Allocation of training slots; Techniques used in past analyses; Before and after; The three parties to training; Who benefits from training?; Effects on output and employment; Vacuum effects; Nonmonetary benefits.

Abstract: This article comprises portions of a study entitled "Training the Poor: Rationale for a Benefit-Cost Evaluation of MITCE" (321). The author points out that it is incorrect to generalize from the results of cost-benefit analyses of MDTA retraining schemes to those training schemes directed towards the War on Poverty. He criticizes some of the techniques used in past analyses of retraining programs: employment may not be the most important aspect of the trainee's experience which we are interested in examining; and before and after comparisons of the records of trainees may be affected by variables such as cyclical conditions. Problems of social and non-monetary benefits are also discussed. The article provides a useful survey of recent work on the evaluation of training programs.

321. SEWELL, DAVID O. *Training the Poor: Rationale for a Benefit-Cost Evaluation of MITCE.* Durham: The North Carolina Fund, 1967. 43 p.

Headings: Introduction; The alternative incomes of participants in past training projects; The MITCE project; The application of benefit-cost techniques in evaluation of training programs; Footnotes and references.

Abstract: The Manpower Improvement Through Community Effort (MITCE) project is the first large-scale project in the U.S. designed to deal exclusively with the needs of the rural poor. This paper outlines the techniques to be used in a benefit-cost analysis of MITCE in the light of past analyses of training programs. The following issues are examined: transfer payments and distribution; discount rates; control groups; conditions in the labour market in which training takes place; and the use of income as the main indicator of the gains to training. The benefit-cost methodology, which provides a comparison of costs of alternative methods of reducing poverty, is an integral part of the PPB System currently being extended to all branches of the Federal Government. It is suggested that the benefit-cost approach is likely to yield results which are favourable to MITCE.

322. SEWELL, DAVID O. "Occupational Training Programs and Manpower Programs for the Disadvantaged: Discussion." In *Cost-Benefit Analysis of Manpower Policies, Proceedings of a North American Conference, May 14-15, 1969,* edited by G. G. Somers and W. D. Wood, pp. 160-169. Published jointly by the Industrial Relations Centre, Queen's University, Kingston, Ontario, and the Center for Studies in Vocational and Technical Education, The University of Wisconsin, Madison, Wisconsin, 1969.

Abstract: The author proposes to apply some of the principles outlined in the paper by Cain and Hollister (258) to the material covered by Hardin (295). This material includes most of the benefit-cost analyses of training programs sponsored by the U.S. Department of Labor under the MDTA, ARA, and earlier schemes. The trainees in these programs represented "the cream" of the individuals available for training. Since the present MDTA programs are geared more towards the "disadvantaged" than earlier, the studies surveyed by Hardin have little relevance. Only one of the studies cited by Hardin does not rely for its results on comparisons between trainees and nonapplicants. Since there are significant differences between trainee and nonapplicant groups it can be argued that the computed benefits from training include the returns

170

to ability and intelligence. Turning to the question of whether training programs raise aggregate output by more than the cost of training, the author asks whether trainees fill skill-shortage jobs thus creating complementary demands for labour (vacuum effect), or whether they simply receive jobs which could have been performed by unskilled workers (displacement effect). A determination of vacuum and displacement effects requires a closer analysis of the effects of training on the two principal components of earnings — the wage rate per hour, and the number of hours worked. We should pay particular attention to the wage effects of training for a number of reasons: hourly earnings are superior to annual earnings since annual earnings reflect unwanted unemployment before training and extra leisure after training; secondly, an increase in the hourly wage rate after training indicates that the worker has moved to a higher productivity job and is not simply displacing less skilled workers; thirdly, the employment effects may have been caused partly by the job placement activities of the authorities — activities which were not duplicated on behalf of the nonapplicant control group. All the studies examined by Hardin have important employment effects, but none of them can be demonstrated unambiguously to have had wage effects. If the benefits of training resulted exclusively from employment effects, it would appear that the trainees did not move into jobs with a higher skill level and that there were no vacuum effects. In addition, it is possible that the employment effects were simply displacement effects and represented no real gains to society. Even if the employment effects were not displacement effects, training appears to have been nothing more than a substitute for a policy of increasing employment by increasing aggregate demand. The prolonged increase in aggregate demand since the observation periods of these analyses may have nullified most of the employment effects by making it easier for nontrainees to get jobs.

323. SEWELL, DAVID O. *Training the Poor: A Benefit-Cost Analysis of Manpower Programs in the U.S. Antipoverty Program.* Research Series, No. 12. Kingston, Ontario: Industrial Relations Centre, Queen's University, 1970.

Headings: Introduction; The applicability of results in past benefit-cost analyses of MDTA-type training projects to training projects in the antipoverty program; The MITCE projects, and the aims of our benefit-cost analysis; The theory of benefit-cost analyses of training programs; The benefits from training; The MITCE project as judged by allocative and distributional investment criteria; Conclusions.

Abstract: This study is a "cost-effectiveness" analysis of training projects in the U.S. antipoverty program. Results from past benefit-cost analyses have often been cited as indicating that such training projects both increase the incomes of the poor and add more to national output than they cost. The present study concludes that these inferences from past analyses are unwarranted. In the first place, it is contended that the training programs analyzed in past benefit-cost studies did not deal with a population of concern to the

171

COST-BENEFIT ANALYSIS

antipoverty program. Secondly, it is argued that insufficiently stringent criteria were employed in past analyses to determine the real benefits and costs of training projects. Applying the more demanding standards adopted for use in our study, it appears that the increases in trainee incomes noted in past analyses were largely achieved at the expense of decreases in the incomes of other members of the labour force, and that the training programs studied may not have raised real output at all. These conclusions constitute the background to analysis of a training project which was felt to deal with a population of central concern to the antipoverty program. This training project was conducted in rural areas of the South, and the average earning levels of the project's predominantly nonwhite clientele fell below the poverty levels adopted by the U.S. Social Security Administration. A sample survey was used to obtain data on the characteristics and earning levels of both trainees and nontrainees who were eligible for training. Multivariate analysis was then employed to determine the increases in average earning levels associated with the training of the project's clients. These estimates of training-related increases in earnings were then compared with the costs of training. The principal findings of the empirical analysis were that the training project, taken as a whole, was associated with significant increases in the average earnings levels of trainees and increased national output by more than it cost. However, some types of training were found which did not appear to be associated with increases in the earnings levels of trainees, and which represented an inefficient use of resources. It was also concluded that in this project at least, the rate of return to society was greater from on-the-job training than from training taking place in a institutional setting. Finally, it was concluded that the results achieved in this training project could be duplicated in other training programs dealing with similar client populations. However, it is pointed out that such training programs for the poor will involve more resources than is commonly supposed.

324. SJAASTAD, LARRY A. "The Costs and Returns of Human Migration." *Journal of Political Economy,* Vol. 70, No. 5, Part 2 (October, 1962, Supplement), pp. 80-93.

Headings: Introduction; Migration too much or too little?; Differences in earnings; The private costs of migration; The private returns to migration; Private versus social costs and returns; Concluding comments.

Abstract: Since migration is an activity which promotes efficient resource allocation and which requires resources, it can be placed in a resource allocation framework. The rate of return on resources allocated to migration provides a criterion to test the effectiveness of migration in reducing spatial earnings differentials. The author prefers the concept of gross rather than net migration for studying the pecuniary and nonpecuniary costs and returns of migration. It is suggested that migration is often accompanied by additional human investment associated with occupational upgrading. If the bulk of this investment must be financed by the individual, this might explain the observed immobility in the face of differentials in current earnings. The social returns

172

to migration tend to exceed the private returns, although, in individual cases, this depends upon the age of the individual and the relevant market structures and government revenue policies.

325. SMITH A. D. "Active Manpower and Redundancy Policies: Their Costs and Benefits." *International Labour Review*, Vol. 95, Nos. 1-2 (January-February, 1967), pp. 49-60.

Headings: Introduction; The inter-relationship and growing importance of active manpower and redundancy policies; The costs and benefits of an active manpower policy; Sharing the costs; Summary.

Abstract: A wide variety of economic and technical forces lead to changes in the structure of jobs in the economy in terms of their geographical, industrial, and occupational distribution. Economic theory holds that the resulting changes in wage differentials will encourage the required labour mobility. Various barriers to labour mobility, however, tend to make the adjustment of the labour force incomplete. This has undesirable economic and social implications. Measures which seek to promote a redeployment of the labour force in terms of occupations, industries, and areas in order to derive economic benefits for society may be termed collectively an active manpower policy. Measures which seek to mitigate the social hardships of structural adjustment may be referred to as redundancy practices. The principles on which the costs and benefits of active manpower and redundancy policies should be assessed and distributed merit consideration. An active manpower policy measure is justified when the "real" benefit is greater than the "real" costs involved. This type of analysis places no limitation upon the financial inducements which might be provided by the policy in order to ensure its success because financial incentives are transfers, not real costs. In addition the active manpower policy will leave residual social problems. These must be tackled by redundancy practices which seek to compensate workers out of the gains which society makes from structural adjustments. The benefits from structural adjustments tend to be spread fairly evenly through society, but employers and workers have been obliged to bear the costs of redundancy practices. Consequently contradictions between redundancy practices, instituted by employers and workers with their own immediate needs in mind, and active manpower policies, promoted by the authorities may exist: the result is impaired effectiveness of active manpower policies. The solution may lie in making adjustments to private policies in return for the assumption of part of their cost by the public sector. As well as taking account of the allocation of benefits, however, the distribution of the costs of active manpower policies must take account of the repercussions on incentives and disincentives.

326. SMITH, RALPH E. "Apportionment of Funds Under the Manpower Development and Training Act of 1962." *Journal of Human Resources*, Vol. 3, No. 4 (Fall, 1968), pp. 499-514.

Headings: Abstract; Introduction; Relevant provisions of the Act; Evaluation of apportionment method; Alternative methods of apportionment.

Abstract: What method of apportioning MDTA funds among states would best fulfil the purposes for which these funds are to be distributed? The present method of computing the apportionment factor for a given State considers only the following factors: the percentage of the U.S. labour force in the State; the percentage of the U.S. unemployed in the State; the lack of appropriate full-time employment in the State; the proportion of insured unemployed to insured employed within the State; and the average weekly unemployment compensation benefits paid by the State. The author demonstrates that this formula is in need of revision. The ideal criterion is one which maximizes the probability that each member of the population group which the MDTA program is designed to assist will have an equal opportunity to receive a given amount of training regardless of his state of residence. The immediate problem is the definition of the target population — those who are structurally unemployed or underemployed. The author suggests that a close approximation to the target population is the unemployed plus low income farm families. The apportionment of funds should be governed by the percentage of the unemployed plus low income farm families in the U.S. residing within the State. The change in the apportionment of funds this formula would entail is examined.

327.   SOLIE, RICHARD J. "Employment Effects of Retraining the Unemployed." *Industrial and Labor Relations Review,* Vol. 21, No. 2 (January, 1968), pp. 210-225.

Headings: Introduction; Placement in training-related jobs; Effects of retraining on labour market status; The effects of retraining on employment over periods of time; Sources of retraining program benefits; The permanence of the benefits from retraining; Conclusions.

Abstract: The empirical findings of this article derive from a study of an Area Redevelopment Act training program in Tennessee. A rough measure of the benefit from retraining can be obtained by comparing the labour force status of those who completed the program with that of three control groups: a group of workers who did not complete the program, a group of workers who applied for the program but were rejected, and a group of nonapplicants. Multiple regression techniques are used to control for differences in socio-demographic characteristics between the completes and the control groups. The entire net employment advantage of the completes may not be derived from the vocational training *per se* since the completes received special placement assistance, some employers regarded training as a screening device, and some of the trainees regained their self-confidence as a result of the program. There is evidence both in this study and in the West Virginian study of Somers and Stromsdorfer (335), that the benefits of training are rather short-lived: the contribution of retraining may consist principally of facilitating a rapid return to gainful employment for unemployed workers.

174

328. SOMERS, GERALD. *Retraining the Unemployed: A Preliminary Survey.* Reprint Series, No. 44. Madison: Industrial Relations Research Center, The University of Wisconsin, 1963. 11 p.

Headings: Introduction; Field surveys in West Virginia; Objectives of retraining; Immediate employment effects of retraining; Attitude of non-trainees; Age as a selective factor; Retraining and relocation; Trainee views on retraining; Employer experience with retrainees; On-the-job and training for specific employers; Human investment in long-run economic growth.

Abstract: The preliminary findings reported in this survey are based primarily on field surveys in West Virginia. Intensive study has been devoted to retraining in West Virginia because of the prevalence of areas of chronic labour surplus in the State. The three major objectives of retraining are a short-run increase in employment, long-run economic growth, and improvement in the welfare and general well-being of the trainees and society. Most of those who have supported recent retraining measures have been more concerned with the current problems of unemployment than with long-run growth and well-being. To date, government-subsidized retraining has achieved only minor reductions in unemployment. Under present selection standards the placement ratio of ARA trainees is 65 per cent and of MDTA trainees, 70 per cent. A crucial issue is whether sufficient job vacancies exist to justify a lowering of standards so as to include more of the hard-core unemployed: such a lowering of standards would probably lead to an even lower placement ratio. Relocation will frequently be necessary if the retraining investment is to bear fruit in job placement: the major role of relocation allowances could be not to induce more outmigration but rather a more rational outmigration. Employers' suggestions for improving the retraining program were longer courses, more effective standards for screening and selecting trainees, and greater efforts to place trainees in the specific jobs for which they were trained. On-the-job training is likely to give a higher placement ratio, but we must ensure that training is extended to unemployed workers and not only to the upgrading of existing employees. The broadening of selection standards is essential if retraining is to make its maximum contribution to the attainment of full employment and long-run economic growth.

329. SOMERS, GERALD G. "Retraining: An Evaluation of Gains and Costs." In *Employment Policy and the Labor Market,* edited by Arthur M. Ross, pp. 271-298. Berkeley: University of California Press, 1965.

Headings: Introduction; Criteria for evaluation of the gains of retraining; Costs and returns; A concluding balance sheet; Appendix: Methodology of the Ford Foundation project to evaluate retraining of unemployed workers.

Abstract: The author points out that an evaluation of retraining is timely because of growing academic interest in investment in human resources and increasing government emphasis on training programs for the unemployed. Retraining may provide gains in productivity, employment, earnings, and social gains. Gains in productivity can be approximated by the impact of retraining on the trainee's employment and earnings. Employment after retraining may be intermittent, and earnings data help to give a more complete picture of the gains from retraining, as well as giving an indication of the quality of the jobs obtained. Some gains to society from retraining programs are a reduction in social payments and an increase in income tax, and possibly an increase in employment. The exact governmental costs of retraining programs for the unemployed are not readily determined, and it is even more difficult to arrive at the opportunity cost involved in forgone wage income during training. Under certain assumptions, however, it can be demonstrated that the economic gains of the trainees, and perhaps of society, derived from retraining outweigh the economic costs. Social-psychological benefits increase the attractiveness of investment in retraining.

330.   SOMERS, GERALD G. "Our Experience with Retraining and Relocation." In *Toward a Manpower Policy,* edited by R. A. Gordon, pp. 215-248. New York: John Wiley and Sons, 1967.

Headings: Introduction; Evaluation of retraining programs; Retraining the disadvantaged; On-the-job training; Retraining and relocation; Conclusions; Discussion by Melvin Rothbaum and Curtis Aller.

Abstract: In order to establish an appropriate relationship between the various U.S. manpower policies, the author suggests that a detailed research evaluation of each is required. The goals of Federal retraining are as follows: for the trainee, reduction of unemployment and underemployment, and increased income through higher skill and productivity; and for society, reduction of transfer payments, reduction of poverty and related social ills, and expansion of output. The paper advocates careful cost-benefit analyses of programs aimed at retraining the disadvantaged, of on-the-job and institutional training programs, and of retraining and relocation programs. The few detailed evaluations made of these programs indicate that they do have a high rate of return. It is hoped that economic analysis will be able to determine how far each program should be expanded, and what is the appropriate program mix to meet specific goals.

331.   SOMERS, GERALD G. "Retraining the Unemployed Older Worker." In *Technology, Manpower and Retirement Policy,* edited by Juanita Kreps, pp. 109-125. Cleveland: World Publishing Company, 1966.

Headings: Introduction; The need for retraining programs; The experience with retraining; Selection and recruitment of trainees; Employment and income; Summary and conclusions; Appendix — Methodology of the Ford Foundation project to evaluate retraining of unemployed workers.

Abstract: It is well established that older unemployed workers remain unemployed for longer periods of time than younger members of the unemployed labour force. The relative lack of education and training among older workers contributes significantly to their unemployment problems. In view of the older worker's limited remaining years in the labour force, private employers are likely to reject the costs of their retraining as an unwise investment. Government subsidized retraining may, therefore, be necessary to alleviate prolonged unemployment among older workers. In spite of this need, the current retraining revolution has largely passed by older workers, primarily because of the patterns of employer discrimination that make older workers difficult to place in employment. Fewer unemployed older workers are found in retraining programs not only because their rate of rejection is higher, but because fewer apply. The reluctance of many unemployed older workers to apply for retraining is rooted in their knowledge of the realities of the labour market. National data on MDTA trainees and data from the Ford Foundation Retraining Project in West Virginia indicate that age, education, and training status each have some independent influence on employment rates; and each of these variables has the power to offset some of the disadvantages in the other variables. Regression analysis indicated that retraining is a more significant predictor of future employment success than either of the variables age and education. Improvement in the employment position of an older worker does not necessarily mean that his income position has improved or that the benefits of retraining exceed the costs. Although the West Virginia data were insufficient for a separate cost-benefit analysis of retraining for older workers, earnings and social payments data suggest that it is a sound social investment.

332. SOMERS, GERALD G. *Evaluation of Work Experience and Training of Older Workers.* Madison: Industrial Relations Research Institute, University of Wisconsin, 1967. 77 p.

Headings: Introduction; The training of welfare recipients; Retraining the unemployed older worker; General conceptual and methodological problems; Study groups, control groups, costs and benefits; Available data and data needs; Appendix: Methodology of the Ford Foundation project to evaluate retraining of unemployed workers.

Abstract: This report seeks to provide the methodological underpinnings of a model which could be used to carry out a full-scale cost-benefit evaluation of training programs for older workers under the Work Experience and Training Program (WE and T). The author mentions some analytical needs of studies seeking to evaluate training programs for welfare recipients. Similar studies covering programs dealing with older workers have additional analytical needs. The cost-benefit analysis of retraining programs for older workers involves peculiar conceptual problems. The solution to some of these problems can be found in the selection of appropriate study and control groups. The costs and benefits of training schemes under the WE and T program are enumerated and various measures of effectiveness are discussed. The conclusion is that the most urgent need in the construction of a benefit-cost model of

177

older worker participation in the WE and T program is an improvement in the data base required for cost and benefit calculation.

333. SOMERS, GERALD G. *The Training and Placement of Older Workers: An Evaluation of Four Community Projects.* Madison: Center for Studies in Technical and Vocational Education, The University of Wisconsin, September, 1967. 210 p.

Headings: Introduction; The older worker project in Baltimore, Garth Mangum; The NCOA older worker project in Boston, David P. Taylor; The older worker project in Buncombe County, North Carolina, Juanita Kreps; The older worker project in Milwaukee, Richard Perlman; Summary and conclusions, Gerald Somers and Graeme McKechnie.

Abstract: This report evaluates four National Council on the Ageing projects designed to test and demonstrate techniques for obtaining employment for hard-core unemployed workers over 50 years of age. The major value of these demonstration projects lies not in their direct economic benefits (which were limited) but in the recommendations derived from these initial experiences for improved projects in the future. A summary of the recommendations contained in the individual reports is as follows: plans and goals should be clearly defined and should be based on careful analysis of the older worker population needs as well as on the labour market demand; the cooperation of the Employment Service, vocational educators, community agencies, and employers should be secured before the project is initiated; the NCOA should play a more active role in providing expertise in older workers' problems to the community agencies charged with local project administration; training programs require prior basic education in some cases, and larger stipends to both trainees and OJT employers to provide motivation and incentive; finally, a multi-service package including testing, counselling, basic education, training, job development, and placement should be provided.

334. SOMERS, GERALD G., and GRAEME H. McKECHNIE, "Vocational Retraining Programs for the Unemployed." In *The Development and Use of Manpower, Proceedings of the Twentieth Annual Winter Meeting,* Washington, D.C., December 28-29, 1967, pp. 25-35. Madison: Industrial Relations Research Association, 1967.

Headings: Introduction; Are we reaching the disadvantaged unemployed?; Are we helping the unemployed?; Some questions and partial answers; References (18).

Abstract: The authors begin by advocating a more vigorous evaluation of the costs and benefits of retraining programs. An evaluation of MDTA should include an appraisal of the changing characteristics of its enrollees; it is suggested that many of the disadvantaged unemployed are bypassed. Follow-up studies constitute another form of evaluation, and the authors survey some of the empirical work in this area. These studies, which vary widely in degree of sophistication, tend to be constrained by a relatively short time-period of follow-up. There is some indication that the advantages gained by retraining may begin to wash out after years of general employment expansion.

335. SOMERS, GERALD G., and ERNST W. STROMSDORFER. "A Benefit-Cost Analysis of Manpower Retraining." In *Proceedings of the Seventeenth Annual Meeting,* Chicago, Illinois, December 28-29, 1964, pp. 172-185. Madison: Industrial Relations Research Association, 1965.

Headings: Introduction; The benefits of retraining; Costs and returns; Conclusions.

Abstract: The authors base their study on sample groups of trainees and non-trainees in West Virginia. Although the trainees had taken courses set up under West Virginia State legislation, the results of this study can probably be generalized for the Manpower Development and Training Act (MDTA) program. The paper discusses the problems associated with using control groups to estimate opportunity costs incurred during training, and gains in income attributable to retraining. The conclusion is that the retraining investment yields high rates of return for the trainee and for society. Retraining, however, is regarded only as a partial answer to the problem of unemployment.

336. SOMERS, GERALD G., and BURTON A. WEISBROD. *The Development of Human Resources,* Reprint Series, No. 97. Madison: Industrial Relations Research Institute, The University of Wisconsin, 11 p.

Headings: Expenditures on human resources: investment, income redistribution, or what?; Evaluation of manpower policies.

Abstract: If certain public expenditures are to be justified on the grounds that they represent profitable investments, should such expenditures be made when they are not profitable? Economic efficiency is only one of the goals which government decision-makers should seek. The government should consider the effects of its actions on the distribution of economic output and on the manner in which the distribution (or redistribution) is brought about. We should not expect that investments will be "efficient" when they are aimed at the disadvantaged-people with whom the private market has chosen not to act. Justification for such investments will often depend on concerns about income — distributional or other social welfare objectives. We should not, on the other hand, disregard economic efficiency. Evaluation of a training program requires at least the following: establishment of the goals of the program; and, in attributing benefits to the program, evidence that these benefits would not have been achieved in the absence of the program or more efficiently in some alternative way. The most important unanswered questions with regard to retraining and relocation policies in the United States are: firstly, is on-the-job training more efficient than institutional training; secondly, can counselling, job development, and placement services achieve the basic objectives of manpower programs more cheaply than vocational training programs; thirdly, what is the appropriate mix in a depressed rural area between retraining programs, relocation subsidies, and area industrial development? Finally, how does the passage of time and the general improvement in the economic climate affect the value of retraining and relocation policies to the worker and to society as a whole.

337.   STIGLER, GEORGE J. "Information in the Labor Market." *Journal of Political Economy,* Vol. 70, No. 5, Part 2 (October, 1962, Supplement), pp. 94-105.

Headings: Introduction; The dispersion of wage rates; The problem of information; The employer's search; Information as capital; Appendix.

Abstract: The paper examines the costs and returns from a search for wage offers by various types of workers, given the observed wide dispersion of wage rates for homogeneous labour. Labour market information possessed by an individual or firm is capital produced at the cost of search. The capital value of this knowledge can be calculated by the usual method of valuing an asset. From the social viewpoint the return from investment in information consists of a more efficient allocation of the labour force.

338.   STROMSDORFER, ERNST W. "Economic Concepts and Criteria for Investment in Vocational Education." A paper prepared for the Conference on Vocational-Technical Education, The Stanford Research Institute, April, 1967. Mimeographed. 30 p.

Headings: Introduction; The relevance of cost-benefit analysis; Basic problems of cost-benefit analysis; Vocational education as a subsidy; Skill shortage; Location incentive; Costs; Investment decision rules and the choice of discount rates; Present value versus internal rate of return; Constraints which invalidate the rate of return criterion; Constraints which invalidate the present value criterion; Conclusion.

Abstract: The paper surveys the concepts of benefits and costs in the evaluation of vocational education programs. Benefits are listed under four headings: economic efficiency; equity; socialization; and consumption. Various problems encountered in measuring benefits are discussed: for example, the problems of control groups, externalities and noneconomic benefits, transfer payments, and unemployment. All costs should be viewed as opportunity costs. There are four main cost categories: current, capital, cost-correction factors, and forgone earnings. The last part of the paper is devoted to investment decision rules. The discount rate should reflect the social opportunity cost of capital: the author lists a variety of rates which have been used in cost-benefit analysis. He outlines the difficulties associated with the present value and internal rate of return decision rules, and lists, for each, the circumstances in which it may be invalidated.

339.   STROMSDORFER, ERNST W. "A Developmental Program for an Economic Evaluation of Vocational Education in Pennsylvania." Mimeographed. University Park: Institute for Research on Human Resources, Pennsylvania State University. xiv + 110 p.

Headings: Preface; A comparative analysis of the goals for vocational education; Current cost-benefit analysis of education and vocational education in the United States, (References (32)); Measuring the costs and benefits of vocational education; Theoretical aspects of cost-benefit analysis: suggested methodologies; Proposals for research in education and public policy for the state of Pennsylvania; Conclusion.

Abstract: Since one of the major characteristics of expenditure on education is that of current investment to gain increased future benefits, and since one of the major goals of education is that of economic efficiency, it is reasonable to use cost-benefit analysis to provide some guidance to decisions of resource allocation in education. The author surveys recent studies of investment in education in general, and examines those works which have dealt with vocational education. He concludes that little of immediate usefulness from a cost-benefit standpoint has been done in the field of vocational education. Several conceptual problems encountered by the cost-benefit analyst in the estimation of benefit and cost data are considered: benefits appear to be conceptually more difficult to measure than costs because of complementarity among the benefits and because of spill-over effects which, in the present state of the art, remain unmeasurable. Once estimates have been obtained for benefits and costs, the proper decision rule is to estimate net discounted benefits and to invest in those projects where this net sum (i.e., net of costs) is zero or positive. One very practical value of cost-benefit analysis is that it uncovers unsuspected problems, implicit assumptions, and preconceptions which would otherwise remain hidden. In conclusion, the author lists thirteen proposals which might serve as the basis for further research into the basic needs of decision-makers in the area of educational and social policy. The three most important proposals, the author feels, are: that the overall institutional effectiveness of vocational education in Pennsylvania should be appraised; that manpower and labour market projections be undertaken to aid the administrator; and that the locational aspects of the vocational schools and community colleges be analyzed.

340.   STROMSDORFER, ERNST W. "Determinants of Economic Success in Retraining the Unemployed: The West Virginia Experience." *Journal of Human Resources,* Vol. 3, No. 2 (Spring, 1968), pp. 139-158.

Headings: Introduction; Description of the variables; Analysis of results; Investment benefits of retraining; Summary and conclusions.

Abstract: This study concerns itself with the labour market experience of some of the first West Virginia workers retrained under the Federal Area Redevelopment Act and West Virginia's own Area Vocational Education Program. Five different types of workers were interviewed: trainees; dropouts; "did not reports" — those who were accepted for a training course but never attended; rejects; and nontrainees. The dependent variables that the models in the study attempt to explain are the percentage of time employed in the 18 month period following the end of retraining, and total before-tax earnings (exclusive of fringe benefits) in the same period. Thirteen independent variables which appear to be conceptually relevant are included: training status; labour market area; prior labour force experience; retraining skill; regular occupation prior to retraining; age; education; sex; marital status; race; course sponsor; geographic mobility after retraining; and the extent to which the trainee tended to have a guaranteed job opportunity at training's end. Prior labour force experience ranks first and second in relative impact on employment and earnings respectively, while training status ranks second in relative impact on employment and third in impact on earnings. When the dropout, reject, and "did not report" categories are dropped from the regression analysis, the net effect of retraining continues to be significant. Three types of measures are used to evaluate the retraining investment: the pay-back period, the internal rate of return, and net present value estimations. Net earnings benefits are estimated from trainee/nontrainee comparisons. Costs include direct training costs, the opportunity costs of wages forgone by trainees, and the differences in transfers paid to trainees relative to nontrainees during retraining (although this is not a social cost). The investment measures indicate that retraining was a worthwhile investment: the pay-back period was approximately 13 months for men and 18 months for women; the internal rate of return is estimated at 90 per cent for men and 64 per cent for women; and discounted at 6 per cent, the aggregate net benefits were over 3 million dollars.

341. STROMSDORFER, ERNST W. "Occupational Training Programs and Manpower Programs for the Disadvantaged: Discussion." In *Cost-Benefit Analysis of Manpower Policies, Proceedings of a North American Conference, May 14-15, 1969,* edited by G. G. Somers and W. D. Wood, pp. 152-159. Published jointly by the Industrial Relations Centre, Queen's University, Kingston, Ontario, and the Center for Studies in Vocational and Technical Education, The University of Wisconsin, Madison, Wisconsin, 1969.

Headings: Capital costs; Problems of valuation; The capital recovery factor; The joint cost problem; Costs and benefits to government units; Negative cost-benefit ratios; The multiplier effect; Vacuum and displacement effects.

Abstract: The author expands upon two main problem areas: the treatment of capital costs and of joint costs. It is difficult to value capital stock in market terms if it existed before the inception of the manpower program now making use of it. There are four possible solutions to this problem: firstly, assume that once the capital stock exists it has no alternative use and hence no social opportunity cost; secondly, use historical cost; thirdly, use replacement cost; and lastly, use an estimate of current assessed valuation. None of these solutions is precisely correct and it is not obvious which price should be attached to capital inputs. The problem of joint costs occurs within two contexts: firstly, at a given point in time when a specific facility is used to produce two or more distinct outputs, and, secondly, when a specific facility is consumed by successive cohorts of subjects. The latter context is familiar in the field of manpower programs where the capital used usually has an economic life longer than the treatment given to each group of trainees. Two solutions are suggested to the problem of joint costs: one is to use imputed rent as a measure of opportunity cost — this involves identifying in the market place capital resources which are substitutes for the resources employed; an alternative is to use a "capital recovery factor" which gives the annual rent needed to recoup the principal and social opportunity cost. The author uses illustrations to demonstrate the arguments for and against proration and points out that the technique for prorating may not be practicable since it is difficult to estimate demand curves for goods and services. In any case, the error which could result from the use of an inappropriate measurement technique may not be large since physical capital cost of manpower programs is usually low relative to other opportunity costs. The author argues against estimating costs and benefits to governmental or other political or social units, since manpower analysis should focus on social and private costs and benefits. He finds it difficult to rationalize Hardin's report of negative benefit-cost ratios for some MDTA programs. This implies that the program actually reduced the subjects' marginal productivity. It is possible that failure to learn a skill could seriously reduce a subject's morale, and that his past skills could deteriorate during the training situation as a result of foregoing on-the-job experience. We might equally well describe this kind of deterioration as a positive cost rather than a negative benefit: if all other benefits were zero, this procedure would yield a zero benefit-cost ratio rather than a negative one. Another possible explanation for the negative benefit-cost ratio is that the control group is inappropriate: in other words the utility weights the trainee attaches to his wage rate are different from those implicitly or explicitly assumed by the analysts. There are two final points to be made. Since the multiplier effect is not unique to manpower programs, only an *increment to* the multiplier impact can be ascribed to the manpower investment. Lastly, the author does not accept Borus's argument that there are no opportunity costs during training or that the entire wage bill after training can be treated as benefits: this implies that the trainee's marginal product is zero. Since members of the control group were employed during the training period there were forgone earnings, and there was not a zero probability of employment without the training.

342. TAUSSIG, MICHAEL K. "An Economic Analysis of Vocational Education in the New York City High Schools." *Journal of Human Resources,* Vol. 3, Supplement (1968), pp. 59-87.

Headings: Abstract; Introduction; Vocational schools and the problems of the school system; Costs and benefits of vocational education; Earnings and employment experience of vocational school graduates; Costs; Other aspects of high school vocational education; Summary and conclusions.

Abstract: The paper gives a brief historical and factual background of the New York City vocational high school system, and follows with an outline of a cost-benefit framework for evaluating the training given in the vocational schools. The benefits we might expect from vocational training are higher earnings, redistribution of income, reduced unemployment, external benefits, and consumption benefits. The available data on the immediate employment experience of vocational school graduates are unreliable. In addition, comparisons of employment rates of graduates of different types of schools implicitly assume that the graduates from one set of schools constitute an appropriate control group for the graduates from another set, an assumption which is patently incorrect. If we hold the structuralist view of unemployment, vocational training can be credited with being the cause of lower unemployment rates; but if we hold the deficient demand view then the net social return from vocational training would arise only from the screening services provided to employers. This issue can be resolved by asking whether there are systematic differentials in wage rates between trainees and nontrainees. The evidence indicates that the skills of vocational school graduates do not command a significant premium in the labour market. The author therefore concludes that the market benefits from high school vocational training have been disappointing. An appropriate measure of the costs of vocational high schools is the difference between the actual costs and an estimate of costs under the most realistic alternative — an expanded system of academic high schools. The difference between per capita costs in academic and vocational schools is multiplied by the average daily attendance at vocational schools to give an approximate figure for the total cost of vocational schools. The conclusion is that measurable returns have been meagre relative to the considerable social investment. Our inability to assess the extent of external benefits and consumption aspects precludes sole reliance on measurable money costs and benefits. Nevertheless the problems of the existing system appear to be of a fundamental nature.

343. THOMAS, BRINLEY, JOHN MOXHAM, and J. A. G. JONES. "A Cost-Benefit Analysis of Industrial Training." *British Journal of Industrial Relations,* Vol. 7, No. 2 (July, 1969), pp. 231-264.

Headings: Analytical framework; Classification of costs; Classification of benefits; A cost-benefit analysis of operative training; Summary of findings.

Abstract: This study examines the costs and benefits to an individual firm arising out of a given once-and-for-all investment in training. Training comprises both specific programs of instruction and "learning by doing". The following costs should be considered: the cost of initiating the training function; the cost of servicing and co-ordinating the training function; the cost of fixed training capital; the cost of working training capital; the cost of providing instruction (a fixed cost); the cost of giving instruction (a variable cost); and the cost of wages of trainees, net of trainee output value. Just as "costs" are the incremental costs of the new system of training being analysed, "benefits" are measured by the increased output (arising from higher performance levels, shorter training periods, and longer retention time) net of any increase in the wages paid. The data used for the analysis were drawn from a Yorkshire firm which initiated a new training scheme in 1965 but resumed its previous training methods in 1967. Of the net benefit due to the training innovation, 25 per cent was accounted for by higher output performance and 75 per cent by a decrease in labour turnover. The training given was "general" rather than "specific" but, contrary to the Becker-Mincer model (4, 313) the trainees did not bear the cost but shared the benefit from higher performance with the firm. The firm's policy in promoting the attachment of the trainees to the firm can be interpreted as introducing a high degree of specificity into the training.

344.   U.S. DEPARTMENT OF LABOR. *Cost-Effectiveness Analysis of On-The-Job and Institutional Training Courses.* Prepared for the U. S. Department of Labor, Manpower Administration, Office of Manpower Policy, Evaluation, and Research by the Planning Research Corporation, Los Angeles, California, and Washington, D.C., 1967. iv + 46 p.

Headings: Introduction; The sample; Costs; Benefits; Findings; Future research; Appendices.

Abstract: This study is an application of the cost-effectiveness techniques outlined in the Planning Research Corporation's *Program Analysis Manual to Support a Planning-Programming-Budgeting System* (64) to the examination of the relative effectiveness of institutional and on-the-job training programs. The data used in the study were derived from reports on the progress of trainees under the MDTA program. It is suggested that institutional courses have the higher average net benefit-cost ratios both per completor and per trainee. It is probable, however, that OJT courses have an appeal to sponsors which is not reflected in these figures. Future research should attempt to accumulate more data and should employ more sophisticated statistical techniques.

345.   U.S. DEPARTMENT OF LABOR. *Illustrative Cost-Goal Analysis in the U.S. Employment Service Area.* Prepared for the U.S. Department of Labor, Manpower Administration, Office of Manpower Policy, Evaluation and Research by the Planning Research Corporation, Los Angeles, California, and Washington, D.C., 1967. iv + 41 p.

Headings: Introduction; Summary; Background; A feasible evaluation design;

Study results; Future research; Appendices.

Abstract: This study illustrates the use of cost-goal analysis (as described in the Planning Research Corporation's *Program Analysis Manual to Support a Planning-Programming-Budgeting System* (64) to identify the cost-effectiveness curve associated with the operations of the U.S. Employment Service. The curve indicates the sensitivity of cost to changes in the program's desired level of effectiveness, and is important in establishing program levels. A detailed analysis of the functions of the U.S. Employment Service is provided, and the statistical procedures used in the analysis are described. The conclusion, given the limitations of the study, appears to be favourable to the extension of U.S.E.S. programs.

346. U.S. DEPARTMENT OF HEALTH, EDUCATION and WELFARE. *Human Investment Programs: Adult Basic Education, Work Experience and Training.* Washington, September, 1966 iii + 32 p.

Headings: An analysis of the benefits and costs of the adult basic education program; An application of cost-benefit analysis to the work-experience program.

Abstract: The basic measure of benefits for each of the two programs examined is the anticipated increase in future earnings representing improved potential for economic independence and self-support. For the Adult Basic Education Program, a number of target populations with different sex ratios, age distribution, levels of educational attainment, and drop-out rates were constructed. The present value of lifetime earnings was calculated for each target population from median income data. The educational characteristics were then changed to represent an increased level of educational attainment and the present value of the anticipated increase in lifetime earnings was calculated. Benefit-cost ratios were calculated for different target populations using an 8 per cent discount rate, and "optimum" values were established for the four population variables considered. The analysis of the Work Experience Program compared the present value of the expected future earnings of program participants after training with that of the same individuals before training, and also with that of non-participants of the same socio-economic and demographic characteristics. The value of output produced by WEP trainees is included among benefits, and savings in welfare payments and increases in income tax were also considered in this analysis, as in the ABE analysis. The estimate of costs used in the WEP study is the incremental cost incurred by the government for an individual participant. The ratio of incremental costs and present value of estimated future earnings per participant without the program is an indication of the percentage increase in future earnings required for the porgram to break even.

347. U.S. DEPARTMENT OF HEALTH, EDUCATION and WELFARE. *An Exploratory Cost-Benefit Analysis of Vocational Rehabilitation.* Washington, August, 1967. vi + 71 p.

Headings: Introduction; Overall summary; Increased lifetime value of earnings and work activity of: rehabilitated wage earners, rehabilitated homemakers and unpaid family workers, rehabilitated self-employed farmers, not rehabilitated wage earners; Cost of vocational rehabilitation services; Some intangible benefits of vocational rehabilitation; Appendices A-V.

Abstract: This study focusses on one among many benefits of vocational rehabilitation — the increase in lifetime earnings of disabled persons attributable to their receipt of vocational rehabilitation services. Since the program is intended to serve all disabled persons who need and can use services, cost-benefit analysis is not intended to select candidates for rehabilitation on the basis of the return to investment. It is expected, however, that differences in benefits per unit of costs between groups of disabled persons will have implications for planning rehabilitation programs. The general procedure for deriving an estimate of the increase in lifetime earnings of rehabilitated clients uses the following data: death and disability rates among clients causing termination of employment; the number of years of work-life for remaining clients until retirement; the earnings associated with clients remaining in employment through the years; the present value of future earnings, and the change in the productivity of workers in the future. Cost estimates included the cost of case services, the business enterprise program, guidance, counselling and administration. Expenditures by private agencies, public agencies other than State and Federal governments, and by individuals were also included. Intangible benefits accrue to the rehabilitated client, to his family and friends, and to the community. These benefits should be taken into account when the figures on costs and benefits presented in the overall survey are used as a basis for policy making.

348. U.S. EXECUTIVE OFFICE OF THE PRESIDENT, COUNCIL OF ECONOMIC ADVISERS. "Economic Costs of Racial Discrimination in Employment." Mimeographed. Washington, 1962, 5 p.

Headings: Introduction; Gain from full utilization of present educational attainment of non-whites; Gains from raising the educational level; Qualitative gains in national welfare; Appendix on derivation of estimates.

Abstract: Discrimination in employment causes inefficiencies in the use of the existing labour force and failure to develop potential skills fully. The paper attempts to estimate how much greater G.N.P. could be if discrimination were eliminated. There are two questions to be answered. By how much would G.N.P. increase if the nonwhite were able to utilize his *present* potential (as measured by years of education) as fully as is the white? By how much would G.N.P. increase if the nonwhite were able to develop his *capacities* as fully as is the white? No attempt is made to calculate the indirect economic

187

costs of discrimination. If nonwhites had the same labour force participation and employment rates as whites, and if they were distributed geographically and occupationally as whites with the same educational attainment, G.N.P. could be increased by 1.8 per cent. If the effect of creation of new capital and increases in the labour productivity of the self-employed is added to this figure, the gain is 2.5 per cent of G.N.P. or $13 billion. If nonwhites had the same educational levels as whites, a further 0.7 per cent of G.N.P. might be added to the cost of racial discrimination making the figure $17 billion. Elimination of discrimination would also reduce the social costs of crime and poor health and lead to a more equal distribution of income among whites.

349. U.S. OFFICE OF EDUCATION. "Guidelines For Adult and Vocational Research." *Journal of Human Resources,* Vol. 1, No. 1 (Summer, 1966), pp. 78-83.

Headings: Introduction; 1966-67 priorities.

Abstract: The Division of Adult and Vocational Research (DAVR) is divided into three branches: the Employment Opportunities Branch, the Human Resources Branch, and the Educational Resources Development Branch. Each Branch is engaged in an area of research and development. Seven areas of special emphasis were selected by DAVR for 1966-67: in order of priority, the areas were program evaluation, curriculum experimentation, personal and social significance of work, personnel recruitment and development, program organization and administration, adult and continuing education, and occupational information and career choice.

350. U.S. OFFICE OF MANPOWER POLICY, EVALUATION, and RESEARCH. "Research on Manpower Policy." *Journal of Human Resources,* Vol. 1, No. 1 (Summer, 1966), pp. 84-85.

Abstract: This paper lists the areas in which research has been sponsored by the U.S. Office of Manpower Policy, Evaluation, and Research (OMPER). The areas of research are: manpower resources and requirements; the nature and conditions of employment and unemployment; the impact of technological change; evaluation and analysis of manpower programs; and methodological studies.

351. ZEISEL, JOSEPH S. "Evaluation of National Manpower Policies: Discussion." In *Proceedings of the Seventeenth Annual Meeting,* Chicago, Illinois, December 28-29, 1964, pp. 152-154. Madison: Industrial Relations Research Association, 1965.

Abstract: The author stresses one of the major differences between U.S. and European retraining programs: the U.S. has not had an adequate structure for providing the initial formal vocational training to the labour force. Consequently, the MDTA is a training *and* retraining program, whereas the European programs emphasize retraining. It is suggested that the two objectives of job creation and training should be combined in the same program.

188

7. HEALTH

352.   ARROW, KENNETH J. "Uncertainty and the Welfare Economics of Medical Care." *American Economic Review,* Vol. 53, No. 5 (December, 1963), pp. 941-973.

Headings: Introduction: scope and method; A survey of the special characteristics of the medical-care market; Comparisons with the competitive model under certainty; Comparison wtih the ideal competitive model under uncertainty; Postscript; References (28); Appendix - On optimal insurance policies.

Abstract: This paper compares the operation of the medical-care industry with the operation of a competitive model. In addition to its descriptive value, the competitive model has implications for economic efficiency: the failure of one or more of the competitive preconditions implies a failure to reach Pareto optimality. The author suggests that when the market fails to achieve an optimal state, nonmarket social institutions tend to arise in an attempt to bridge the gap. He contends that the special structural characteristics of the medical-care market are largely attempts to overcome the lack of optimality due to the nonmarketability of the bearing of suitable risks, and the imperfect marketability of information.

353.   BARLOW, ROBIN. "The Economic Effects of Malaria Eradication." *American Economic Review,* Papers and Proceedings, Vol. 57, No. 2 (May, 1967), pp. 130-148.

Headings: Introduction; Malaria and its eradication; A classification of the economic effects of eradication; A model for measuring the economic effects of eradication; The model applied to Ceylon; Appendix: Equations for the determination of income.

Abstract: The author presents a method for measuring the effects of malaria eradication on long-run per capita income. There are four categories of effects to be considered: effects on population size; effects on labour inputs; effects on capital inputs; and other effects on output. In order to study the impact of malaria eradication in this way, a model of the entire economy must be specified; this is an approach somewhat more elaborate than that typically used in benefit-cost analyses of health programs. The reason for taking this kind of approach is that malaria eradication can cause quite marked changes. The equations of the model are estimated for the case of Ceylon and the model is applied to the question of what the course of Ceylonese per capita income would have been after 1947 if the successful eradication campaign of that year had not been undertaken. The conclusions are that in the short-run eradication proved beneficial but that, in time, the gain in per capita income tended to be eroded by population increase. A final set of simulations examines the consequences of a twin program of malaria eradication and birth control.

354. ENKE, STEPHEN. "The Gains to India from Population Control: Some Money Measures and Incentive Schemes." *Review of Economics and Statistics,* Vol. 42, No. 2 (May, 1960), pp. 175-181.

Headings: Introduction; Threat of population to Indian progress; The economic value of preventing one birth; Alternative schemes and bonus scales; Some practical considerations.

Abstract: The marginal production eventually occasioned by an extra million of population born in 1961 is far less than its total consumption. The savings in consumption can be discounted to give the present value of a permanently prevented birth. This value is increased if the released resources are invested. Some alternative schemes for reducing the number of births are discussed. The criterion of the size of an incentive bonus aimed at preventing births is its effectiveness as an inducement, not the estimated value of a prevented birth, since the bonus is a transfer payment, not a resource cost. The resource costs of a dual program consisting firstly of bonuses to nonpregnant women and, secondly, of a million vasectomies a year performed on men having wives in their twenties would be relatively small. The author suggests that the rate of return would be fifty to one.

355. FELDSTEIN, MARTIN S. "Economic Analysis, Operational Research, and the National Health Service." *Oxford Economic Papers,* Vol. 15, No. 1 (March, 1963), pp. 19-31.

Headings: Introduction; Quantitative methods and government policy: cost-benefit analysis and operational research; The concern with efficiency in the National Health Service; Operational research for health service management; Conclusion.

Abstract: The author surveys the application of cost-benefit analysis and operational research to the problems of water resource development and national defence. He cites the attempts to use operational research in the British National Health Service as another example of the growing interest in improving the efficiency of public expenditure. The problem of allocating resources within the health service and between health and other wants of society should be considered in terms of optimal allocation rather than in terms of "meeting needs". Economic reasoning can suggest the proper questions, and, providing that data on the costs of particular services and the benefits of treatment can be obtained, cost-benefit analysis can provide useful answers.

356. HOLTMANN, A. G. "Estimating the Demand for Public Health Services: The Alcoholism Case." *Public Finance,* Vol. 19, No. 4 (1964), pp. 351-360.

Headings: Introduction; A benefit-cost model; The alcoholism case; Conclusions; Résumé.

Abstract: The author feels that the community's demand curve for a public health service can be developed by identifying and measuring the benefits which accrue to various groups in society. This procedure would make benefit estimates available to compare with the marginal cost of the service, and would give some indication of who should pay for the service. The marginal costs and marginal benefits of treatment of alcoholics are compared, and it is suggested that expenditures can be justified on grounds of economic efficiency with a probability of success of treatment as low as .10. There are substantial external effects connected with alcoholism, although most of the benefits from successful treatment accrue to alcoholics and their families.

357. HOLTMANN, A. G. "Alcoholism and the Economic Value of a Man." *Review of Social Economy*, Vol. 23 (September, 1965), pp. 143-153.

Headings: Introduction; The economics of alcoholism; The economic loss of premature death; Conclusions.

Abstract: The paper describes the costs associated with alcoholism, and explains that the market does not operate efficiently in providing treatment for alcoholics because of external benefits from treatment, and irrational consumption decisions on the part of alcoholics. The author uses life expectancy tables and median earnings figures to calculate the economic loss of premature death among alcoholics. He compares the present value of this future loss with the estimated costs of rehabilitation and concludes that investment in treatment is potentially a good investment if at least thirteen out of every one hundred alcoholics treated is rehabilitated.

358. KLARMAN, HERBERT E. *The Economics of Health*, New York: Columbia University Press, 1965. 200 p.

Headings: Overview; Factors influencing demand; Demand by business, philanthropy, and government; Supply of personnel; Supply of hospital services; Organization, cooperation, and regulation; Selected problems; Selected bibliography (230).

Abstract: The author defines the economics of health as those aspects of the health problem that deal with the determination of the quantity and prices of the scarce resources devoted to health and related purposes, and with the combinations in which these resources are employed. He gives a description of the health and medical care industry and lists the major distinctive economic characteristics of health and medical services as follows: the uneven and unpredictable incidence of illness; external effects; health and medical care as a need; lack of knowledge; the mixture of consumption and investment elements; the large component of personal service; a nonprofit motive; and medical service and education as joint products. The author's approach follows the traditional framework of economics, classifying data and hypotheses under the factors comprising the demand for and supply of the product of the health industry. Consumers' demand for health services is a function of prices, income, and preferences, and the quantity demanded varies inversely with the price of the product. In paying for health services, however, the consumers' position is not the dominant one. Other sources of demand examined by the author are business, government, and philanthropy. The supply of hospital services can be analyzed in conventional terms by inquiring into the natures of the short- and long-term marginal cost curves. In the case of physicians' services, it would seem artificial to analyze the market for the product separately from the market for physicians: on the demand side, demand can be said to be for a physician; and on the supply side, the quantity of services offered depends largely on the number of physicians in practice and little on the price per unit of service rendered. Although solo practice is the most common form of medical practice in the United States, the group practice form of organization has received extensive treatment in the literature: the author includes group practice in his discussion of certain aspects of organization and coordination in the health and medical care field. In his final chapter, the author selects the following three problems for examination: the construction and application of the medical care price index; the evaluation of health and medical care programs by means of cost-benefit analysis; and the question of how much a nation can afford to spend on health and medical care.

359. KLARMAN, HERBERT E. "Syphilis Control Programs." In *Measuring Benefits of Government Investments,* edited by Robert Dorfman, pp. 367-414. Washington: The Brookings Institution, 1965.

Headings: Introduction; Concepts and techniques; Incidence of syphilis; Economic costs of cases infected in 1962; Economic benefits; Comments by Selma Mushkin.

Abstract: The author examines the concepts and techniques employed by economists in measuring the costs of a disease. From this survey emerge the decision rules adopted for the study. The incidence of syphilis and the various costs attributable to the disease are calculated. These costs include medical care expenditures, production loss, and reduction in earnings owing to the stigma attached to having contracted venereal disease. The economic benefits of total eradication, and, as a more feasible alternative, the benefits obtained from control programs at alternative levels of intensity are calculated. Mushkin argues that more vigorous efforts at quantifying the "non-measurable" components are required.

360. MARSHALL, A. W. *Cost-Benefit Analysis in Health.* Santa Monica: The Rand Corporation, 1965. 18 p.

Headings: Introduction; A view of relevant research; Program budgeting of government health programs; A program budget for health; Problems of cost-benefit analysis; Final comments.

Abstract: The author points out that health is a consumption good as well as an investment good. Recent research has tended to focus on the latter aspect since output loss or gain is measurable in money terms. Some method must be found to reflect the consumption value of improved health, and a more realistic reflection of the options open to investment in better health should be included in cost-benefit studies. A sample program budget for health is given, and promising areas for cost-benefit analysis are enumerated. Various aspects of research strategy are discussed.

361. MUSHKIN, SELMA J. "Health as an Investment." *Journal of Political Economy,* Vol. 70, No. 5, Part 2 (October, 1962, Supplement), pp. 129-157.

Headings: Introduction; Education and Health: similarities and differences; Measuring capital formation through health care.

Abstract: This paper discusses the economics of health and education programs and the interrelations between the two areas of human investment. The author summarizes various measures of capital formation through health programs. The central problem in assessing investment in health is the measurement of the labour product added through health care. An attempt is made to estimate the contribution to economic growth resulting from the enlargement of the work force through reductions in death rates. The paper concludes with a survey of applications of cost-benefit analysis to the human resource field.

362. MUSHKIN, S. J., and B. A. WEISBROD. "Investment in Health — Lifetime Health Expenditures on the 1960 Work Force." *Kyklos,* Vol. 16 (1963), pp. 583-598.

Abstract: Recent attempts to explain the sources of economic growth have emphasized the influence of qualitative changes in resources. An increasing amount of economic research has been directed to the changes occurring in the quality of labour resources. Health and education expenditures are principal means by which the quality of labour resources can be improved. This paper considers health expenditures made for or by members of the work force throughout their lifetime to have been investment in health. An estimation of the stock of health investment in human capital would be needed either to determine the percentage rate of return being realized on the resources required to produce the stock, or to determine the amount of economic growth which is attributable to the stock. The definitions of stock for the two purposes are different: the first includes not only the value of investment which was successful in raising productivity but also the value of unsuccessful investment including that on persons who subsequently were not part of the labour force; the second definition, which is the one used in the present paper, includes only the investment which was medically successful in influencing the number and productivity of workers. On this definition, the health stock in the 1960 work force of the U.S. at 1960 prices is estimated at $204 billion. This compares with an estimated $535 billion of educational capital in the 1957 labour force. Thus, about 38 cents of health capital is embodied in the labour force for each $1 of educational capital.

363.   REDER, M. W. "Economic Theory and Non-Profit Enterprise — Some Problems in the Economics of Hospitals." *American
Economic Review,* Papers and Proceedings, Vol. 55, No. 2 (May,
1965), pp. 472-480.

Headings: Introduction; The socially optimal stock of hospital facilities; The
optimal use of facilities; Efficiency and cost differentials; Duplication of facilities and efficiency.

Abstract: Because of the intercorrelation of demand and supply of hospital
beds we have no way of determining the "medical need" for hospital facilities
from observations on their use. Utilization is a difficult matter requiring
medical decisions. It is suggested, however, that there is a lack of financial
incentive to avoid over-utilization. It is unlikely that the ratios of prices of
various hospital services and their marginal costs of production are equal.
The prestige motives for expanding and improving hospitals are likely to
generate excess capacities.

364.   REYNOLDS, D. J. "The Cost of Road Accidents." *Journal
of the Royal Statistical Society,* Series A, Vol. 119, Part 4 (1956),
pp. 393-408.

Headings: Introduction; Effects of road accidents; Cost of road accidents;
Basis of the estimates of the cost of road accidents in 1952; Total cost of road
accidents to the community in 1952; The cost of various consequences of road
accidents; Conclusion; Summary; Appendix A — The costs of various consequences of road accidents; Appendix B — Examples of the economic return
to be gained from road-safety measures; References (13).

Abstract: The author confines his estimates to concrete and ascertainable
costs in the form of net loss of output of goods, and expenditure of resources
necessary to make good the effects of accidents. Among the costs considered
are the following: damage to property; cost of medical treatment; administrative cost of motor insurance; net loss of output due to deaths; and loss of
output due to injury. It is demonstrated that expenditure on various types of
road-safety measures can lead to savings in real resources as well as increased
human welfare. The introduction of pedestrian crossings and of improved
rear lighting can be justified on purely economic grounds, and *a fortiori* on
humanitarian grounds.

365.   SCHELLING, T. C. "The Life You Save May Be Your Own."
In *Problems in Public Expenditure Analysis,* edited by Samuel B.
Chase Jr., pp. 127-176. Washington: The Brookings Institution,
1968.

Headings: Introduction; Social interest in life and death; Economic interest
in lost livelihoods; Consumer interest in reduced risk; Conclusion; Comments
by Martin J. Bailey and Gary Fromm.

Abstract: This paper discusses approaches to the question of what it is worth to reduce the statistical frequency of death within some identifiable group of people. If a death occurs the most obvious loss is that of the person who dies, although we are not sure exactly what he loses; death also involves the welfare of people close to the person who dies; and, finally, society in general may lose or save money as a result of a death. When the economic impact of untimely death is being calculated, it is important to distinguish between the life and the livelihood that goes with it: evaluation of the worth of the latter to the family unit and to other members of the economy can be based on market evidence. How much of the loss of livelihood falls on the family depends on institutional and market arrangements. The author looks at various elements of the accounting procedure necessary to assess the costs of a death: insurance; noncontractual claims; and taxes and fiscal policy. What is a program to save lives worth to those who stand to benefit from it? This question could be answered by observation of market behaviour, or by interviewing the people concerned but neither method yields very satisfactory results. Nevertheless, decisions have to be made about death-reducing programs. The gravity of such decisions can be dispelled by letting the consumer express himself on the subject of small increments in small risks. Bailey points out that existing economic theory provides an adequate treatment of Schelling's subject and that the practical problems can be solved fairly simply. Fromm holds that Schelling's essay is misleading in certain logical, statistical, and economic grounds.

366. SEWELL, DAVID O. "The Cost-Effectiveness of Family Planning as an Anti-Poverty Measure." Mimeographed. Durham: The North Carolina Fund, 1966.

Headings: Introduction; Procedure; Footnotes.

Abstract: Since the output-increasing effects of family planning in the U.S. are likely to be less important than the distributional effects, the project has been designated a "cost-effectiveness" rather than a "cost-benefit" study. The "poverty level" is measured on a sliding scale relating family income to family size. If, as a result of family planning programs, realized family size in lower-income groups were brought closer to desired family size, a certain proportion of the population would automatically be raised above the "poverty level". There is reason to believe that family planning programs for the poor would produce results of a greater than marginal nature and, consequently, allowance has to be made for the use of shifting rather than fixed relationships in the analysis. The paper concludes by examining some of the objections usually raised to the use of cost-effectiveness analysis to quantify the social effects of government investments.

367. SIMON, JULIAN L. "The Health Economics of Cigarette Consumption." *Journal of Human Resources*, Vol. 3, No. 1 (Winter, 1968), pp. 111-117.

Headings: Costs of cigarette smoking; Conclusions; Appendix A: The effect of smoking on male life expectancy; Appendix B: Decrease in life before age 65 for average smoker.

Abstract: The extent of the danger of smoking is crucial to social decisions about the cigarette hazard. The calculations in Appendix A indicate that the average smoker's life is four years shorter than if he had not smoked. The author examines price elasticity of demand and elasticity of demand with respect to advertising, and with respect to adverse publicity. He suggests that abolition of cigarette advertising is the best way to reduce consumption. The savings to the economy from keeping productive people alive outweighs the negative social effect of a reduction in cigarette consumption on wages, salaries, and farm earnings in the cigarette industry. The author claims that the trade-off is between an incremental short-run decrease of one dollar of wages, and an increase of 99 hours of human life (± 20 per cent error).

368. VILLARD, HENRY H. "A Note on the Economics of Birth Control." *Review of Economics and Statistics,* Vol. 40, No. 1 (February, 1958), pp. 78-79.

Abstract: The author surveys the costs and benefits of promoting widespread birth control in developing areas. He concludes that such areas would benefit substantially from population limitation under existing techniques.

369. WEISBROD, BURTON A. "Some Problems of Pricing and Resource Allocation in a Non-Profit-Industry — The Hospitals." *Journal of Business,* Vol. 38, No. 1 (January, 1965), pp. 18-28.

Headings: Introduction; The structure of hospital room prices; Utilization instability for a hospital and for the industry.

Abstract: The paper argues that the insulation of the hospital industry from some important market pressures permits pricing and investment practices which appear to be nonoptimal. The lower cost of ward accommodation as compared with semi-private rooms should be reflected in the implicit prices established by Blue Cross plans so that users will consider not only their preferences, but also the resource costs involved. The author demonstrates that hospitals are confronted by fluctuating demand while supply is fixed in the short-run. Thus it might be possible to reduce the amount of idle capacity without reducing the level of medical care.

370. WISEMAN, JACK. "Cost-Benefit Analysis and Health Service Policy." *Scottish Journal of Political Economy,* Vol. 10, No. 1 (February, 1963), pp. 128-145.

Headings: Introduction; Investment in health; Characteristics of health services; Measuring the return to health services; The policy problem; Conclusions and suggestions.

Abstract: The author examines the problem of calculating the efficient size of a health program, and of deciding on the optimal allocation of medical resources among different uses. The application of cost-benefit analysis to this problem involves peculiar problems of identifying costs and benefits, as well as the familiar problems of externalities and the social discount rate. It is suggested that the analyst must take account of the value system of the policy maker if the analysis is to be of practical value. Two methods of relating the results of the analysis to the policy maker's value system are outlined — the welfare approach and the direct-evaluation approach.

371. BESEN, STANLEY M., ALAN E. FECHTER, and ANTHONY C. FISHER. "Applications of Cost Effectiveness Analysis to the 'War on Poverty'." Internal Note N-245 (R). Arlington: Institute for Defense Analyses, 1965. 15 p.

Headings: Introduction; Evaluating training programs; Evaluating regional development programs; Conclusion.

Abstract: This paper explores the use of cost-benefit analysis in the evaluation of anti-poverty programs. The discussion covers two programs intended to increase earnings and employment: investment in education, and investment in highways and other public facilities. The returns from these programs can be measured by the change in the real output of the economy which they bring about. The authors examine evaluations of training programs by Page (316) and Somers and Stromsdorfer (335). The nature of the benefits and costs of highway construction under the Appalachian Regional Development Act is outlined. The correct method of evaluating the returns to the construction of a road is to determine the increase in real output which the introduction of the road generates. It has been suggested that the indirect benefits of highway construction may exceed the direct ones several times. Some key questions must be answered before a complete evaluation is possible.

8. POVERTY and SOCIAL WELFARE

372. GORDON, MARGARET S. *The Economics of Welfare Policies.* New York: Columbia University Press, 1963. xi + 159 p.

Headings: Introduction; Welfare programs in the United States; Some international comparisons; Welfare programs and income redistribution; The old-age, survivors, and disability insurance program; Unemployment compensation; Conclusions; Appendix: The federal OASDI system and the federal-state unemployment insurance system — description of provisions at end of 1961; References (226).

Abstract: This book discusses the treatment of some of the major economic issues associated with welfare programs in the economics literature. Welfare programs are defined as social programs designed to transfer income to those whose capacity for self-support has been impaired, interrupted, or (in the case of children) has not yet reached maturity. In other words, the study deals almost entirely with income-maintenance programs, although certain public subsidy programs designed to benefit low-income consumers are also included. The author traces the growth of public welfare expenditures, refers briefly to private welfare expenditures, compares public welfare expenditures in the United States with those in other countries, and presents some data on the income-redistribution effects of welfare programs. She then considers the economics of two major American public welfare programs — OASDI and unemployment insurance — which are described in an appendix. There are indications that the OASDI program may have a significant effect on economic growth, partly through its impact on human resources and on the adjustment of the labour force to economic change. There is also evidence that OASDI transfers could be timed so as to act as a countercyclical device. In addition, the program's role as an automatic stabilizer is likely to become more important as the program matures. It is not clear whether OASDI has had any longer-run effects on consumer behaviour. The unemployment compensation program is not making as effective a contribution to restoring the wage losses of unemployed workers or to maintaining economic stability as it might. The present financing system and fears that higher benefits will enhance disincentives to work are hampering proposals to strengthen the system. Possibilities which should be studied are cyclically graduated compensation, variations in maximum duration of benefits on the basis of previous employment records, and a broader tax base in the form of employee or government contributions. The relationship between unemployment insurance and unemployment assistance should also be investigated. The author concludes that, while the negative income tax proposal seems impractical, it does highlight the need for greater attention to the overall impact of the complex array of U.S. welfare policies on the present distribution of real income and on the stability and growth of the economy as a whole.

373.   HODGES, EMORY F. "New Light on Delinquency Through Operations Research." Paper given at a joint meeting of the Socieadad Mexicana De Neurologia Y Psiquiatria and the American Psychiatric Association, Mexico City, May, 1964. New York: Community Research Associates, 1964.   8 p.

Abstract: Operations research is a scientific method of providing executives with a quantitative basis for decisions regarding the operations under their control. The techniques of operations research, including observations of results, data analysis, operational experiments in part of the system and evaluation results, can, in the opinion of the author, help stem the rising tide of delinquency in the U.S. Operations research has made possible, among other things, a delinquency prediction device of reasonable accuracy, and a scientific methodology for social casework. The paper concludes with a short bibliography and a plea for more interdisciplinary research.

198

374. LAMPMAN, ROBERT J. "Approaches to the Reduction of Poverty." *American Economic Review,* Papers and Proceedings, Vol. 55, No. 2 (May, 1965), pp. 521-529.

Headings: Introduction; The poverty rate and the poverty income gap; Why poverty persists; Countering "events"; Breaking down barriers; Improving abilities and motivations; Summary.

Abstract: The author claims that the U.S. poverty rate is diminishing at the rate of one percentage point per annum and that the poverty income gap is down to two per cent of GNP. If this trend continues, poverty in the U.S. can be eliminated in this generation. Social scientists should use cost-benefit analysis in the appraisal of various anti-poverty programs. Such programs involve countering the "events" which select people for poverty, breaking down social barriers which restrict opportunities, and increasing human investment.

375. LAMPMAN, ROBERT J. "The Guaranteed Minimum Income: Is It Worth What It Would Cost? A paper presented at the Conference on the Guaranteed Minimum Income, School of Social Service Administration, University of Chicago, January, 1966. Mimeographed. 20 p.

Headings: Introduction; Transfer payments and the poverty-income gap; Schwartz-Wade Plan A; Cost of Plan A; Cost of some alternative GMI plans; The basis for choice.

Abstract: What would it cost the U.S. to implement a guaranteed minimum income of the kind outlined by Professors Schwartz and Wade? The Schwartz and Wade plan is a simple plan to fill each family's poverty-income gap, that is to pay the difference between their original income and the poverty-line income for their family size. Two alternative poverty lines for a four-person family are examined — $3,000 and $4,000 per annum. The net cost of these schemes is estimated at $10.7 billion and $18 billion respectively. Some other variants of the scheme are also considered. The principal dilemma is between keeping the initial cost of the scheme down by having a low break-even point (and thereby having high penalty tax rates on the near-poor) or extending the break-even point in an effort to avoid high tax rates on low incomes (and thereby pushing the initial cost up and placing it on the richer part of the population who already have relatively high marginal tax rates). Are the benefits of the GMI worth its cost? The benefits include an end to poverty as defined, increased freedom of choice for many low-income persons, greater participation in community affairs by lower-income groups, and a long-run reduction of dependency through better education and health for the children of the poor.

199

376. LAMPMAN, ROBERT J. "Towards an Economics of Health, Education and Welfare." *Journal of Human Resources,* Vol. 1, No. 1 (Summer, 1966), pp. 45-53.

Headings: Introduction; HEW economics as a sub-discipline; Descriptive inquiry; Normative inquiry; Predictive inquiry.

Abstract: The paper argues that the range of activities pursued by the U.S. Department of Health, Education, and Welfare (HEW) constitute a sub-discipline in economics. The author outlines three modes of enquiry: descriptive, normative, and predictive. The HEW "school" is characterized by "persuasive predictions". It is centred on an overlap of reallocation and redistributive questions, and links the goals of efficiency and equity.

377. LEVINE, ABRAHAM S. "Cost-Benefit Analysis and Social Welfare." *Welfare in Review,* Vol. 4, No. 2 (February, 1966), pp. 1-11.

Headings: Introduction; Significance for current policy makers; Essential elements; Some cautionary words; Levels of application; The focus is on the future; An illustrative study; Commentary; In conclusion; Selected bibliography (29).

Abstract: This paper provides a general survey of cost-benefit analysis, and examines some of the specific problems involved in its application to welfare programs. As an illustration, the author examines the study by M. E. Borus (250) on the economics of retraining the unemployed. It is pointed out that this study did not explicitly take psychological and sociological benefits into account. It may not be possible to ignore such values in the appraisal of a social welfare program. An attitude scale might be used to measure psychological and sociological variables. Borus's study is cited as a useful example of the conceptualization and analysis involved in a specific cost-benefit study.

378. LEVINE, ROBERT A. "Evaluation of Office of Economic Opportunity Programs: A Progress Report." A paper presented at the 126th Annual Meeting of the American Statistical Association, Los Angeles, California, August, 1966. Mimeographed. 26 p.

Headings: Introduction; Training; Education; Community action.

Abstract: This paper is a report on what the OEO is doing to evaluate the impact of vocational training, educational, and community action programs on poverty. Training programs are conceptually the most simple to evaluate. Attention has been directed towards identifying control groups which will allow comparison of "before-and-after" experience of trainees with the similarly time-phased experience of nontrainees. An inventory of Federal educational programs for the poor is outlined in tabular form: this inventory identifies programs, estimates the number of beneficiaries and the amount of funding, and states briefly what is known about the impact of these programs on the rate of learning. "Head Start", the major education program operated by the OEO, has been evaluated for its effects on educational achievement, but an anti-poverty evaluation has not been undertaken. The ultimate measure of effectiveness of community action programs is the change in the number of people in poverty who came originally from CAP target areas. This information will be obtained from the Current Population Survey. Short-run evaluation will be accomplished through the CAP monitoring function which will examine individual projects.

379. LEVINE, ROBERT A. "Manpower Programs in the War on Poverty." In *Cost-Benefit Analysis of Manpower Policies, Proceedings of a North America Conference, May 14-15, 1969,* edited by G. G. Somers and W. D. Wood, pp. 170-183. Published jointly by the Industrial Relations Centre, Queen's University, Kingston, Ontario, and the Center for Studies in Vocational and Technical Education, The University of Wisconsin, Madison, Wisconsin, 1969.

Abstract: The author is skeptical about the use of cost-benefit analysis as a major policy instrument at present. In the first place, cost-benefit analysis is a very partial tool in decision-making in manpower programs whereas the decisions which have to be made at this time are at a fairly high level of aggregation. Secondly, as the record of cost-benefit analysis of the Job Corps demonstrates, the technique is subject to a number of difficulties — problems of constructing control groups, predicting program results, and comparing results for different programs. Manpower programs are regarded as part of an overall anti-poverty strategy, complementing other anti-poverty measures. Recently anti-poverty programs seem to have made an impact upon the capable poor: we now need a complementary program aimed at the incapable poor. This conclusion raises the "equity/effectiveness" dilemma: we cannot concentrate our anti-poverty efforts upon the capable poor without contravening equity considerations, but neither can we concentrate our manpower programs upon the incapable poor without sharply lowering the effectiveness of our efforts. The author feels that the solution to this dilemma is the negative income tax. The negative income tax is the first part of the anti-poverty strategy, while manpower programs constitute the second. If unemployment remains low, the Job Opportunities in the Business Sector program is probably the greatest hope for successful large scale operations in the manpower field. A complementary program is the Job Opportunities in the Public Sector program which the author would like to see becoming an "employer of last resort". It is impossible to say how large these programs will have to be. We know of no way to measure the needs of the poor for manpower programs — either in terms of the number of slots or of the kinds of programs. A hierarchy of programs which allowed a fall-back from one program to another, the final fall-back position being the negative income tax, would enable us to feel our way to an optimum program-mix, and at the same time would prevent a lot of poor people suffering while the planners experiment with refined techniques like cost-benefit analysis.

380. MacDONALD, JOHN STUART. "Benefit-Cost Analysis of Social Welfare Programs." In *Proceedings of the Seventeenth Annual Meeting,* Chicago, Illinois, December 28-29, 1964, pp. 186-194. Madison: Industrial Relations Research Association, 1965.

Headings: Introduction; Clear criteria of effectiveness; Comparison of alternatives; Hierarchies of sub-projects and stages of suboptimization; Time streams of costs and benefits over the life of the project; Shadow prices and opportunity costs; Primary indirect costs and benefits; Secondary costs and benefits; Rates of interest for future inputs and outputs; Non-linear relations between inputs and outputs; The distinction between average cost and incremental cost; Summary conclusion.

Abstract: The paper suggests the possibility of evaluating all projects from a three-tiered, socio-economic, cost-benefit standpoint, i.e. from the particular firm's standpoint, from the national income standpoint, and from the social development standpoint. Social development is defined as a raising of the level of living; it cannot be fully expressed in economic terms. However, the author argues that the problem lies not in questions of intangibility or quantifiability, but in the use of commensurable units. He poses the question of whether social development indices can be treated like financial flows in cost-benefit analysis.

381. MUTH, RICHARD. *The Evaluation of Selected Present and Potential Poverty Programs.* Arlington: Institute for Defense Analysis, 1966. xii + 86 p.

Headings: Summary; Introduction; Education and training programs; Direct measures to increase family income; The effect of changes in wage rates, transfer payments and taxes; The Federal cost of direct measures to increase family income; Comparison of programs; Appendix A: The Federal cost of education and training; Appendix B: Determination of family income; Appendix C: The Federal cost of raising average family incomes by $100 through wage, tax, or transfer programs; Appendix D: Interstate regression results.

Abstract: This study attempts to appraise the effectiveness of education and training programs, measures to increase the demand for low-wage workers, and tax and transfer payments in increasing the incomes of poor families. The basis for comparison of the effectiveness of these programs is the average annual cost to the government of raising income by $100 per year over the working life of the family head. It is argued that the increase in the worker's future earnings rather than the change in the unemployment rate is the relevant criterion for judging the benefits of training programs because the increase in employment tends to be temporary and because higher earnings rates may be the more important effect of training. The effects of wage rate, tax, and transfer payment changes on income were estimated using regression analysis. These estimates were combined with information on program costs to determine the efficiency of various programs. Under the criterion of efficiency adopted, changes in marginal tax rates and training programs for young workers appear to be the most effective. The comparisons suggest that direct hiring by the government at prevailing wage rates and transfer payments to families with earnings are among the least efficient means of achieving the desired goal.

382. RIBICH, THOMAS I. *Education and Poverty.* Washington: The Brookings Institution, 1968 xii + 163 p.

Headings: Education as an investment; Poverty lines and the criteria of policy choice; Job training and dropout prevention; Compensatory and preschool education; Increased per-pupil expenditures; Education's role in a war on poverty; Appendix A: Selection of poverty lines; Appendix B: Evaluation of compensatory education; Appendix C: The option value of education; Appendix D: Bibliography (52).

Abstract: The author feels that benefit-cost analysis is an appropriate tool for measuring the contribution of education to the War on Poverty: benefit-cost computations can measure the economic impact of education on the directly affected individuals; and the context of a war on poverty gives the economist a guide to income distribution preference. The single poverty line and the poverty income gap are inadequate measures of poverty when the effectiveness of an anti-poverty program is being ascertained. As an alternative, a dual poverty line technique is suggested: the first line represents the highest standard of living low enough to arouse social concern; the second line is the income level which, at the going cost of anti-poverty programs, society is indifferent about altering upwards. These two lines form guideposts for weighing dollar gains experienced by the poor in various income ranges. Ideally, the effectiveness of anti-poverty programs would be guaged by *weighted* benefit-cost ratios. Five different types of educational improvement are considered: job retraining; dropout prevention programs; compensatory education programs for "culturally deprived" children; preschool programs; and increasing the quality and magnitude of resources put into formal education. The author's own benefit-cost computations are made under uniform assumptions, and the ratios calculated by other authors are adjusted to make them comparable. The paucity of observations and the conceptual and measurement difficulties encountered in calculating (unweighted) benefit-cost ratios make conclusions about the relative payoff rates of different types of educational investment very tentative. Three conclusions are worth noting: vocationally oriented training has a higher rate of payoff than general education; secondly, the payoff-rate evidence gives no strong indications that special emphasis should be placed on the very early school years or on the preschool years; thirdly, rates of payoff appear to be higher from adding expenditures in those school districts which are now spending relatively little. Despite the tentative nature of the empirical results, the benefit-cost ratios calculated raise serious questions about the payoff from investment in education as an anti-poverty weapon. The intergenerational effects and supramarginal changes are phenomena which may increase the anti-poverty potential of education: the author's analysis, however, indicates that these factors do not add much to the "case for education" in the reduction of poverty. Other aspects which are examined — nonpecuniary returns, dependency, equality of opportunity, externalities, and economic growth — are social benefits distinguishable from the poverty reduction goal. On the assumption that a heavy emphasis on general education is not the most efficient way to approach poverty alleviation, the author outlines six alternative policy conclusions.

383.   ROSENBERG, LAURENCE C. "On Costs and Benefits of a National Television System for India." *Indian Economic Journal,* Vol. 14, No. 1 (July-September, 1966), pp. 1-17.

Headings: Introduction; Methodology; Technologies and system costs; Potential net benefits from National Television; Summary and conclusions.

Abstract: Three system components are distinguished: programming — the production of programs and delivery to the point of initial transmission; transmission; and reception. Costs associated with the programming and reception components are common to all systems discussed in this paper. Comparative system costs, therefore, are determined by the transmission element. Three transmission elements are considered — satellite transmission, airborne transmission, and ground broadcasting stations with microwave links. The estimates of the present values of the costs of the various systems are calculated for 6 and 12 per cent discount rates and for 15 and 20 year economic lives. Low and high estimates are presented. Two kinds of potential benefits are considered: television for formal education; and television for information and other purposes. The estimates of the benefits of educational television are based on the costs of training and paying enough teachers to fill India's teacher deficit, given the goal of providing universal education from Grades 1 to 8. Although the analysis explores the full range of neither costs nor benefits, two important conclusions are reached. Firstly, for broad areas of geographical coverage the satellite is the least costly method of transmission. Secondly, while the kinds of benefits of television systems for education and information are likely to exceed those calculated in the paper, the analysis suggests that nation-wide coverage of India may be worth the costs of these few benefits alone.

384.   ROY, ROBERT H. "An Outline for Research in Penology." *Operations Research,* Vol. 12, No. 1 (January-February, 1964), pp. 1-12.

Headings: Introduction; The Patuxent concept; Procedure; Institutional organization and operation; Inadequacy of the present penal system; Proposals for research; Summary.

Abstract: Under the present penal system an offender is confined for the duration of his sentence less possible time off for good behaviour and with some chance of early release on parole. Almost every inmate can look forward to a day of release. Of those who are released, 70 per cent are back in prison within five years. The cycle of crime, detection, apprehension, trial, judgement, confinement, attempted rehabilitation, release, crime etc. is a costly one. The author proposes an alternative system based upon the concept of the "indeterminate sentence", and having as its objective the minimization of the sum of all costs associated with the whole system over time. At any point in time, the decision as to whether to release an inmate would depend upon the costs of continued incarceration and rehabilitation, the probability of his committing another crime, the costs of the judicial process connected with that crime, the cost of the crime itself, and the value of the work done by the individual after release. The concept of the indeterminate sentence is applied in Maryland and has been found constitutional. The author argues that it is merely the legal acknowledgement of a probabilistic principle that a *defective* delinquent may be confined indefinitely as long as the likelihood of his committing another crime, if released, is deemed sufficiently high. The present decision-making model would extend this principle to other classes of criminals.

385. SCHULTZ, THEODORE W. "Investing in Poor People: An Economist's View." *American Economic Review,* Papers and Proceedings, Vol. 55, No. 2 (May, 1965), pp. 510-520.

Headings: Introduction; Two applications of demand theory; Three hypotheses; Implications.

Abstract: The author examines the various sources of income streams and relates them to observed changes in poverty. The decline in poverty is largely a consequence of increases in income from labour. A substantial part of the remaining poverty is a consequence of disequilibria. Three examples of disequilibrium are given: the market for agricultural skills; the market for the skills of Negroes; and the regional disequilibrium existing in the Southern States. The conclusion is that increased investment in human resources will hasten the decline of poverty.

386. SMOLENSKY, EUGENE. "Investment in the Education of the Poor: A Pessimistic Report." *Amecian Economic Review,* Papers and Proceedings, Vol. 56, No. 2 (May, 1966), pp. 370-378.

Headings: Introduction; The poverty line as a signal; The historical record points toward full employment; Full employment and declining wage differentials: the trickle-down mechanism; Increased schooling as an anti-poverty policy; References (18).

Abstract: This paper proposes the "consensus" approach as an alternative to the "needs" approach in measuring poverty. The "consensus" approach serves as an index of the disutility to the community of the persistence of poverty. Under this approach, a fall in the proportion of families in poverty would probably require a decline in income inequality. The conditions for declining income inequality are discussed, and it is suggested that a program of "trickling-down" from growth to poverty reduction would be politically unattractive. Emphasis has been placed on less aggregative policies such as encouraging students to complete high school. The two basic reasons for a federal policy to add financial incentives to education — that the marginal social benefit of schooling exceeds that marginal private benefit, and that the capital market is imperfect — are, however, made largely irrelevant by the "irrational" behaviour of the poor: although the high unemployment levels among young people provide an economic incentive to remain in school, the drop-out rate is high.

387.   THUROW, LESTER C., and CARL RAPPAPORT. "Law Enforcement and Cost-Benefit Analysis." Discussion Paper No. 19. Mimeographed. Cambridge, Mass.: Harvard Institute of Economic Research, Harvard University, March, 1968. 23 p.

Headings: Introduction; Benefit measures; The discount rate; Actual benefits; Costs; Net benefits; Strategies for maximizing net benefits; Conclusions.

Abstract: This article focuses on economic crimes although the cost-benefit framework could be applied to personal crimes provided a method is found to translate reduced injuries and deaths into economic benefits. Specifically the authors seek to formulate methods for finding the best techniques for enforcing the provisions of the Fair Labor Standards Act. The data is derived from a compliance survey undertaken by the Wage and Hour Division of the Department of Labor. Benefits consist of "back-wages found due" which were paid, and the difference between wages owed in establishments which were not investigated and in those which were. Minimum wage and equal pay benefits were multiplied by an arbitrary factor of 1.5 to allow for distributional aims. The discount rate is composed of two factors — the interest rate and a risk premium reflecting the declining deterrent effect of a previous investigation. Investigatory benefits could be calculated for different enforcement techniques as well as for different areas of investigation. Suggested areas of investigation are as follows: different sizes of establishments; different industries; and different regions. From the data available, it is possible to calculate the expected benefits from investigating an establishment of a given size in a given industry, and in a given region. The results assume however, that there are no interaction effects among these categories. The per worker cost curve for investigation of establishments of various sizes is constructed on the assumption that there are economies of scale in investigations. From the matrix of net benefits, the paper attempts to answer two questions: if WHD investigated the same number of workers as at present and attempted to maximize benefits, how large could the average net benefit be? If WHD spent the same amount of money and attempted to maximize net benefits, how large could the net benefit be?

206

388. TWEETEN, LUTHER G. *The Role of Education in Alleviating Rural Poverty*. Agricultural Economic Report No. 114. Washington: U.S. Department of Agriculture, June, 1967. iv + 56 p.

Headings: Introduction; Dimensions and costs of rural poverty; Education in low-income rural areas; The contribution of education to income and economic growth; Education and earnings in rural areas; education and migration; Goals and values; Inducement for greater educational attainment; Integrating education with other measures to combat rural poverty; Research proposals for appraising the potential contribution of education to area growth; Conclusions; Bibliography (162).

Abstract: This study examines the role of education in raising income and living standards in rural areas characterized by low incomes. The review of literature on past research (cited in the extensive bibliography) establishes several conclusions: education is a necessary, although not always a sufficient, condition for sustained social and economic progress in rural areas; youth tends to lag in education in low-income rural areas where attitudes are often inimical to educational attainment; and education is a profitable economic investment for society, especially where rural youth is assimilated into the nonfarm economy. The author suggests that public policy decisions may be made on the basis of benefit-cost ratios, although he emphasizes that educational inputs and outputs are difficult to measure.

389. WILSON, R. A. "An Application of Systems Analysis to War on Poverty Budget Planning and Evaluation." A paper presented at the 11th Annual Meeting of the Operations Research Society of America, Western Section, September, 1965. Mimeographed. ii + 20 p.

Headings: Abstract; Introduction; The Economic Opportunity Act of 1964; War on Poverty program planning and evaluation; Program budget optimization technique — cost/effectiveness; Summary and recommendations; Bibliography (11).

Abstract: The paper examines the elements and applicability of cost/effectiveness analysis with respect to the War on Poverty as expressed in the Economic Opportunity Act. The measure of effectiveness, or benefit, established is the negative "cost-to-society concept": this involves calculating the cost of **not** operating a program. The use of the negative cost-to-society does not imply that other benefits will be disregarded. Evaluation of poverty programs cannot be relegated to a time when all information as to benefits is available. Consequently, an economic model is formulated which will provide allocation simulation capability. The model uses dynamic programming because the allocations involve multi-stage decisions subject to nonlinear constraints, and the objective function presented is also nonlinear. The paper concludes with some specific recommendations with respect to establishing a cost-effectiveness approach to the War on Poverty.

AUTHOR INDEX
by entry number

210